CLASSIC
AMERICAN
STREAMLINERS

MIKE SCHAFER AND JOE WELSH

Motorbooks International
Publishers & Wholesalers ®

DEDICATIONS

To my mom, who took me for a ride on my first streamliner, Illinois Central's *Land O' Corn,* and who from then on encouraged my passion for passenger trains.

—*Mike Schafer*

To mom, who took me west on the *General* and the *California Zephyr* and helped a little boy develop a lifelong interest in railroading.

—*Joseph M. Welsh*

ACKNOWLEDGMENTS

INDIVIDUALS

Richard Allen; Chris Baer; Marshall Beecher; Jim Boyd; Seth Bramson; Bill and Joann Caloroso; Bill Connolly; Richard Cooley; George Drury; Arthur Dubin; John Dziobko; Steve Esposito; Fred Frailey; Linda Frysztacki; Wes Frysztacki; Deb and Ron Goldfeder; Sandy Goodrick; Larry Goolsby; Bruce Heard; Bill Howes Jr.; Robert W. Jones; Dee Joseph; Paul Joslin; Bill Kratville; John H. Kuehl; Mark Llanuza; Mitch Markovitz; Keith Mathiowetz; Jim McClellan; Bill Middleton; Joyce Mooney, Jon Nelson; Dave and Jill Oroszi; Bob Penisi; Elvis A. Presley; Dave Randall; David Salter; Don Sarno; Jack Savage; Bill Schafer; Max T. D. Schafer; Bob Schmidt; John Signor; Don Snoddy; Jana Solberg; Brian Solomon; George Speir; Carl Swanson; Greg Stout; John Strauss; J. W. Swanberg; Ross Tabor; Peter V. Tilp; Bob Wayner; Janis Welsh; John J. Welsh; Katie Welsh; Kellie Welsh; Margaret Welsh; Lawrence Williams; Doug Wornom; Bob Yanosey; J. J. Young Jr.; Karl Zimmermann.

ORGANIZATIONS

Hagley Museum and Library; Pentrex Publishing; RPC Publications; Southern Pacific Lines; St. Louis Mercantile Library; Union Pacific Railroad Museum.

First published in 1997 by Motorbooks International Publishers & Wholesalers, 729 Prospect Avenue, P.O. Box 1, Osceola, WI 54020 USA. ©Andover Junction Publications, 1997.

Book design and layout by Mike Schafer/Andover Junction Publications, Andover, New Jersey, and Waukesha, Wisconsin

Library of Congress Cataloging-in-Publication Date Available
ISBN 0-7603-0377-0

Classic American Streamliners/Mike Schafer and Joe Welsh

On the front cover: Chicago, Burlington & Quincy was one of the leading pioneers in the development of the streamliner and by the mid-1950s played a major role in speeding travelers to their destinations aboard *Zephyr*s and other fine trains. On an autumn afternoon in 1963, CB&Q Electro-Motive E-units roar toward the village of Lee, Illinois, with the *Empire Builder* en route to the West Coast. Between Chicago and the Twin Cities, this is really two streamliners in one, as the *Builder* is combined with the *Afternoon Zephyr* as far as St. Paul. *Jim Boyd.*

On the endsheets: Illinois Central's newly streamlined *Land O' Corn* flies over Pierpont Road just west of Rockford, Illinois, in the spring of 1947 during its daily trip between Waterloo, Iowa, and Chicago. *T. V. Maguire, Mike Schafer Collection.*

On the frontispiece: Twilight is settling over northern Illinois as the raucous wail of multi-chime air horns warns of the approach of Burlington's northbound *Afternoon Zephyr* at a lonely country crossing along U.S. 30 near Shabbona in March 1969. The photographer claims the train was cruising at 100 mph—which *Zephyr*s certainly had a penchant for. *Jim Heuer.*

On the title page: One of the greatest streamliner fleets ever launched was that of Southern Pacific, whose stunning *Daylight* trains brought passenger transport to new, sophisticated levels. Initially pulled by powerful, stream-styled 4-8-4 steam locomotives, the red, orange, and black *Daylight*s were considered by historians and public alike to be the epitome of streamlined passenger trains. The *Daylight*s of that genre disappeared by the end of the 1950s, but their inspiration lived on, and in the early 1980s a recreation of the classic, steam-powered *Daylight* of that earlier era emerged, thanks to hundreds of dedicated volunteers and other individuals, the City of Portland, Oregon, and the Southern Pacific Railroad. On its way from Portland to the 1984 World's Fair at New Orleans, the "Louisiana World's Fair Daylight" exhibition train provides a later generation with a glimpse of what it might have been like to watch a *Daylight* thread its way along the Sacramento River in Northern California. *Mike Schafer.*

Foreword photo: Chasing the sun, the combined *City of Denver/City of Portland* accelerates out of Chicago at the start of its transcontinental journey on an evening in 1970. *Mike Schafer.*

On the back cover: A color-tinted postcard from the 1940s shows how streamlining was even applied to railroad buildings, such as the Las Vegas (Nevada) depot, shown with the streamliner City of Los Angeles. *Mike Schafer Collection*

A promotional folder for New York Central's 1938 20th Century Limited. A world-class train, the streamlined Century was one of the ultimate monuments to Art Deco and streamlining. *Joe Welsh Collection*

Santa Fe's Chicago-Los Angeles Chief roils the snow on the outskirts of Chicago on a wintry day in the 1960s. *Jim Boyd*

Dining-car patrons sample the special of the day aboard Rock Island's experimental Talgo streamliner of the mid-1950s, the Jet Rocket. *ACF Collection, St. Louis Mercantile Library*

Printed in Hong Kong through World Print, Ltd.

CONTENTS

FOREWORD

My railroading began in the early 1960s and all too soon involved overseeing the demise of three venerable institutions steeped in the traditions of the "golden age" of rail travel; namely, the passenger departments of the Baltimore & Ohio Railroad and the Chesapeake & Ohio Railway and the Pullman Company. I was a youngster in a business populated with proud, yet dispirited veterans who grasped for signs of hope even as they resigned themselves to a continuing erosion in traffic and a quickening pace of train discontinuance petitions. Streamlined equipment, which had been so enthusiastically touted and received when it entered service on our premium trains beginning in the late 1930s, now filled out our shrinking consists on even the slowest "milk runs."

I struggled to relate all this to a time, just a generation earlier, when railroads dominated the intercity travel market and were embracing new technologies and bold designs of Henry Dreyfuss, Raymond Loewy, Otto Kuhler, Paul Cret, and others in response to threatening competition in the air and on the highways. Then, one evening, while in the diner of B&O's *Capitol Limited* after the dinner hour, I spotted crewmen feasting on a dish not offered on the menu. "Mush" (a cornmeal con-

coction) was the chef's response to my inquisitive look. This exchange led to a discourse with the crew on life and work aboard the cars of the road's passenger fleet and, for me, a blossoming appreciation of the intimate relationship between man (trained and motivated personnel) and machine (safe, reliable, and comfortable equipment) that produces superior service. I came to realize that the contoured lines of stainless steel and colorful carbodies, the designer interiors, and the sleek, swift-moving diesels and shrouded steam locomotives could not, in of themselves, describe the rail travel experience of the streamliner era. What really defined this period, as well as distinguished one railroad from another, was the strength of each road's commitment to service and the attention passengers received from the men and women who worked aboard these glamorous new trains. This is just one of the stories being told in the pages that follow, but it is an important lesson for today as Amtrak tries to restructure the nation's rail passenger service.

—William F. Howes Jr., June 4, 1997
former Director Passenger Services, C&O/B&O
former director, The Pullman Company

INTRODUCTION AND GLOSSARY

The American streamlined passenger train evoked many emotions and left indelible memories for those who had a chance to ride it or witness its passing. As individual as the memories are, it's still possible to say what it all meant in a few important ways.

Economic recovery: The streamliner was created out of necessity. In the teeth of the worst recession the country had ever seen, America's railroads found themselves wondering how to reconstruct their shattered passenger business. Once a secure source of revenue, the passenger trains' market had been slowly eroded during the 1920s as more Americans discovered the freedom of the private automobile. Further, the economic downturn of the late 1920s and early 1930s curtailed folks' ability to travel at all.

These two forces had a dramatic effect. By mid-Depression, the nation's railroads' passenger earnings had been cut in half. The conservative railroad industry at first responded by taking marginal steps, most of which focused on cost control. Some amenities were introduced to attract new passengers, the most notable of which was air conditioning, a technological marvel of its day. But clearly something more dramatic was needed to attract passengers back to the rails.

Enter the streamlined train. Although streamlining had been around for some time in other fields, the 1930s represented the first time that the concept held center stage. Nowhere was this done more dramatically than by the railroad industry. Visionary carriers such as the Burlington, Union Pacific, and Rock Island heavily promoted their early streamliners, taking dead aim at potential customers in an all-out gamble to stop the slide in revenues.

It worked. New shapes, vibrant colors or shining stainless steel which replaced stodgy heavyweight equipment attired in somber Pullman green proved irresistible. Early rider surveys indicated that a healthy number of the patrons flocking to the new trains had shifted their allegiance from other forms of transportation. The public was hooked.

Technological advancement: If the average citizen responded to the new shapes and colors, the industry was swayed by the technology. There were skeptics, and some conservative railroads at first resisted the sirens' call of lightweight construction wary of the safety of the new equipment. Others knew better. Most never would have guessed that those trains constructed of stainless steel would last at least twice as long as a normal railroad car.

Up front, changes in motive power were making even greater strides. Diesels replaced steam engines, in many cases doubling the efficiency of trains as they were able to operate at higher sustained speeds and required significantly less maintenance. As if sensing the threat, steam engines rose to the challenge, reaching the pinnacle of their performance and beauty. Few would argue that Norfolk & Western's sleek J class 4-8-4s or New York Central's streamlined Hudson steam locomotives were not the perfect companions for the streamlined trains they pulled.

What was perhaps most impressive about the new revolution was its scope and speed. This was no incremental improvement but wholesale change. New propulsion, new engineering, new metallurgy, and a whole new art form—industrial design embracing Art Deco—combined to dazzle professional and amateur alike. To the public, it seemed to happen overnight.

Pride: Community pride played a major role in encouraging streamlining. To leaders in larger communities such as Miami, Atlanta, or Pittsburgh, being served by a streamliner was a sign that you had arrived. Not having one was a major rallying point to convince the business community to lobby the local railroad to install a new train.

For small-town America, the pride was evident in the murmurs of approval voiced on the platform by those who'd just seen their *Hiawatha* or *Zephyr* or *Chief* rocket through at 90 miles per hour plus. The railroaders returned this affection with a sense of civic and personal duty. Despite the schedule, for example, *Powhatan Arrow* engineer Alonzo Carter always seemed to have enough time to distribute candy to the flock of children waiting on the platform each Sunday morning at Lynchburg, Virginia.

Diversity: Once upon a time before passenger railroading was nationalized, it was possible to learn about the character of a region by riding its trains. It came to you subtly in the way the station agent announced your train's arrival. It was there in the drawl of a crewmember or the food in the dining car where no two railroads ever seemed to offer the same entree. The streamliners enhanced this tradition, adding local color to the mix. The Monon Route, for example, painted its streamliners in the school colors of home state Indiana's two largest universities.

The streamliner was much more than a new mode of transportation or an advertising gimmick; it was the best that Americans had to offer. It represented the diversity of America in an era when every place was different and proud of it.

AUTHORS' NOTE:

As much as we would like to have featured every streamliner that ever ran, doing so would have nearly doubled the size (and price and production time) of this book. Rather, we've chosen some of the most well-known streamliners as well as a cross section of lesser-knowns to provide an overall look at how streamliners were once very much a way of American life.

GLOSSARY

ACF: American Car & Foundry, a railcar builder once based at St. Charles, Missouri, near St. Louis.

Alco (American Locomotive Company): A principal builder of American steam and diesel-electric locomotives from the late nineteenth century to 1969.

Articulated train: A train whose component cars—sometimes including the power car as well—are permanently joined and which share trucks (i.e., one truck [wheel assembly] supports the ends of adjoining cars), thereby reducing overall train weight and improving ride quality by allowing the train to flow through curves.

Budd: Originally the E. G. Budd Manufacturing Company and later known as the Budd Company, this Philadelphia-based firm was considered a world-class builder of lightweight, streamlined cars.

Buffet-lounge: A lounge that features a counter for serving refreshments and snacks.

Coach: A term often used to describe any passenger car, but technically should refer only to those cars equipped with rows of seats in a common area to serve as "coach class" seating.

Consist (KON-sist): With emphasis on the first syllable, this word becomes a noun that in railroadspeak refers either to the makeup of a train in terms of types of locomotives and cars assigned or the set of assigned cars itself comprising the train.

Double bedroom: A private room for two occupants, with a chair and sofa or two chairs by day and two fold-down beds at night.

Electro-Motive (EMC or EMD): The principal builder of U.S. diesel-electric streamliner power cars and passenger locomotives from 1934 to the 1990s. Initially Electro-Motive Corporation, EMC in 1941 merged with and became the Electro-Motive Division of General Motors.

Head-end cars: Any cars that carry baggage, mail, and/or express. These cars are usually—but not always—carried at the head end of the train between locomotives and passenger-carrying cars.

Heavyweight: A passenger car of standard (heavy) all-steel construction, which became vogue around the time of World War I. Such cars usually had riveted sides, squared-off windows, and a clerestory roof and rode on heavy-duty six-axle trucks.

Observation car: Often confused as being a dome car, the term really refers to a car designed for end-of-train use. As such, end windows permit a full view of the receding countryside. Heavyweight observation cars usually had a "back porch" open-air platform on which travelers could roost. Streamliner observation cars were either round-end or square end. Some observation cars also featured dome sections.

Pullman: A sleeping car staffed and operated by the Pullman Company. The term has achieved almost a generic status by being used in reference to any sleeping car, but this can be misleading, as not all sleeping cars were owned and/or operated by the Pullman Company.

Pullman-Standard (P-S): At one time a subsidiary of the Pullman Company that had merged with Standard Steel Car Company and other builders to form Pullman-Standard. P-S became one of the leading passenger- and freight-car builders in America.

Roomette: A popular sleeping-car accommodation for individual travelers featuring a built-in overstuffed chair that folds down into a bed, covering the toilet.

RPO (Railway Post Office car): A car set up for enroute mail sorting by U.S. Postal Service employees.

Section: Open facing seating for two by day that is transformed at night into upper and lower wide berths made private by heavy curtains.

"Ten-and-six" (10-6) sleeper: After World War II and until the 1990s, the most common configuration for sleeping cars built between World War II and 1956, featuring 10 roomettes for individuals and six double bedrooms for one or two people.

Transcontinental train: By strict definition, a train operating from coast to coast; i.e., from Atlantic to Pacific. However, in the history of U.S. rail passenger transportation, only one regularly scheduled train has met that criteria, Amtrak's *Sunset Limited*. For purposes of this book, "transcontinental" refers to trains operating between Chicago, St. Louis, or New Orleans and the West Coast.

Truck: A rotating, sprung wheel assembly that carries a freight or passenger car. Freight or passenger cars of conventional design each have two trucks.

Vista-Dome: A car of a standard roof height but with a raised, glassed-enclosed, upper-level seating area that permits a nearly 360-degree view. The term "Vista-Dome" is usually associated with dome cars built by the Budd Company, but it has often been generically used to describe any dome car of any manufacturer.

CHAPTER 1

FIRST GENERATION STREAMLINERS

Union Pacific's M-10000-series trains
Chicago, Burlington & Quincy's shovel-nose Zephyrs
Boston & Maine/Maine Central's Flying Yankee
New York, New Haven & Hartford's Comet
Baltimore & Ohio/Alton's Royal Blue and Abraham Lincoln
Chicago, Milwaukee, St. Paul & Pacific's original Hiawatha
New York Central's Mercury

Burlington *Denver Zephyr*, 1936
Optimism and modernism almost burst from from the confines of two dimensions in this calendar art dating from 1942. In it, Chicago, Burlington & Quincy's new 1936 *Denver Zephyr* speeds away from the sparkling skyline of a nighttime Chicago at the start of the streamliner's overnight dash to the foot of the Rocky Mountains. Meanwhile, an archaic steam locomotive appears to pause in its tracks, humbled by the new king of the rails. *Collection of Mike Schafer*

ith the Roaring Twenties but a fragrant memory of self indulgence, Americans faced an altogether different situation as the dusty pall of the 1930s unfolded. The Depression hung heavy over the land, and the nation's economy had slowed to a murmur. The overall mood, however, was one of resolution. People and industries were looking for ways to pull themselves out of the mire; something that would jump-start national pride and the economy. In the middle 1930s, that began to happen. Streamlining was a part of the movement.

The Century of Progress exposition held in Chicago in 1933-34 bolstered the optimism of America and helped popularize the emerging movement known as streamlining, of which Art Deco style was an integral part. Streamlined shapes were simple, rounded, smooth, and friendly. Suddenly, everything was getting streamlined: toasters, automobiles, buildings, vacuum cleaners, and, of course, passenger trains. And, in fact, America's first two internal-combustion-powered lightweight, streamlined trains were stars at the Century of Progress. Together, Union Pacific's M-10000 streamliner and Chicago, Burlington & Quincy's little stainless-steel *Zephyr* 9900 would revolutionize rail passenger travel, and a new era in transportation was off and running.

The Very First

The streamliner era of American railroading was in some ways a paradox: the advent of streamliners was the direct result of the decline of passenger train travel in general. Although popular belief holds that the U.S. passenger train began its fall from grace when the first commercial jet airliner flew off into the friendly skies in 1958, that event in reality only heralded a resumption of an alarming decline that had begun some thirty years earlier.

UP M-10000 brochure
Above, the cover of Union Pacific's promotional brochure for its new streamliner capsulized the evolution of over-land travel, from conestoga wagon to the latest wonder of the ages—the M-10000. The inside of the brochure (facing page) featured a floor plan of the entire train and revealed that "exhaustive tests" helped the railroad choose a color scheme for the new train. *Collection of Don Sarno.*

M-10000 on tour
(Facing page) Before entering regularly scheduled public service, UP's new speedster barnstormed from coast to coast, stopping at selected cities for exhibition. Outside the train shed of Chicago & North Western's lakefront depot at Milwaukee in the spring of 1934, residents of Wisconsin's largest city mill about to check out what was in a sense a visitor from another world. *Courtesy Union Pacific Museum.*

Although U.S. rail travel peaked during the 1920s, the almost overnight proliferation of privately owned automobiles riding on a mushrooming network of government-funded highways and byways spelled trouble for the passenger train. Arguably the ultimate virtue of the auto—its flexibility—would prove stiff competition for the passenger train, which through the 1920s remained much a stalwart operation. Nearly all passenger trains of the period were coal-fired and steam-powered—not a particularly tidy way to travel, especially in warm weather when "cooling," such as it was, was usually accomplished by opening windows. Travel in something more comfortable than the ubiquitous day coach—such as in a parlor car or a sleeping car—was, due to its high price, usually reserved for the elite.

True, passenger trains—lots of them—served just about every nook and cranny of U.S. soil in the late 1920s and at virtually all hours of the day. Still, it wasn't enough to lure Americans away from their new and increasingly affordable Fords and Chevys, which were relatively clean, quiet, and always ready to go when you were and take you exactly to where you wanted to be.

Railroads became concerned. Until this time, they had been blessed with a largely captive market. There were few fast, reliable alternatives to rail travel. Commercial air travel was an iffy proposition, subject to the whims of Mother Nature, and bus or jitney transport was only as good as the road system and not particularly fast.

Complicating matters, not only for railroads but all transportation companies, was the stock market crash of 1929 and the onset of the Depression, during which Americans became homebound on a nationwide scale. By 1934, the railroads' passenger earnings had been been cut in half. The industry needed a new "hook" to attract passengers back to the rails.

Credit for launching such a reversal of fortunes goes to two railroads—Union Pacific and Chicago, Burlington & Quincy—and a cadre of manufacturers: Pullman-Standard (P-S), Electro-Motive Corporation (EMC), Winton Engine Company, and the Edward G. Budd Manufacturing Company. Pullman-Standard, the manufacturing arm of the Pullman Company which for nearly a century operated most sleeping cars in America, was already an established builder of freight and passenger cars; EMC and Winton, both subsidiaries of General Motors, were builders of railroad motorcars and internal-combustion engines respectively; Budd produced automotive parts and specialized in carbody construction.

UNION PACIFIC'S M-10000

Burlington and UP did not invent the streamliner concept per se. Rather, UP and Burlington ushered the streamlined concept into adulthood. Streamlined railroad passenger equipment had made isolated appearances since the start of the twentieth century, but it was really UP and Burlington which refined the concept by combining lightweight construction, futuristic styling, internal-combustion power, and high-speed capabilities.

With this formula, UP was the first to introduce a true streamliner, which it ordered early in 1933 and took delivery of on February 25, 1934. Looking like a creature out of a Jules Verne novel with a face that only a mother could love, the new lightweight featured an aluminum carbody built by P-S and was powered by a Winton spark-ignition gas engine. UP was leery of diesel-engine designs of the time, even though their refinement was close to making them viable for locomotive power, and thus opted for a distillate engine to ensure that it would be first to unveil a streamliner.

Designated as the M-10000, the little 204-foot-plus caterpillar-like train comprised three "articulated" sections; that is, the component cars were semi-permanently coupled, sharing a common truck at the joints. Aside from the high, turreted crew cab and the power plant below, the power car also contained a Railway Post Office and a baggage compartment. The second

car had seating for 60, and the third car featured seats for 56 and a buffet-kitchen nestled in the car's bulbous, windowless posterior.

The train's "fishbelly" form (sides slightly bowed out)—tested with a wooden model in a wind tunnel at the University of Michigan—added strength, and the aluminum, of course, provided light weight. It stood at about 12 feet high from the railhead, some three feet shorter than standard rolling stock. At 124 tons, the three-car streamliner weighed not much more than a single heavyweight Pullman sleeping car. The modest 600-hp engine could cruise the train at 110 mph. Passengers rode in air-conditioned comfort in a modern interior featuring fluorescent lighting.

The train's riveted exterior was clad in what the railroad termed as "canary yellow" and "golden brown," the yellow having been chosen for safety reasons. (Even in the 1930s, autos were wanton to wander into the paths

of approaching trains.) This was apparently the first application of what became known as "Armour yellow" to Union Pacific equipment—a color which serves UP to this day. Enhancing the safety aspect, the power car featured a siren, electric gong, and a ten-inch-wide vertical beam of light that shot straight up into the night sky.

Shortly after delivery, the M-10000 embarked on a phenomenally successful tour of the U.S., drawing huge numbers of Depression-weary Americans—including President Franklin Delano Roosevelt—down to trackside for a glimpse at the speedster that rode a wave of new optimism. (Wary of the train's reliability, the Secret Service advised FDR against riding an exhibition trip). Initially, UP had intended to use the M-10000 as a test train, planning to operated it at sustained speeds of 100 mph on a remarkably ambitious Chicago-West Coast schedule of about 24 hours. Billed simply as *The Streamliner* when it finally entered regular service on January 31, 1935, its duties were considerably more modest: it made two daily round trips, one between Kansas City and Salina, Kansas, 187 miles, and one between Kansas City and Topeka, Kansas, 68 miles. Generally, its schedule called for an average speed of under a mile a minute, including stops. The train was an instant hit with the pubic, and it made Union Pacific happy as well, for it produced handsome revenues at considerably reduced cost compared to the operation of a regular steam train.

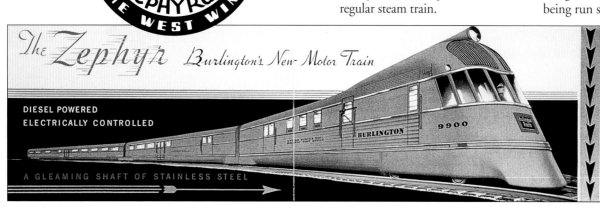

Budd had been impressed by the reliability and economy of stationary diesel engines he had first seen in active service during the late1920s and felt they could be applied to locomotion. He collaborated with Winton on the idea and Winton produced a diesel engine which could fit within the confines of a locomotive carbody—and the carbody in this instance would be the *Zephyr*, which was to be constructed by the Budd Company (no relation to Ralph Budd) near Philadelphia.

Like Winton, Budd itself had been pioneering new ground in the railroad field, experimenting with stainless-steel railcar construction. Hailed as a miracle metal, stainless steel was incredibly strong, lightweight, attractive, and virtually corrosion free. However, some of these properties made stainless steel difficult to fabricate, short of loading it up with rivets and bolts; the metal could not be welded by conventional methods. The answer came in the form of a process developed and patented by Budd called "shotwelding," which utilized a jolt of high-amp electric current to fuse stainless-steel components, creating a joint that was stronger than the stainless-steel itself.

Despite its initial high cost, stainless steel essentially has no known life expectancy other than "long," thus the Burlington expected that use of stainless steel and its associated costs would be offset by lower maintenance and a carbody's increased longevity. Burlington's assessment was right on the mark. Sixty years later in the 1990s, new Amtrak passenger cars were still being built using Shotwelded stainless-steel components—and were being run shoulder to shoulder with Budd stainless-steel cars built 40 years earlier.

On June 17, 1933, the Burlington placed an order with Budd for a three-car stainless-steel streamliner to be powered by a 660-hp Winton diesel engine. What emerged nine months and 21 days later on April 7, 1934 was a slope-browed, shovel-nosed silverly slip of of fluted stainless steel called the *Burlington Zephyr*.

The 197-foot-long articulated train featured a power car that included a Railway Post Office and mail-storage compartment, a baggage-coach which included a boiler room (for the train's heating system), and a coach-parlor observation car. Total seating capacity was 72, 44 less than the M-10000. Nonetheless, the *Zephyr* was 9 feet, 8 1/2 inches wide, 8 1/2 inches wider than the M-10000.

On April 9, the *Zephyr* made its first test run (it took two days to finally get the Winton engine to fire up) over the Reading Company, reaching a top speed of 104

CB&Q'S *ZEPHYR* 9900

Though Burlington's renowned *Zephyr* 9900 arrived on the scene about a month and a half after UP's M-10000, it was still first rate in many respects. For one thing, it was America's first diesel-powered streamliner; for another, it popularized the use of stainless steel in carbody construction.

In essence, the *Zephyr* was the brainchild of Ralph Budd, Burlington's visionary president since 1932.

Zephyr brochure, 1934
(Facing page) "A gleaming shaft of stainless steel" proclaimed one of several promotional pieces put out by Chicago, Burlington & Quincy for its new chariot on rails. This brochure apparently pre-dated the train's release from Budd, as it shows the train with traditional Roman-style lettering rather than the Art Deco gothic style with which it was delivered. The *Zephyr* name came from Burlington's president, Ralph Budd, who at the time of the train's developmental stages in 1933 had been reading Chaucer's CANTERBURY TALES which featured Zephyrus, the God of the West Wind. The name was a natural, and the railroad developed the theming to transcend all of its future streamlining endeavors. *Brochure, Don Sarno Collection.*

Zephyr 9900
(Left and above) The new *Zephyr*, which carried the number 9900, introduced the "shovel nose" design on the power car which would be a signature on several of the train's progeny. The large, red Mars safety light, whose beam moved in a figure-8 pattern, was added above the train's regular headlight during the 1940s. Upper right: The train was truly an art form from head to tail, and its exterior design was largely the work of Albert Dean, an aeronautical engineer who worked for the Edward G. Budd Manufacturing Co. Originally, the train was named *Burlington-Zephyr*, but late in 1935 it was renamed *Pioneer Zephyr* to differentiate it from other *Zephyr*s that were being added to the fleet. The observation lounge area at the train's end reveals the smart interior design work of John Harbeson, who worked for a Philadelphia architectural firm run by Paul Cret. *Three photos, John H. Kuehl.*

13

Read the book; see the picture

(Below) While on its 1934 exhibition tour, *Zephyr* 9900 starred in a n RKO-Radio Pictures movie entitled *"Silver Streak,"* which Whitman Publishing Company of Racine, Wisconsin, published in book form as part of its children's The Big Little Book series. *Mike Schafer Collection.*

Pioneer Zephyr at four

(Bottom) Operating as the *Pioneer Zephyr* between Kansas City and Lincoln, the 9900—its consist expanded with an additional 40-seat coach added in June 1935—coasts off the Missouri River bridge and into Omaha, Nebraska, on May 5, 1938. *Collection of William A. Raia.*

mph. On April 18, the train was officially christened at Philadelphia's Broad Street Station as it was unveiled to press and public. (The *Zephyr* moniker, which means "west wind"—Zephyrus being the mythical Greek god of the West Wind—had actually been chosen late in 1933; the new equipment carried the number 9900, so it was sometimes also referred to as *Zephyr* 9900.) On April 19, the *Zephyr* embarked on a remarkable nationwide exhibition stint that would last into the fall season.

On May 10, the *Zephyr* arrived on home rails in Chicago by way of Philadelphia, Washington, D.C., Buffalo, Detroit, Cleveland, Pittsburgh, Cincinnati, and Louisville, among many other stops. From Chicago, it was exhibited at points on the Burlington all the way to Denver where it would be poised for its finest day in history. At 5:05 A.M. on May 26, a green flag which had commenced numerous Indianapolis Speedway races signaled the start the the *Zephyr*'s nonstop dawn-to-dusk run between Denver and Chicago. At 7:10 P.M. that same evening, 1,015.4 miles farther east and having averaged almost 78 mph, the *Zephyr* reached downtown Chicago and at 8:09 P.M. rolled right onto the stage of Edward Hungerford's "Wings of a Century" pageant under way at the Century of Progress World's Fair Exposition

on Chicago's lakefront. The crowds went wild.

For most of the rest of the year, the *Zephyr* toured the West and Texas, partaking in the filming of the RKO movie "Silver Streak" during September. By the time it entered regularly scheduled service in November, it had been toured by more than 2 million people, had traveled 30,437 miles, and had exhibited at 222 cities.

From the start, it had been Burlington's intention to use the *Zephyr* on relatively short passenger runs where steam-powered trains were experiencing losses due to low patronage and high operational costs—but where service had to be continued account of public necessity. One of these was the 250-mile Lincoln-Omaha-Kansas City route on which the *Zephyr* entered daily service November 11, 1934, becoming America's first regularly scheduled, diesel-powered, stainless-steel streamliner.

Burlington had high hopes for the little speedster: expecting the *Zephyr* to reduce operating losses on whatever run it was assigned at least to break even. Despite its initial investment being twice that of a heavyweight three-car train powered by a steam locomotive, the *Zephyr* was half as costly to operate, and because of its comfort and appeal, it immediately began to attract new patronage. Further, it turned out that its high speed and lower maintenance requirements enabled it to do the work of *two* heavyweight, steam-powered trains. As a result—and to Burlington's aston-

For New England, a "Yankee Zephyr"

Although Burlington held the spotlight as the first, then another, and then still more *Zephyr*s came on line from Electro-Motive/Budd, there were two other players peripheral to the early *Zephyr* story, Boston & Maine and Maine Central. Following the 1934 fanfare of *Zephyr* 9900 and before Burlington took delivery of *Zephyr* sets 9901 and 9902 in April 1935, New England allies B&M/MEC in February 1935 took delivery—from Budd and EMC—of trainset 6000. From an exterior standpoint, it was nearly identical to CB&Q's 9901 and 9902 that would, within weeks, be delivered for *Twin Zephyr* service. On the inside it differed in featuring a baggage-buffet, a full coach, and a coach-observation; the 9901 and 9902 would have a baggage-buffet, diner, and coach-observation.

The B&M/MEC train did not adopt the *Zephyr* title, however, as that name originated with Burlington. In Boston (Massachusetts)-Bangor (Maine) service, this train became known as the *Flying Yankee* and was New England's first true streamliner, beating New Haven's *Comet* by several months. The train reduced Boston-Bangor travel time by 65 minutes to just under 4½ hours. No surprise, the *Yankee* was an overnight sensation, attracting nearly 50 percent new patronage and earning a tidy profit.

It was pulled from Boston-Bangor service account of not being able to handle wartime crowds and placed in service between Boston and Littleton, New Hampshire, via MEC and B&M lines. Eventually, ownership of the little train was transferred entirely to B&M, and during the ensuing years it operated on various B&M routes and under other names including *Cheshire* and *Minute Man*. The train was retired in 1957 and today is on display as the *Flying Yankee* near Crawford Notch in New Hampshire's White Mountains playground.

B&M's *Flying Yankee* is shown in its twilight years at Troy, New York, on June 20, 1953, running as the Boston-Troy *Minute Man*. *Railroad Avenue Enterprises.*

ishment—the train showed a profit. So successful was the *Zephyr* that in June 1935 a dinette-coach was added to its consist, upping train seating to 112.

The impact this little train would have on U.S. rail transportation was remarkable. Consider this: In 1997, most U.S. intercity rail passenger routes operated by Amtrak were being served by diesel-powered passenger trains built of stainless steel, and two of them still carried the *Zephyr* name!

Zephyr and M-10000 progeny

The astonishing success of the two new streamliners almost immediately spawned new trains for both their owners. In fact, before the M-10000 had even been completed, confident UP had already ordered, in June 1933, a second streamliner from EMC/P-S. Deliv-ered in October 1934, the M-10001 was a lengthened version of the M-10000, featuring a diesel power car pulling five aluminum-alloy passenger cars: baggage-dormitory, three sleeping cars, and a coach-buffet. The homely turret cab, grille-nose design prevailed.

Not to be outdone by Burlington's famed dawn-to-dusk nonstop *Zephyr* run, UP almost immediately sent its M-100001 on a 56-hour, 55-minute Los Angeles-Chicago-New York test run; the L.A.-Chicago portion was done in a record-breaking 38 hours and 50 minutes. Chicago & North Western handled the train between Omaha and Chicago while New York Central forwarded it to Manhattan's Grand Central Terminal. With the addition of a diner-lounge and a new 1,200-hp diesel engine which had replaced the original 900-hp power plant, the M-10001 entered Chicago-Portland (Oregon) service as the *City of Portland* on May 5, 1935, operating

Original *City of Portland*

Looming like a spectre out of the fog, the M-10001 trainset treads past onlookers at Breman Avenue in St. Louis, Missouri, on November 17, 1934, during a test run. One car appears to be missing during this run; the original *City of Portland* was a seven-car train when it later entered regular service. The M-10001 power car originally contained a 900-hp power plant which was found to be inadequate for hauling a seven-car train at high speeds, so the power car was returned to Electro-Motive for modification. It re-emerged with a 1200-hp power plant and a modified carbody and paint scheme. It entered regular service in the spring of 1935. *Collection of J. M. Gruber.*

Streamliners under construction

A peek inside the Electro-Motive plant at LaGrange, Illinois, on May 10, 1936, reveals an M-series locomotive set (probably the M-10004), both cab unit and (behind it) booster, under construction for UP, breaking up the monotony of an army of diesel switchers also being built. *EMD.*

jointly with C&NW, whose tracks the *City* used east of Omaha. It made ten "sailings" (as non-daily streamliner schedules were then marketed) per month, five each from Chicago and Portland on pre-announced dates. The *City of Portland* became the first transcontinental streamliner and the first to offer sleeper and full dining-car service. Public response was overwhelming, and each trip was often sold out well in advance.

There was now no question that more was better, and early in May 1936 UP took delivery of its M-10002 streamliner. The M-10002, which entered 39-hour, 45-minute Chicago-Los Angeles service on May 15 as the *City of Los Angeles*, carried on the turret-cab styling and tapered car sides found in the M-10000 and M-10001, but featured a 900-hp booster power unit in addition to its 1200-hp cab power car. The train's nine cars (a tenth car came later) were articulated only in pairs, thus marking a departure from earlier streamliners, *Zephyr* 9900 included, whose trainsets were in essence a single entity—that being a significant drawback. If a problem developed on even just one car, the whole train had to be pulled from service.

The *City of Los Angeles* featured a baggage-mail car, baggage-dormitory-kitchen car, diner-lounge, five sleepers, a coach, and a coach-buffet car. By the time this train entered service, the M-10000 had been christened as the *City of Salina* to help differentiate it from the growing fleet of "City" trains.

The M-10004 nine-car trainset came next, ahead of the M-10003, and entered service on June 14, 1936, as the *City of San Francisco*, making five round trips per month between Chicago and Oakland, California; the one-way trip was scheduled at 39 hours and 45 minutes. UP jointly operated its *City of San Francisco* with C&NW and, between Ogden, Utah, and Oakland, the Southern Pacific. The M-10004 power set featured a styling of radically new design, appearing somewhat like a automobile front, with a raised cab that was set back high above a grilled nose. This styling, complete with generous applications of chrome trim, was retained for all subsequent M-series streamliner locomotive sets.

Only four days after *City of San Francisco* service began, trainsets M-10005 and M-10006—both with two power cars and ten passenger cars—were introduced as the *City of Denver*; at the same time, UP took delivery of a spare motive-power set, the M-10003. The M-10003 served as back-up power. Two trainsets allowed daily service between Chicago and Denver via C&NW-UP with enroute stops at Cedar Rapids, Iowa, Omaha and Grand Island, Nebraska, Sterling, Colorado, and other points. The *City of Denver* was the fastest of the new *City* trains, averaging 66 mph.

Through all the UP streamliner inaugurals, Burling-ton was hardly idle. During *Zephyr* 9900's "test-and-tour" period following its May 1934 delivery to CB&Q, one of its test trips included a Chicago-Twin Cities run on July 30 of that year. *Zephyr* 9900 did the 431 miles between Chicago and St. Paul in just over six hours—almost twice as fast as regularly schedule steam trains on the route! Five days after the test trip, Burling-ton ordered more *Zephyr*s from Budd and EMC.

In March and April 1935, Burlington became the proud owner of two more *Zephyr*s, Nos. 9901 and 9902. Like their 9900 prototype, kin 9901 and 9902 were three-car articulated trains, but with a slightly different interior arrangement: power-baggage car, diner coach, and observation coach. Each train seated 88.

Sets 9901 and 9902 went to work as the new *Twin Zephyr*s on April 21, 1935, between Chicago and Minneapolis/St. Paul, but not without considerable—and unique—fanfare. The railroad invited 44 sets of identical twins to ride a special run of the 9901 set on April 14 from Chicago to Aurora, Illinois, 38 miles. At Aurora, the 9901 was turned and met up with set 9902. All the twins were then split up, with each half riding each train back to Chicago—with both trains running side by side all the way back to Union Station! The following day, both trains were christened (by champagne bottle-wielding twin sisters, of course) as the *Twin Zephyr*s and departed Chicago side-by-side for the Twin Cities. Regular service began on April 21, initially with each set doing a one-way trip each day. Demand out-

Having a great time; wish you were here
Colorized postcards were all the rage when streamliner fever hit. Color was added to a black & white publicity photo to bring this scene of the M-10006 *City of Denver* to life. Later M-series power cars such as this illustrate how automotive stylists influenced train design. *Joe Welsh Collection.*

1110—Union Pacific Streamline Train. Overnight Service to the Rockies from the Mississippi

6A480

Mark Twain Zephyr
Delivered in 1935, *Zephyr* 9903's original assignment was as the *Mark Twain Zephyr* running between St. Louis and Burlington, Iowa. Reflecting that service, its baggage-mail power car was named *Injun Joe*; its baggage car, *Becky Thatcher*; its dinette-coach, *Huckleberry Finn*; and its coach observation car, of course, *Tom Sawyer*. The view at left at Macon, Missouri, in July 1957 shows the train operating not as the *Mark Twain Zephyr* but as the westbound St. Joseph (Missouri) connection to the new *Kansas City Zephyr*. *Sandy Goodrick*.

General Pershing Zephyr
The last shovelnose to be built was the 9908–*Silver Charger*. Technically it was not a train per se but a powered passenger car and therefore considered more of a Budd product than an EMC locomotive—the latter being the case for the shovelnose power units built for the *Denver Zephyr*. Initially, it powered the non-articulated three-car (two coaches and a diner-parlor observation car; one of the coaches is missing in this view) *General Pershing Zephyr*, a joint Alton-CB&Q operation between St. Louis and Kansas City. The 9908 was the last shovelnose to operate in regular service, serving as a locomotive for branchline freight locals in the 1960s. Today, *Silver Charger* resides at the St. Louis Museum of Transport. *William A. Raia Collection*

stripped this assignment however, and in June each set began making one round trip each day, thereby providing double-daily Chicago-Twin Cities service as the *Morning Zephyr* and *Afternoon Zephyr*.

In October 1935 a fourth *Zephyr* train joined the fleet, No. 9903, a four-car train. In keeping with Burlington's original intention of using little streamliners to replace heavyweight trains on short-distance runs, the 9903 went to work as the *Mark Twain Zephyr* on the 221-mile St. Louis-Burlington (Iowa) route.

Meanwhile, back on the *Twin Zephyr* route, demand continued to burgeon, prompting Burlington to order two new *Twin Zephyr* trainsets, Nos. 9904 and 9905. With only two passenger-carrying cars in each set, the original *Twin Zephyrs* were simply too small. The new *Twin Zephyrs* were each six-car trains—baggage-lounge, two coaches, a full dining car, a parlor car, and a parlor-observation car—pulled by an 1800-hp. shovelnose power car. The locomotive and cars of the "male" set (9905) carried names of Greek gods: *Zephyrus, Apollo, Neptune, Mars, Vulcan, Mercury,* and *Jupiter*. The "female" set (9904) was thus named for goddesses: *Pegasus, Venus, Vesta, Minerva, Ceres, Diana,* and *Juno*. These trains entered service on December 18, 1936, bumping the original *Twin Zephyrs* to less-demanding routes. The 9901 became the *Sam Houston Zephyr* between Fort Worth and Houston, Texas, while the 9902 became the *Ozark State Zephyr* on the Kansas City-St. Louis route.

Undoubtedly, the fact that UP was now dabbling in long-distance streamliner service did not go unnoticed by Burlington. After all, if the streamliner concept worked so well on short- or medium-distance runs, there was little reason to believe it couldn't be made to work on runs of a thousand miles or more. For Burlington, its premier route—Chicago-Omaha-Lincoln-Denver—would be an obvious stage for the next level of *Zephyr* service.

Such came in the form of two more *Zephyr* sets, Nos. 9906 and 9907—the renown *Denver Zephyrs*. Two EMC power/booster locomotives generated 3000 hp. to power two ten-car stainless-steel trains built by Budd (see the artist's rendition of this train appearing at the start of this chapter). The trains themselves represented a slight departure from the norm: rather than the whole train being articulated and therefore an entity, only selected car pairs were articulated. Now consist length could more easily be adjusted to meet travel demand. As delivered, each *DZ* included a baggage-mail car, baggage-dormitory-lounge, two coaches, diner, four sleepers, and a parlor-observation car. These were the first Burlington *Zephyrs* to have locomotives and cars named with a "Silver" prefix; e.g., *Silver King, Silver Lake,* etc. Thus started a Burlington tradition that would last to the road's final *Zephyr* equipment delivery in 1956.

Before they even entered service, power car set 9906A&B and its train broke *Zephyr* 9900's dawn-to-dusk Denver-Chicago run, when on October 23, 1936, it made the 1,017-mile run west from Chicago in 12 hours and 12 minutes at an average speed of more than 83 mph, its top speed peaking at 116 mph in eastern Colorado. The two trains went into regular Chicago-Denver service on Nov. 8, 1936.

One more shovelnose *Zephyr* would join Burlington's ranks as the CB&Q and other railroads took a decidedly new approach to streamliner equipment. In 1939, power-baggage car 9908–*Silver Charger,* coaches *Silver Leaf* and *Silver Eagle,* and diner-observation car *Silver Star* were delivered from Budd. Unlike previous *Zephyr* trains, no articulation was involved, thereby providing maximum flexibility and ease of maintenance. If there was a problem with any one car including the power car,

it could easily be substituted with a standard car or locomotive, steam or diesel. The 9908 and its cars entered St. Louis-Kansas City service—operated jointly with the Alton Railroad—as the *General Pershing Zephyr*.

NEW HAVEN'S *COMET*

More than any other railroad, Burlington and UP advanced the streamliner concept from infancy into adulthood—and they did it fast and in a big way. By the end of 1936—only two years after *Zephyr* 9900 and the M-10000 appeared—the two roads were operating more streamliners to more points than any other company.

Not that other lines weren't interested in boarding the streamliner bandwagon. Indeed, the *Zephyrs* and the *City* trains weren't the only streamliner creatures roaming U.S. rails. UP and Burlington's efforts influenced other carriers to begin experimentation. One of these was the fabled New York, New Haven & Hartford Railroad.

Ironically, streamlining got its start on the New Haven partly as the result of a zeppelin crash. In 1933, the wreck of the U.S. Navy's *Akron* signaled the decline in popularity of the airship. This turn of events forced the Goodyear-Zeppelin Corporation, an American-German joint venture founded in 1923, to seek other markets. In 1934, with the Federal Government's Public Work's Administration assisting in the financing, the New Haven purchased its first lightweight streamliner

New Haven *Comet*
A rare color view of Goodyear-Zeppelin's one and only venture into streamlined trains shows New Haven's *Comet* in local service early in the 1950s. It's one-of-a-kind nature notwithstanding, the train was reasonably successful mechanically speaking, but suffered the same problems inherent in fixed-consist, articulated trains—a lack of flexibility, which is how it got bumped from its original assignment, Providence-Boston, during World War II. *Leon Onofri.*

the route. Inside, 160 passengers could be accommodated in an environment which featured air conditioning and indirect lighting.

From an engineering standpoint, the experimental train was largely viewed as a success, chalking up nearly a 90 percent reliability ratio. However, New Haven's bankruptcy in 1935 precluded the addition of any siblings.

B&O AND ALTON—THE *ROYAL BLUE* AND THE *ABRAHAM LINCOLN*

In 1934, a government assisted project funded the construction of two non-articulated lightweight streamliners by the American Car & Foundry of St. Louis. One trainset, built of Cor-Ten steel and dubbed the *Abraham Lincoln*, was assigned to Chicago-St. Louis service on Baltimore & Ohio subsidiary Alton Railroad in 1935. The second, an aluminum alloy train named the *Royal Blue*, was placed in service over the B&O and the Central Railroad of New Jersey between Jersey City, New Jersey and Washington, D.C., in June 1935. Both rivet-clad trainsets were nearly identical save for the type of metal used in construction.

Pulled at first by unique Hudson Class 4-6-4 steam engine *Lord Baltimore*, the *Royal Blue* was significant not just because it was the first true streamliner to operate within what is today known as the Northeast Corridor (Boston-New-York-Philadelphia-Washington-Richmond), but also because it was powered by the first self-contained passenger diesel locomotive in the U.S., Electro-Motive-built box-cab No. 50, which supplemented the *Lord Baltimore* shortly after the train's introduction. Other contemporary diesel application involved power cars integral with trainsets, whereas the 50 could be coupled to and power any conventional train.

The *Royal Blue* and *Abraham Lincoln* each included a baggage mail car, three coaches, a lunch counter-diner, two parlor cars, and a parlor-lounge observation. As would be expected, the trains and their locomotives were cloaked in Royal Blue with gold striping. Height-

B&O-Alton *Abraham Lincoln*
The original *Abraham Lincoln* streamliner is northbound at the Alton Railroad's Bloomington, Illinois, depot circa late 1930s. Motive power on this rainy day is B&O No. 50, an 1800-hp box-cab diesel-electric locomotive built by Electro-Motive in 1935. Its quasi-streamlined sloped face was added after delivery when it was sent west to work the *Abe Lincoln* on B&O-controlled Alton. *Mike Schafer Collection.*

Abraham Lincoln folder
B&O/Alton issued an informative brochure about the new *Abraham Lincoln* which, unfolded, showed interior views and a floor plan. *Don Sarno Collection.*

from the former airship manufacturer.

The Goodyear-Zeppelin *Comet* was a lightweight, low-slung, three-car articulated speedster. The bi-directional train featured two porpoise-nosed power cars sandwiching a non-powered coach. The three-car train rode on only a total of four trucks, its carbodies clearing the rails by a mere 10 inches. Power was provided by two 400-hp Westinghouse diesel engines, one in each power car. The total weight of the three-car train was an amazingly low 126 tons. With its center of gravity 25 inches lower than a standard train, the speedster was well suited for New Haven's curvaceous main line.

Introduced in Providence-Boston service in June 1935, the little blue-and-aluminum streamliner completed five round trips daily, offering a 45-minute one-way carding while hitting speeds of up to 95 mph on

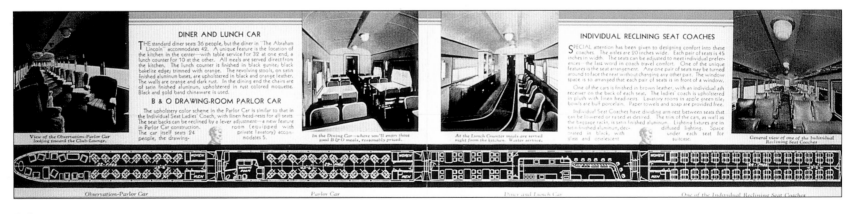

wise, the cars were slightly shorter than standard-size passenger cars of the period, and they featured full-width diaphragms versus the more-common door-width style. Full-width sprung diaphragms enhanced streamlining by camouflaging the break between cars.

Unimpressed with the general ride quality and performance, B&O removed the train from the Jersey City-Washington route in 1937, sending it to the Alton to join its sister *Abraham Lincoln* and renaming it—yes—*Ann Rutledge* (Abe's first true love, for readers who have forgotten their American history). The trains' shortcomings must not have been as critical to Alton and successor Gulf, Mobile & Ohio, for at least one of the trainsets remained in use well into the 1960s.

THE GM&N *REBELS*

For a little railroad, the 734-mile Gulf, Mobile & Northern—which connected Jackson, Tennessee, with Mobile, Alabama, Jackson, Mississippi, and New Orleans, Louisiana—was ahead of its time. The railroad began experimenting with internal-combustion power as early as 1924. By the end of 1935, all of the railroad's passenger services were operated by internal-combustion power. Although most of these were "doodlebug" (motorcar) trains, two trainsets delivered in the summer of 1935 were true streamliners.

In fact, the *Rebels* were billed as the South's first streamliners. The red-and-silver trains, styled by notable industrial designer Otto Kuhler, had been built by American Car & Foundry. The *Rebels* were constructed of high-strength, lightweight Cor-Ten steel. As built, each train had a baggage-power car with a prime mover supplied by American Locomotive Company (Alco) and two cars. Herein was another first for GM&N: Unlike their contemporaries, save for B&O's *Royal Blue* and *Abraham Lincoln*, the *Rebels* were not articulated, avoiding a feature of early streamliners that eventually would backfire. Rather, each train was comprised of separate cars—a buffet-coach and a sleeper observation-lounge. An extra coach was built later on.

The trains entered service on July 29, 1935, between Jackson (Tennessee) and New Orleans on an overnight schedule, hence the sleeping accommodations. The extra coach bolstered each train south of Jackson (Mississippi) where ridership was heaviest. The trains were very well received, some 40 percent of the passengers having been enticed from their autos. The success warranted the construction of a third trainset of four cars in 1938. This set ran between Mobile and Union, Mississippi, where connection was made with the original *Rebels*. The Mobile section did not do well and was discontinued in 1941 by Gulf, Mobile & Ohio, GM&N's successor. The now-surplus *Rebel* set was used to extend *Rebel* service north to St. Louis.

The *Rebels* were quite stylish and featured a train hostess—another first to the credit of GM&N. Despite their luxurious appointments, the railroad charged the same per-mile fare to ride the *Rebels* as its other trains, and the little streamliners became a welcome fixture in the Deep South.

Gulf, Mobile & Northern *Rebel*
GM&N's *Rebel* streamliners bore a family resemblance to other railroads' streamliners of the mid-1930s (shovel nose, smooth lines) but the *Rebels* had one important difference: they were non-articulated trains. GM&N took advantage of such flexibility factors, having one *Rebel* operating out of Mobile transfer a coach-sleeping car at Union, Mississippi, to a *Rebel* set operating out of New Orleans to Jackson, Tennessee. Following the GM&N-Mobile & Ohio merger of 1940, the new Gulf, Mobile & Ohio extended *Rebel* service to St. Louis. The *Rebel* set shown at left is at Murphysboro, Illinois, on the St. Louis end of the railroad on April 7, 1945. By this time, the train's crimson stripe had faded to pastel. *C. V. Simon, Monty Powell Collection.*

THE *GREEN DIAMOND*

Another early entry in the great race to acquire streamliners was Illinois Central, a respected Midwest carrier stretching from Chicago to the Gulf and to Iowa. In March 1936 (just before UP's M-10002 *City of Los Angeles* was delivered), IC became the recipient of a five-car streamliner from Pullman-Standard, with power plant by Electro-Motive. In deference to IC's time-honored diamond logo and the fact that the railroad's star train on the Chicago-Springfield-St. Louis line was the *Diamond Special*, the new arrival—also slated for Chicago-St. Louis service—was christened the *Green Diamond*.

The train, which was indeed green (in two tones), bore a striking resemblance to the early UP *City* trains, possibly because IC at the time was controlled by UP. Only slightly less homely than the early M-10000-series UP streamliners, the *Green Diamond* featured a raised crew cab which sat high above an ominous grilled nose. The four cars that trailed the 1200-hp power car included a baggage-express-RPO, a coach, coach-dinette, and a dinette-kitchen-observation parlor car. The train seated 100 in coach seats and 22 in first class (parlor). Unlike the UP trains, the *Green Diamond* was built of Cor-Ten steel. IC's claim was that its *Green Diamond* was the first *standard-size* diesel-powered streamliner.

During April and May 1936, the train did a 7,000-plus-mile tour of the Midwest and South Central states on and off the IC, including such cities as Milwaukee, Wisconsin; San Antonio, Texas; Detroit; and Oklahoma City, Oklahoma, as well as most important on-line IC

The *Green Diamond*

What would be a long-term love affair with streamliners for Illinois Central began with the *Green Diamond* of 1936, whose floor plan (below) was featured in its inaugural brochure. The train is shown at Springfield, Illinois, in 1937 while working its original assigned route, Chicago-St. Louis. It remained in this service until 1947 when IC introduced a conventional streamlined *Green Diamond* and reassigned the original train to Jackson, Mississippi-New Orleans service under the name *Miss Lou*. It remained on this run until 1950, shortly after which the historic train was scrapped. *Ad, Don Sarno Collection; photo, W. Reugger, Cal's Classics.*

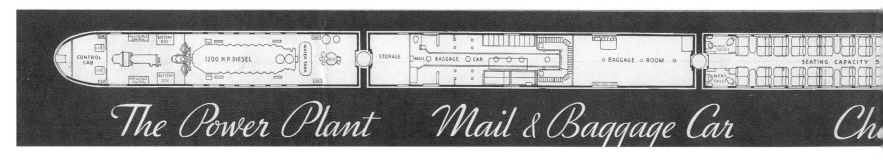

The Power Plant   Mail & Baggage Car   Ch

points. More than 414,000 visitors walked through its Art Deco interior.

The train went to work on May 17, 1936, on a 4-hour, 55-minute schedule between Chicago, Springfield (Illinois), and St. Louis—faster than today's Chicago-St. Louis trains—making one 588-mile round trip each day.

MILWAUKEE ROAD'S *HIAWATHA*

The last two early streamliners featured here represent a departure from the others in that they were largely designed and built by their owning railroads.

In 1933, as production was under way on Burlington's *Zephyr* and UP's M-10000, the Chicago, Milwaukee, St. Paul & Pacific—The Milwaukee Road—was quietly experimenting with lightweight passenger rolling stock in its famed Milwaukee Shops. The result was the February 1934 unveiling of two lightweight, modernistic, all-welded (i.e., no visible external rivets) "Luxury Lounge Progress Coaches."

Pleased with the results of this experiment, the Milwaukee ordered its skilled shop forces to build more than enough new lightweight cars to equip a pair of new "speedliners" slated to vie with Burlington's new *Twin Zephyr*s, which were scheduled to enter Chicago-St. Paul/Minneapolis service in April 1935. Despite recent advances in internal-combustion technology, the Milwaukee opted for the tried-and-proven steam locomotive for its new speedsters, ordering two Atlantic-type (4-4-2) engines from Alco—but with a twist: the locomotives would sport streamlined shrouding and be painted in a livery that would match the new trains.

Milwaukee Road was among the first to recognize the drawbacks of articulation, and its new trains represented conventional wisdom in terms of overall carbody design; i.e., a center-silled car floor supporting walls and roofs, with each carbody—equipped with conventional couplings—riding on two sets of four-wheel trucks. (In other streamliners of the period, particularly the *Zephyr*s, the car sides in part provided support for the entire car.) The Milwaukee felt that passengers would be more comfortable in standard-size cars than in a "small, cramped articulated train," as the railroad summed it up.

Enough equipment for two trains was rushed to completion so the Milwaukee would not to be left high and dry in the race for new trains to the Twin Cities. Early in May, a partial *Hiawatha* trainset embarked on test runs, during one in which the train cruised at a sustained 112.5 mph for 14 miles. Then a *Hiawatha* consist was dispatched on an exhibition tour along its intended route as well as in a few nearby cities.

The "*Hi's*" hit the rails in regular service on May 29, 1935, only 39 days after Burlington's inauguration of its *Twin Zephyr*s and nearly five months after Chicago & North Western introduced its *"400"* on the Chicago-Milwaukee-Twin Cities corridor. (The saving grace here was that the *"400"* was but a reconditioned steam-powered heavyweight train on an accelerated schedule.)

The original *Hiawatha*s, as they were christened (in honor of the "swift of foot" Indian hero immortalized by Longfellow), in one sense represented a level of technology that lay somewhere between the *"400"* and the *Zephyr*, but they were so well-executed, astutely marketed, and so fast that they created a sensation among the public that rivaled that inspired by the *Zephyr* and M-10000. For months following the *Hi's* introduction, it was common to see crowds lining the tracks to watch its passing. One newspaper publisher estimated that, if placed end-to-end, the people who thronged to trackside to watch the daily passage of the *Hiawatha*s would stretch from Chicago to a point 75 miles beyond the Twin Cities.

As a homemade train—and steam-powered, at that—the *Hiawatha* had nothing to apologize for. Each of its two consists featured a restaurant buffet car with a Tip Top Tap lounge (in honor of the Tip Top Inn at the top of the Pullman office building in Chicago), three coaches, a parlor car, and a "Beaver Tail" parlor-observation car—the train's signature car, so-called because of its wide, flat, sloped back end. The Indian-themed trains wore a handsome livery of orange, maroon, and gray. They made the 410-mile Chicago-St. Paul trip in 6 hours, 30 minutes—the same as the *Twin Zephyr*s on a 431-mile route. (The *"400,"* with a 396-mile route, did the trip in as little as 6 hours, 15 minutes.)

Like the *Zephyr*s, *Hiawatha* capacity was soon stretched to the limit. During the first ten months of

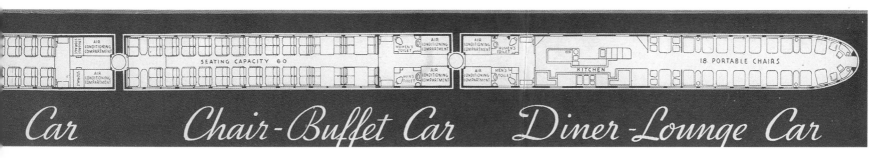

Car   Chair-Buffet Car   Diner-Lounge Car

The *Hiawatha*, 1935

Posing on the Milwaukee Road's Chicago-Milwaukee main line at Techny, Illinois, for the company photographer, the original *Hiawatha* represented a new era in passenger service for its proud owner. The A-class Atlantic (4-4-2) locomotive was no slouch when it came to speed, routinely reaching 100 mph with its stylish train, which included the distinctive Beaver Tail parlor observation car. Amtrak trains which still plied these same tracks in the late 1990s still carried the *Hiawatha* name. *Both photos, the Milwaukee Road.*

service, the *Hi*'s carried 200,000 passengers. Accordingly, CMStP&P added a fourth coach in June 1935 and then a fifth in August the same year. Eventually the Milwaukee had to introduce larger-capacity *Hiawatha*s, which it did in October 1936 with new nine-car trains.

The *Hiawatha* moniker became a household name in the Upper Midwest as additional Chicago-Twin Cities *Hi*'s were born as well as *Hiawatha*s on other routes, some of which will be highlighted in Chapter 6.

NEW YORK CENTRAL'S *MERCURY*

The last streamliner featured in this chapter was born to what in the 1930s was one of the nation's largest and most-powerful railroads, New York Central. Despite that status, the Central was still feeling the pinch of the

Depression and wound up going the route that Milwaukee Road had: it would create its own streamliner and power it with a proven steam locomotive.

Unlike the Milwaukee, though, Central built its new train out of existing heavyweight equipment—surplus commuter cars built in the 1920s—rather than from the ground up. Work on the rolling stock was done at subsidiary Big Four Route's Beech Grove Shops near Indianapolis while Central's West Albany (New York) Shops added a rather thorough streamline shrouding to one of NYC's Pacific-type (4-6-2) locomotives.

The *Mercury* debuted at Indianapolis on June 25, 1936, and then embarked on a systemwide tour. The tour concluded in Cleveland, Ohio, destined to be the train's home terminal in regular service. From here, the *Mercury* made a daily round trip to Detroit on a schedule that allowed Clevelanders nearly a full business day in the Motor City. The 164-mile one-way run was covered in about 2 hours and 45 minutes.

Like nearly all the other streamliners discussed so far, the two-tone gray *Mercury* was an instant hit. Cars were added to the train, and heavier locomotives assigned. By the end of the decade, Central was building a second *Mercury* trainset and *Mercury* service was extended west of Detroit to Chicago. The streamliner concept had been proven to conservative NYC, a railroad destined to become operator of not only one of the largest streamliner fleets in all of North America, but also of what was arguably the greatest streamliner ever, the world-class *20th Century Limited*—a principal topic of the following chapter.

A NEW STREAMLINER EPOCH

The trains featured in this chapter pioneered new territory for the nation's railroads. Many of the trains described were of experimental nature, and in all cases the experiment was an unequivocal success. The streamliner concept was here to stay.

As fast as new trains were delivered, they were being filled with passengers, many of whom had earlier forsaken rail travel altogether. This was particularly important, for it proved that new concepts like streamlining could entice folks back to the rails. For example, Burlington conducted revealing surveys aboard its *Zephyr* fleet during the early years of operation. Of 4,700 *Twin Zephyr* patrons tallied, nearly 23 percent said they would have used auto, bus, or plane had the *Zephyr*s not been available.

Such discoveries, coupled with the greatly increased operational and maintenance savings realized by streamliners, was a breakthrough, and basically it all happened within a three-year period—1934 through 1936. To the skeptics that had largely remained spectators—among

them such industry powerhouses as the Pennsylvania Railroad, Santa Fe, and Southern Pacific—such findings were a revelation. This was a period when railroads still valued passenger transportation, despite the decline that had started during the 1920s, and any solution that would stem—or better yet, reverse—that slide while slashing operational costs was one to be seized upon.

The result? In the closing years of the 1930s, fueled by the easing of the Depression and a new era of optimism, a new wave of streamlining began to wash across America. For the purposes of this book, 1937 was the arbitrary starting point of this second wave.

This new era reflected a revised approach to the concept. The idea of streamliners being single entities whereby the power unit and its trailing cars were articulated as one integral unit was on the wane. Most early streamliner experiments proved what railroads really should have known all along: that a train's length should be readily adjustable to accommodate the peaks and valleys of customer demand; therefore, some degree of standardization was necessary. This second-most important lesson of streamliners was quickly picked up on by railroads and car and locomotive builders.

What we've seen so far is why and how the streamlining movement got under way. What follows is a look at how the growth of streamlining brought exciting new choices to travelers all over America. Happily, far more trains were developed than can be documented in this volume, so the following chapters feature selected streamliners or streamliner fleets using them to tell the story of how streamliners left their marks on the pages of U.S. travel history.

New York Central" *Mercury*
New York Central's original *Mercury* featured a smoking-lounge combine, three coaches, a coach-kitchen, full dining car, a buffet-lounge, full parlor car, and an unusual parlor-lounge observation car (above) that sported extra-large, wraparound windows. All in all, it resembled a "gunner's blister on a bombing plane," as noted passenger-train connoisseur Lucius Beebe once remarked. Rising-star industrial designer Henry Dreyfuss was commissioned by Central to handle the train's interior appointments. Additional *Mercury* equipment was built (again, from surplus commuter cars) and *Mercury* service expanded. The above view circa 1955 at Dayton, Ohio, shows the *Cincinnati Mercury*, which ran between Detroit and Cincinnati. *Al Schultz.*

CHAPTER 2

ATLANTIC TO THE HEARTLAND

The east-west streamliners of:
New York Central
Pennsylvania Railroad
Baltimore & Ohio
Chesapeake & Ohio
New York, Chicago & St. Louis (Nickel Plate)
Norfolk & Western

Century-on-Hudson
As evening drifts in over a region romanticized by author George Washington Irving, New York Central's *20th Century Limited* cruises northward along the Hudson River near Cold Spring, New York, on a summer's evening in 1964. Tomorrow morning will find the *Century* along a different shore line, that of Lake Michigan on the approach to Chicago. *Richard J. Solomon*

The United States was born on the Atlantic seaboard. America clung to those shores during adolescence, anchoring itself with wise and prospering cities and ports—New York, Boston, Philadelphia, Baltimore, and Washington. It didn't take long, however, for restless Americans to venture westward, breaching the formidable Appalachian range in search of a heartland to serve as the new nation's breadbasket. Farmlands blossomed in newly settled "West"—today's Midwest, territories became states, and trading posts grew into great cities like Chicago, Detroit, Cincinnati, and St. Louis.

The frail links that joined the Atlantic seaboard with the heartland—early transportation arteries like the National Road and the Erie Canal—quickly turned into strong bondings of steel as railway transportation boomed in late nineteenth century America. Soon passengers were traveling back and forth in droves between Eastern cities and the Middle West. Benchboard seating gave way to gracious travel early in the twentieth century when exceptional trains like Pennsylvania Railroad's *Pennsylvania Special* and New York Central's *20th Century Limited* hit the rails. And when the streamliner era emerged from a Depression-weary America, rail travel between the Atlantic Seaboard and America's heartland rose to new and unprecedented levels of style, speed, and comfort.

2 7

New York Central's Great Steel Fleet

The ultimate streamliner?
In the view below near Garrison, New York, on the morning of June 24, 1939, New York Central's eastbound *20th Century Limited* speeds toward an on-time arrival at Grand Central Terminal in Manhattan. Many historians consider this—Central's first streamlined edition of the *20th Century Limited*—to be the ultimate streamliner. *Chris Burger Collection.*

Commodore Vanderbilt
Right, the *Century*'s sister train, the exclusive *Commodore Vanderbilt*, pauses at Elkhart, Indiana, during its Chicago-New York run in late afternoon of the Fourth of July 1952. Sleeper-lounge-observation *Manhattan Island* on the rear was built in 1937 originally for *20th Century* service. *Sandy Goodrick.*

As Chapter 1 revealed, New York Central was among the very first U.S. railroads to enter the streamliner era with its Cleveland-Detroit *Mercury* of 1936. Rebuilt from humble surplus commuter cars, the train was an economical but successful venture—and an interesting precursor to what legions of transportation historians would claim to the the world's ultimate streamliner: NYC's *20th Century Limited*.

As a service, the *Century* was hardly new; the train had been clipping the miles between New York and Chicago since 1902. But with streamlining suddenly becoming all the rage as the Depression-ridden 1930s belatedly blossomed, the *Century*—as NYC's top-ranking conveyance—was a natural candidate now that NYC had convinced itself of the viability of streamlining through its *Mercury*.

The 1938 streamlining of *Century* and PRR's rival *Broadway Limited* was in reality a behind-the-scenes joint affair. The new cars for both trains in essence represented a single bulk order for Pullman-Standard, allowing PRR and NYC to enjoy economies resulting from lower unit costs.

Although the basic car structures and configurations were virtually the same on both railroads' orders—both roads ordered, 10-roomette 5-double-bedroom sleepers, and sleeper-lounge-observation cars, for example—the railroads wound up with two trains of distinctly different personalities. That was because the two roads had hired separate industrial designers—Henry Dreyfuss for

NYC and Raymond Loewy for PRR—to style their rolling works of art.

Dreyfuss' approach was that of understated elegance, done largely in cool tones—outside and in. The exterior of the 1938 *Century* was light gray with dark gray window bands edged in Mercury blue and highlighted with aluminum stripes. Interiors likewise relied on cool colors—largely grays and blues—to exude an air of sophistication, but offset by complementary tans, copper trim, and rust colors.

Dining and lounge interiors were the ultimate in swankiness, but without being too pretentious. Smooth, rounded, simple shapes and surfaces—which Dreyfuss referred to as "cleanlining"—added to the elegant club-like atmosphere that was a *Century* hallmark. The *Century's* diner was as fine as any Manhattan restaurant, serving such exotica as planked Peconic Bay weakfish and "Roast Shrewsburn Squab with Guava Jelly." Like several streamliners of the era, the *Century* featured its own dining-car crockery. Following the regular dinner seatings, the dining car was transformed into an elegant night club, its lights turned down to a soft rose-colored glow as contemporary music was piped into the restaurant-turned-"Cafe Century."

The *Century* was among the first "all-room" trains in the U.S. whereas nearly all other all-Pullman trains offered at least a few "section" accommodations—the economy sleeping accommodation that featured curtained upper and lower berths. Rather, the *Century* (and the *Broadway*) offered double bedrooms, compartments, drawing rooms, and the popular new roomette for individuals.

The *Century's piece de resistance* was its Dreyfuss-style Hudson-type (4 pilot wheels, 6 driving wheels, 4 trailing wheels) streamlined steam locomotive, ten of which were ordered from American Locomotive Company. Dreyfuss, fortunately, resisted temptation to overdo the streamlined shrouding, leaving the locomotive's impressive driving wheels fully visible for trackside admirers of steam locomotion. The result was the ultimate example of streamlined steam.

Some 65,000 and 40,000 people walked through the exhibition *Century's* on display at New York and Chicago respectively prior to inauguration. The first streamlined *20th Century Limited's* departed from Chicago's La Salle Street Station and New York's Grand Central Terminal at 5 p.m. on June 15, 1938—at the same moment that PRR's new *Broadway Limited* streamliners were pulling out of Pennsylvania Station in Manhattan and Chicago Union Station. Their destination arrival times the following morning were likewise identical, despite the fact that NYC's "Water Level Route" along the Hudson River and Great Lakes was 961 miles long versus

Pennsy's 908 miles—but NYC didn't have a climb over the Allegheny Mountains to hamper train speeds.

On-board services were as impeccable as the train's design. One of the streamliner's most distinguished features was its train secretary, who assisted passengers with correspondence, hotel and theater reservations, return-trip ticketing, and dictation. The train also had telegraph, valet service and a barber shop. Prior to departure at Chicago and New York, a red carpet with the *20th Century* logo was rolled out from trainside into the concourse for boarding passengers.

Typically, the extra-fare train operated with 13 cars (mail-baggage, buffet-lounge, five sleepers, two diners, two more sleepers, and the sleeper-lounge observation car), but it often swelled to 16-17 cars and at other times operated in two sections (i.e., as two trains). Even before streamlining, the *Century* had earned the status of an American institution, one utilized by movie stars, financial tycoons, and other elite members of society.

The train has even been a star itself, subject-wise serving as a center-piece for the Broadway play "20th Century" and in reality serving as props in the 1959 Hitchcock thriller "North by Northwest," starring Cary Grant. Some on-board scenes were filmed in a Hollywood studio which faithfully reproduced *Century* car interiors; the famous dining-car scene was indeed filmed on real NYC equipment, and the passing scenery outside the dining-car windows, although filmed separately and matted into the dining-car sequence, correctly shows the *Century's* post-departure cruise along the Hudson River.

Central waited nearly three years before it would fully and officially streamline another New York-Midwest run—the *Empire State Express*—although it had taken delivery of enough new streamlined cars in 1938-

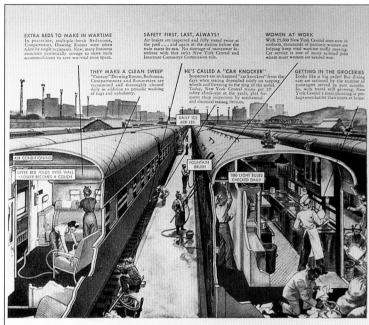

"Behind the scenes" ad, World War II
In this war-era magazine ad, NYC provided a glimpse of what it took to service the *20th Century Limited* between runs. The illustration was one of a series presented in a booklet called BEHIND THE SCENES OF A RAILROAD AT WAR in which cutaway views of railroad rolling stock and structures were presented to familiarize people with various aspects of railroading. In mid-century America, the railroad industry was quite astute on keeping the public "railroad aware." *Mike Schafer Collection.*

41 to begin re-equipping other trains. The *Empire* had been in service since 1891, and in 1941 NYC transformed it into a streamliner with new cars built by the Budd Company and steam locomotives shrouded in streamlining. News of the train's modernization, though, was eclipsed by a much more significant event which occurred on the very same day: the bombing of Pearl Harbor, December 7.

At the time, the *Empire State Express* was a New York-Cleveland train on a day schedule with a Buffalo-Detroit connection that operated through southern Ontario. The train featured a baggage-mail car, baggage-tavern-lounge, coaches, diner, parlor car, and an observation-tavern-lounge. The *Empire State Express* brought daytime streamliner service to cities like Syracuse, Rochester, Buffalo, and Cleveland which the *Century* normally passed through in the middle of the night.

World War II interrupted New York Central's (and most other railroads') streamlining efforts, but once the war was out of the way, NYC jumped back into streamlining with a vengeance. On December 13, 1945, Central placed what was then the largest single order for passenger equipment ever: 420 cars at a cost of $34 million. These postwar cars would join some 300 cars that had already been ordered, but not delivered, prior to the war. Together, both orders were expected to cost NYC a total of $56 million and would theoretically result in 52 new sets of streamliners.

When new equipment did start to arrive, the *Century* received priority and in 1948 was re-equipped with a raft of new cars, including a twin-unit diner and a mid-train lounge car offering a barber shop and shower. The upgraded *Century*'s rededication at Grand Central Terminal was presided over by New York Mayor William O'Dwyer and U.S. President-to-be Gen. Dwight D. Eisenhower—father of the interstate highway system.

The 1938 streamlined equipment bumped from the *Century* in 1948, together with newly delivered cars from Budd, Pullman-Standard, and American Car & Foundry,

Observation lounge, 1948 *Century*
The sleeper-lounge observation cars, above, built for the 1948 rendition of the *20th Century Limited* featured high windows and a raised-floor lounge area partitioned from the adjacent lounge section by narrow glass panels. The car was always a fashionable meeting place before or after dinner. *Ed Nowak, ©Morning Sun Books, Inc.*

***Century* dining a la 1948**
It was one of the finest restaurants in Manhattan, but by early evening it had left town . . . The 1948 *Century* dining cars were Pullman-Standard products whose interior appointments were elegant yet unpretentious. *Ed Nowak, ©Morning Sun Books, Inc.*

enabled NYC to assign lightweight cars to the other star players in the East Coast-Midwest market in 1947-49, notably the *Commodore Vanderbilt* and the *Pacemaker* (New York-Chicago), the *New England States* (Chicago-Boston), *Southwestern Limited* (New York-Cleveland-St. Louis), *Ohio State Limited* (New York-Cleveland-Cincinnati), and the *Detroiter* (New York-Detroit).

Central's overnight New York-Chicago "Dreamliners" were in the most demand on NYC's east-Midwest lines, and there were several parallels in services. The *Commodore Vanderbilt*—named for Cornelius Vanderbilt, the rail baron who almost single-handedly developed the NYC from infancy—was Central's answer to the PRR's New York-Chicago *General*. A no-extra fare all-Pullman train, the *Commodore* made stops not made by the *Century*, including Cleveland, where the *Century* totally bypassed Union Terminal by way of the lakefront line. The *Pacemaker* was the all-coach competitor to Pennsylvania's New York-Chicago *Trail Blazer*; the *Southwestern Limited* competed with PRR's "*Spirit of St. Louis*" while the *Ohio State Limited* was

the Central's answer to PRR's *Cincinnati Limited*.

Because of its strategic position in the Northeast and Midwest, serving many large cities, NYC operated a comprehensive network of passenger trains. As the 1950s got under way, nearly all of Central's intercity passenger trains, both long-distance and regional, carried streamlined equipment. With such a large armada of trains, most of which now carried stainless-steel equipment, Central was referring to its passenger-train network as the "Great Steel Fleet."

Unfortunately, the 1950s and the 1960s weren't kind to NYC's passenger department. Despite the massive postwar investment in equipment, the return on that investment in terms of ridership was disappointing. One of the first signs of trouble was the 1950 combining of the all-coach *Pacemaker* with the all-Pullman *Advance Commodore Vanderbilt*. In 1955, the *Advance Commodore* name was simply dropped as the *Pacemaker* officially became a coach-and-sleeper operation.

For the 1957 summer season, NYC dropped the regular *Commodore Vanderbilt*, now a coach-and-sleeper oper-

Twilight of the *Century*
As the midnight hour approaches, patrons aboard train 25, the westbound *20th Century Limited*, enjoy their nightcaps in the observation lounge while the train makes its station stop at Syracuse, New York. It's July 1967, and the *Century* is enjoying its last months of existence. By the end of the year, the train will have been hastily discontinued—a move by NYC that made front-page news throughout the U.S. *David W. Salter.*

3 1

Ohio State Limited

The popularity of Central's overnight New York-Cincinnati *Ohio State Limited* is underscored by this view of its seemingly endless consist arriving at the Queen City in August 1956. Powering the train is one of NYC's unusual Baldwin passenger diesels coupled to a more-familiar Electro-Motive F-series locomotive. Aside from New York-Cincinnati coaches, diner, and sleeper-lounge, the train also carried Boston-Cincinnati, New York-Columbus, and Buffalo-Cincinnati sleepers. *John Dziobko.*

Empire State Express

Star daylight train between New York and the Midwest was the *Empire State Express*, launched on December 7, 1941. The Budd-built streamliner is shown climbing West Albany (New York) hill in May 1948. Tavern-lounge observation car *Franklin D. Roosevelt* is serving on today's westbound run; undoubtedly its mate, the *Theodore Roosevelt,* is serving on the eastbound counterpart. *William D. Middleton.*

ation, adding the *Commodore* coaches to the *Century* and breaching that train's all-Pullman status. In the spring of 1958, the *Commodore* was combined with the *Century* on a year-round basis. There simply was no longer a need for two luxury overnight trains on similar schedules. The *Commodore* name finally disappeared in 1960.

In 1959 NYC introduced "Sleepercoach" service to the *Century* and *New England States*. These new cars were in fact Budd Company's "Slumbercoaches"—high-capacity, all private-room cars with compact single and double bedrooms sold at a surprisingly economical surcharge above the coach fare. The Budd Slumbercoach, introduced in 1956, was purchased by a number of railroads and was well-received by the traveling public.

By the 1960s, passenger services were well into the downward spiral being experienced by most U.S. roads. As with other railroads which operated multiple passenger schedules on given routes, consolidation became the keyword for a number of trains. For example, for a time the St. Louis-New York *Southwestern Limited* was combined with the Cincinnati-New York *Ohio State Limited* between Cleveland and New York.

On November 5, 1967, the *New England States* and the *20th Century Limited* were combined. Less than a month later on December 2, 1967—with virtually no warning—Central terminated the *Century,* a move

which resulted in considerable public outcry and bad publicity for NYC. Shortly thereafter, Central radically restructured its passenger service, concentrating on short- or medium-distance corridors such as New York-Buffalo and Chicago-Detroit. Through services were reduced to a minimum, with through service between the East and St. Louis dropped altogether. Gone, too, were most train names.

On February 1, 1968, NYC and PRR merged to form Penn Central, a railroad whose titanic failure became legendary. By the time of Amtrak's commencement on May 1, 1971, the only through New York-Midwest services on former NYC lines were three nameless New York-Chicago runs and a Boston-Chicago train which was combined into one of the New York trains at Albany. The Great Steel Fleet had been "stolen"!

Pennsylvania Railroad's Fleet of Modernism

Long a leader in the Northeast-to-Midwest passenger market, the Pennsylvania Railroad first entertained the idea of operating a true streamlined intercity passenger train in February 1934. Nearly concurrent with the introduction of the Union Pacific's M-10000 articulated lightweight train, which made a tour of cities on the PRR, railroad officers met to consider how to modernize passenger service in line with the "Chrysler theory," which espoused offering modernized interiors and exterior streamlining.

In March of the same year, at the instigation of then-Vice President Martin Clement, the railroad hired industrial designer Raymond Loewy. It also directed the prominent engineering firm of Gibbs & Hill to consider the development of a high-speed multiple-unit (MU) electric train based on the design of the UP streamliner.

It would be over 30 years before a high-speed MU "streamliner" was actually born, for PRR determined instead that a locomotive-hauled train would be more practical. In August 1934, after ten weeks of testing, the PRR chose the GG1—a bidirectional electric locomotive being developed by General Electric—as its primary electric passenger locomotive, and Loewy got his most important design commission: to streamstyle the GG1. The results were a complete success and the railroad ordered 57 production-model GG1s in November. Now all PRR needed was a streamlined train for the new "Gs" to pull.

By January 1935, Loewy and the engineering firm would be working together with representatives of Pullman, GE, and Westinghouse on PRR's newly formed "Unit Train Committee." Over the next two years, the committee would consider the development of lightweight trains, focusing heavily on day trains to be used in the New York-Washington corridor. It also explored the concept of creating a 13-car New York-Chicago articulated streamliner.

The idea for a New York-Chicago articulated PRR train hadn't gone far when an event on the New York Central changed PRR's strategies. Rival NYC introduced it first streamliner on July 15, 1936. The *Mercury*, a home-built non-articulated train created by industrial designer Henry Dreyfuss, began operating between Detroit and Cleveland (see Chapter 1). Dreyfuss had skillfully re-styled lowly commuter coaches to produce a striking new train. When teamed with a futuristically styled streamlined 4-6-2 steam locomotive, the results were magic. The *Mercury* captivated public and press alike. Before long, the NYC was candidly admitting to Chicago newspapers that it was considering streamlining its flagship, the incomparable *20th Century Limited*, contender to Pennsylvania's New York-Chicago *Broadway Limited*. Had you been in a firehouse, the alarm bells wouldn't have been any louder. PRR responded immediately, proposing to NYC that both roads build and introduce the two trains jointly. New York Central acquiesced and the railroads announced the project in March 1937.

The odd concept of rival roads introducing trains

Broadway Limited, 1938 edition
Three passengers are still enjoying cocktails and conversation in the sleeper-lounge observation car as the westbound *Broadway Limited* curves into Pittsburgh's east end during the small hours of the morning. It's war time and U. S. Steel's J. Edgar Thomson Works is in full swing, lighting the sky as the *Broadway* passes under the Westinghouse Bridge in this opaque water color rendering by artist Mitchell A. Markovitz. *Mike Schafer Collection.*

jointly had its roots in the fact that both the *Century* and the *Broadway* were largely comprised of Pullman cars which both railroads leased from the Pullman Company. Both railroads had jointly negotiated their contracts to operate Pullman cars on their trains, and Pullman's manufacturing arm Pullman-Standard was selected to construct the new streamlined cars. Pullman itself would operate the cars once they were in service. Pullman was concerned about manufacturing costs for the new cars and maintained a "waste management" committee to oversee construction and encourage standardization in the new lightweights—hence it was in Pullman's interest to build the trains jointly and in the PRR's interest to ensure that rival NYC didn't steal a march on it in the New York-Midwest market.

In spite of the construction similarities of the equipment, the presence of Raymond Loewy (for PRR) and Henry Dreyfuss (for NYC) gave the new *Century* and *Broadway* distinctive identities. While NYC's train was cloaked in conservative two-tone gray, Loewy's exterior color scheme for the Pennsylvania featured warm shades of Tuscan red and maroon. Interiors were equally attractive. Vibrant tones of yellow and blue highlighted the Pennsylvania cars' public rooms which were also finished in light woods.

Since the popular train often ran in two sections in each direction to accommodate demand for travel, Central's approach was order enough new cars to introduce four *Century* trainsets. The PRR chose a more egalitarian approach, spreading the newly streamlined equipment around its fleet. While initially only the *Broadway* would be completely streamlined, the New York-St. Louis *"Spirit of St. Louis,"* the New York-Chicago *General*, and the Washington-Chicago *Liberty Limited* would

---

Streamlinings of Note

Pullman: "The World's Greatest Hotel"

The earliest on-board sleeping facilities for railroad passengers were probably the crudely built bunks in a remodeled coach operated by the Cumberland Valley Railroad between Harrisburg and Chambersburg, Pa., in the late 1830s. Sensing a demand for more comfortable overnight accommodations, and drawing liberally upon the ideas of others, George M. Pullman and his partner, Benjamin C. Field, devised a positionable upper-berth construction which, along with lower berths from hinged seat backs, permitted a day coach to be quickly converted for night travel. Pullman and Field remodeled two coaches of the Chicago, Alton & St. Louis Railroad into sleepers. The first of these, car No. 9, entered service September 1, 1859, between Bloomington, Ill., and Chicago.

Popular acceptance of the Alton sleepers, and recognition that further improvements were needed, prompted Pullman and Field to build an entirely new car. Completed in 1865 and named *Pioneer*, it incorporated design features and amenities which, with continual refinement, would define railroad sleeping-car service for the next hundred years.

Important as George Pullman's technical advances were, it was his vision of an enterprise providing a nationwide pool of deluxe equipment and a well-trained staff to maintain the cars and offer a high level of passenger comfort, coupled with his single-minded drive and marketing acumen, that propelled Pullman's Palace Car Company over the other sleeping-car companies spawned by the popularity of early sleepers and growth of the railroad network. By the end of 1899, Pullman's Palace Car Company had a virtual monopoly in the sleeping-car business except where roads operated their own cars. That year, the firm changed its name to The Pullman Company.

At its zenith in the late 1920s, Pullman had a fleet of nearly 10,000 sleepers and carried 100,000 guests nightly, maintaining consistently high standards for passenger safety and comfort.

In 1924, Pullman reorganized its car-building activities—which now included a wide variety of railroad rolling stock—as the Pullman Car & Manufacturing Corporation. A holding company, Pullman Incorporated, was formed in 1927 to control both the PC&MC and The Pullman Company. Following its merger in 1934 with several small car builders including the Standard Steel Car Company, MC&MC became the Pullman-Standard Manufacturing Company.

By 1940, sleeping-car service agreements typically called for Pullman to own, perform repairs and interior maintenance on, supply, and staff all sleepers operating on the contracting railroad. Railroad agents sold tickets for travel in Pullman cars, with the railroad retaining the first-class rail fare while the seat, berth, or room charge revenue went to Pullman.

In addition to the monopoly it enjoyed in providing sleeper service, Pullman rebuffed efforts of other car builders (principally its arch competitor, the Budd Company) to furnish equipment for its operations—which is to say that if a railroad wanted to offer Pullman service, it had to be in Pullman-Standard-built cars. This prompted Budd to initiate anti-trust litigation and a 1944 Federal Court decision forcing Pullman Incorporated to dispose of either its manufacturing business or its sleeping-car operations. The Pullman Company was thus sold to a group of 57 railroads in 1947. Nearly all of Pullman's lightweight sleepers, plus many of its heavyweight cars, were sold to the railroads on which they had been regularly assigned; the rest were retained in a Pullman-owned pool. Railroad-owned cars needed for line operations were leased back to Pullman. In most other respects, the contracts between individual railroads and Pullman remained much as they had been.

Declining patronage and increasing costs caused some of the railroads to reduce or eliminate sleeping-car service or to consider alternatives to its handling by Pullman. Starting with the New York Central in 1958, several roads took over all or part of their sleeper operations. In 1968, as it became evident that Pullman could not efficiently provide full-service operation of cars for just a limited number of carriers, the remaining roads prepared for their takeover of staffing and revenue collection on January 1, 1969, and the total termination effective August 1, 1969, of Pullman's car leases and its role in U.S. sleeping-car operations. Some railroads reacted by simply cutting sleeping-car services altogether, overnight transforming some streamliners into coach-only secondary trains.

be partially re-equipped. Pennsylvania called them its "Fleet of Modernism" inaugurating the trains on June 15, 1938. The new *20th Century Limited* went into service the same day.

For the next three years, the PRR would supplement its fleet with new equipment and new trains. On July 28, 1939, the railroad introduced the *Trail Blazer*, a fast all-coach streamliner between New York and Chicago; later, Washington cars would be added. The *Jeffersonian*, a deluxe all-coach streamliner between New York and St. Louis, debuted on April 27, 1941. Both new coach trains were rebuilt by PRR from existing heavyweight cars.

After World War II, the PRR continued to streamline its trains and upgrade earlier streamliners, completely re-equipping the *Broadway*, the *General*, the *Liberty Limited*, the *Spirit*, the *Jeffersonian* and the *Trail Blazer*, while introducing a newly streamlined *Cincinnati Limited* (New York-Pittsburgh-Cincinnati) and adding new cars to still other trains. Dressed in a scheme of solid Tuscan red with black roof, the new fleet reflected the design features of the time—with a surprise or two thrown in for good measure. The *Jeffersonian*, for example, incorporated a recreation car which featured a variety of diversions including a newsreel theater and a playroom for children. Diesel locomotives arrived in the postwar period from Alco (American Locomotive Company), Baldwin, Electro-Motive, and Fairbanks-Morse. Diesels first appeared on the New York-Detroit *Red Arrow* then quickly replaced steam locomotives on other top trains. Between New York and Harrisburg, the fleet was still pulled by Pennsy's dependable GG1 electrics.

The immediate postwar period saw the birth of a short-lived phenomenon—the transcontinental passenger-car line. Although Chicago and St. Louis were major western passenger terminals for the PRR, its trains carried cars destined for points beyond. The *Broadway* began hosting a New York-Los Angeles sleeper via Santa Fe's *Chief* at Chicago. The *General* and other trains handled sleeping cars for the *California Zephyr* and Chicago & North Western-UP trains bound for the Bay area. For a short time between 1946 and 1948, the Missouri Pacific *Sunshine Special* operated as a through train from the Southwest—with cars from as far away as Mexico City—to St. Louis and New York via the PRR. In August 1948, when the through operation was discontinued, PRR inaugurated the *Texas Eagle* (renamed shortly thereafter the *Penn Texas*), and this train continued to carry a bevy of through sleeping cars destined for Midwestern

and Southwestern points on the Missouri Pacific, the St. Louis-San Francisco ("Frisco"), and the Missouri-Kansas-Texas ("Katy") railroads among others. The *Penn Texas* would handle through sleepers longer than any other PRR train with the last MP through cars being discontinued in the summer of 1961.

To be sure, there were clouds looming as the 1950s unfurled. The optimism about passenger service bolstered by high ridership during World War II was unfounded. The postwar increase in auto and air travel between PRR's major market cities had a profound effect, and Pennsy's long-distance passenger operations failed to turn a profit from 1946 through the merger with NYC in 1968. By 1951 the railroad was openly

Recreation on the Jeffersonian
The social center of PRR's postwar streamliner *Jeffersonian* between New York, Pittsburgh, and St. Louis was the recreation car, which offered something for everyone. This feature car was heavily promoted, as in the above magazine ad appearing in 1948. The cutaway artwork revealed the car's game and reading lounge, a "sunken" buffet-lounge, a movie theater (far end), and—a concept way ahead of its time—an enclosed children's playroom, left, complete with play pen. *Ad, Mike Schafer Collection; photo, ACF, St. Louis Mercantile Library.*

Cincinnati Limited

Fifteen cars strong, Pennsy's *Cincinnati Limited* eases out of Cincinnati Union Terminal on July 25, 1948, at the start of its 755-mile overnight run to Gotham. A pair of handsome Alco PA-type passenger diesels—the lead unit equipped with train-phone antenna—lead the Tuscan Red streamliner. *R. D. Acton Sr.*

Trail Blazer brochure

When the PRR introduced the new all-coach *Trail Blazer*, the railroad spared no expense in letting the public know about it, publishing a handsome color brochure (right) that detailed each of the train's cars and services. *Mike Schafer Collection.*

referring to the situation as "the passenger problem" and meeting with consultants to address the crisis. As the largest rail passenger operator in the nation, PRR's colossal financial commitment to personnel, rolling stock, stations, and other passenger-related infrastructure meant that, when it lost money, it had a huge financial liability to underwrite. This prompted the railroad to take quick steps to economize.

Beginning in 1950 the all-coach *Trail Blazer* was combined with the all-Pullman *General* during certain non-peak travel periods. By 1951 the consolidation would become permanent. The *Jeffersonian* was discontinued in the spring of 1953 and its coaches added to the all-Pullman *"Spirit of St. Louis."* The *Liberty Limited* was dropped in 1957 and in its place the *General* began carrying Washington-Chicago cars.

Despite these rationalizations, the *Broadway Limited* was actually experiencing a rebirth in popularity. The

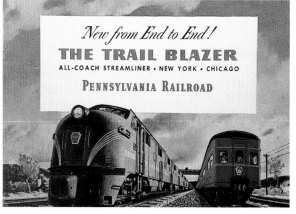

downgrading of NYC's *20th Century Limited* in 1958 to a coach-and-sleeper operation resulted in many first-class riders transferring their allegiance to the still all-Pullman *Broadway*. PRR maintained the train in fine tradition as an exclusive first-class operation until December 12, 1967, when the *General* was discontinued and its coaches transplanted to the *Broadway*. The merger of NYC and PRR as the Penn Central in February 1968 resulted in the wholesale elimination or downgrading of duplicate services. The *Broadway* maintained some semblance of dignity, still carrying multiple sleeping cars, offering fine meals and even having some its assigned equipment refurbished, but the rest of the fleet was allowed to fall even further into disrepair. PC made an unsuccessful attempt to discontinue virtually all of its long-distance east-west passenger service and limped along until the start of Amtrak on May 1, 1971, when nearly all the remnants of PRR's once-great Fleet of

Modernism were discontinued. Amtrak's miniscule startup budget only allowed the *Broadway* and a revised version of the *"Spirit of St. Louis"* to survive on the former-PRR Northeast-Midwest routes.

Gone are the days when a businessperson could board Pennsylvania's *Broadway* in New York or Philadelphia and enjoy a drink in the observation lounge before dinner as the train raced down the New York-Philadelphia main. Lingering at table in the diner, the traveler could watch collegiate rowers leave a gentle wake on the picturesque Schuylkill River or ponder Philadelphia's attractive Main Line suburbs after the train departed North Philadelphia along PRR's historic "Main Line" route to Pittsburgh. Later, there was a ritual not to be missed as riders peering from lounge windows or curled up in a cozy Pullman bed watched the twinkling lights of their train as it negotiated famous Horseshoe Curve near Altoona, Pennsylvania. Awakening after a sound night of sleep, passengers preparing for a hearty breakfast in the diner found a surprise under their door—a slip noting the day's weather for their destination, one of the many little extras *Broadway* customers came to expect from one of the best trains in North America. It was all part of a more relaxed age when Americans had the time to enjoy the journey as much as the destination and the railroads were anxious to oblige.

Broadway at Chicago Union Station
Below, the *Broadway* stands ready for departure from the dim confines of Chicago Union Station's train sheds on a winter afternoon in 1965. This is the 1948 edition of the train, still going strong 17 years later—and still all-Pullman, too. *Ron Lundstrom.*

. . . and at speed
Bottom, the eastbound *Broadway*, train 28, cruises along PRR's four-track "Broad Way' (for which the train was named) through the Susquehanna River valley near Harrisburg in the early morning hours of a spring day in 1965. *John Dziobko.*

The regal streamliners of Baltimore & Ohio

Throughout the streamlined era, passenger services on the Baltimore & Ohio Railroad bore the imprint of a man who retired in 1941 after 31 years at the helm of America's first passenger railroad: Daniel Willard. For Willard—his road locked in competition with the much larger and stronger Pennsylvania and New York Central railroads—safety, courtesy, on-time performance, cleanliness, and exemplary dining-car service were more important and more readily attainable than state-of-the-art equipment and speed.

Not that B&O management was old fashioned. The road had, in fact, been among the first to embrace air conditioning (1930), streamlined styling (1935), and the diesel-electric passenger locomotive (1935). "Uncle Dan" simply focused on passenger comforts, a philosophy which, along with B&O's often tenuous financial condition, guided the line's passenger services until the arrival of Amtrak in 1971.

Flagships of the B&O's east-west passenger fleet were the *Capitol Limited* operating between Jersey City, New Jersey (gateway to New York City across New York Harbor), Washington, and Chicago and the *National Limited* linking Jersey City, Washington, Cincinnati, and St. Louis. Both trains were introduced as all-Pullman services west of Washington, the *Capitol* in 1923 and the *National* in 1925. Northeast of Washington, the trains were, in reality, comprised of just a few through cars integrated into B&O's schedule of local trains serving the urban corridor between Washington, Baltimore, Philadelphia and, via operating rights over the Reading and Central Railroad of New Jersey, metropolitan New York. B&O dropped its passenger service east of Baltimore in 1958.

As the PRR and NYC invested in streamlined equipment of lightweight construction in the late 1930s and early 1940s, B&O turned to Pullman and its own Mount Clare Shops at Baltimore for the upgrading of conventional heavyweight rolling stock. New ride-enhancing running gear and modest streamlined styling were the result. The styling was inspired by designer Otto Kuhler who also could claim the B&O's strikingly handsome blue-and-gray color scheme accented by gold striping as his creation. Kuhler's interior decor hinted at Art Deco, employing light color tones, tubular chromium furnishing, and indirect lighting.

In 1938 each *Capitol Limited* received a remodeled nine-car consist of combination baggage-crew dormitory-club car, six sleepers, diner, and a sun room sleeper-lounge observation car. All had been restyled with rounded roofs, skirting, and full-width diaphragms. In a typical B&O nod to tradition, the diners retained their Georgian Colonial interior motif. The train was powered by locomotives from B&O's 1937 order of Electro-Motive model EA and EB diesels.

The *National Limited*, which now carried coaches as well as sleepers, received a similar streamlining in 1940. A new all-coach overnight Jersey City-Washington-Chicago service, the *Columbian*, was added to the schedule in December 1941 using heavyweight rolling stock upgraded and streamlined at Mount Clare.

First streamlined *Capitol Limited*
B&O chose famous Thomas Viaduct near Relay, Maryland, for this wonderful publicity photo circa 1938 of the first streamlined rendition of the *Capitol Limited*, which featured heavyweight cars smartly remodeled by the road's Mount Clare Shops. Leading the new streamliner was an Electro-Motive EA (cab) and EB (booster) locomotive set, that company's first E-series passenger diesel models. B&O had begun receiving its EA/EB locomotives in 1937 and they were already in service when the *Capitol* received its new equipment. Electro-Motive continued production of E-series passenger diesels until 1964, although with less-streamlined surfaces, the look of later models was not quite as elegant as B&O's EAs and EBs. *B&O, Collection of William F. Howes Jr.*

Offering a service pioneered by B&O in 1937, both the *National* and the *Columbian* carried a stewardess-nurse catering to the needs of all passengers. The statesmen and industrialists who populated the *Capitol Limited* had the services of a male secretary, while the women and children aboard were attended by a maid manicurist. Valet service was available to Pullman passengers of both the *National* and the *Capitol*.

Following World War II, B&O embarked on a three-pronged approach to updating its fleet: (1) rebuilding heavyweight cars into streamlined cars at its own shops, (2)

contracting with carbuilders for state-of-the-art equipment, and (3) acquiring surplus lightweight cars from other railroads.

The road initially concentrated on the development of two all-coach streamliners, one linking Baltimore and Washington with Cincinnati on a daylight carding and the other an East Coast-Chicago service. Racing against rival Chesapeake & Ohio's plans for a new Washington-Cincinnati day service and unwilling to take its place in the postwar backlog of orders at the commercial carbuilders, B&O once again turned to the Mount Clare Shops for two

National at St. Louis

(Below) With a billow of diesel exhaust, the eastbound *National* accelerates away from St. Louis on a summer morning in 1965. The *National* still sported an observation car complete with *National Limited* drumhead, but by the end of the summer, they will have been pulled from service. *Jim Boyd.*

Dining on the *National Limited*

(Bottom right) passenger Grace Joseph is about to enjoy some of B&O's widely applauded dining-car cuisine aboard the *National Limited* during a 1961 journey between St. Louis and Washington. As was B&O tradition for many years, the fare is being served on B&O's famous blue Centenary china, original pieces of which today command top dollar. Note, too, behind Mrs. Joseph the bottled Deer Park spring-water pitchers. *Oliver "Dee" Joseph.*

streamlined trainsets constructed from heavyweight car-bodies. Drawn by Pacific-type steam locomotives now sporting bullet-nosed shrouding, the *Cincinnatians* entered service in January 1947. Each train contained three coaches, a baggage-coffee shop car serving light meals, and a round-end observation car containing a full-service dining room and cocktail lounge.

Meanwhile B&O had placed an order with Pullman-Standard in late 1945 for two eight-car lightweight trainsets initially intended to operate on a daylight run between Washington and Chicago. By the time of their delivery in May 1949, it had been decided to use this equipment to replace the heavyweight *Columbians* on an overnight schedule comparable to the all-Pullman *Capitol Limited*. Behind new EMD F3 diesels, each train included a baggage-dorm-coffee shop car, five coaches, a dine,r and a bar-lounge-observation car. Most notable among the train's many modern features was the glass-enclosed dome on one of the coaches. Dubbed a "Strata Dome" by the B&O, the cars were the first dome cars to operate in the East. Budd-built Slumbercoaches offering thrifty overnight sleeping accommodations at near coach prices were introduced

in 1958, another B&O first in the East.

The eight coaches and two dome coaches built for the *Columbian* would be the only lightweight coaches on the B&O postwar roster. The road continued to use its own shops to rebuild 1920-30 era heavyweight cars into streamlined diners and coaches for the *Capitol* and the *National Limited*s a well as most of its other long-distance trains. Finally in 1957, a pair of lightweight twin-unit diners was purchased from the New York Central and assigned to the *Capitol*.

As for first-class sleeping accommodations, B&O gradually re-equipped both the *Capitol* and the *National* will all-room lightweight cars by 1958. Much of this equipment, including dome-sleepers for the *Capitol* and sleeper-observation-lounge cars for the *Capitol* and *National*, was acquired from C&O and NYC.

A trip from New York on a B&O streamliner began with a B&O motor bus and or a Jersey Central ferry boat ride across the Hudson River to the CNJ's terminal at Jersey City. The run down the Northeast corridor was just a prelude to the "main event" beginning at Washington. Here the *Capitol* and *National*'s Pullmans filled with the leaders of government, the armed forces, business, and labor. Coach patronage on the *National* and *Cincinnatian* was more reflective of the rural and industrial blue-collar population in B&O's territory.

Strata-dome or observation lounge seats were the favorite spots for witnessing a B&O train's westward progress along the picturesque Potomac River and the neighboring C&O Canal. Suddenly, you popped through a tunnel and crossed the white waters of the Potomac at its confluence with the Shenandoah River in Harpers Ferry, West Virginia. Next, the rails traversed hallowed Civil War battlegrounds en route to Martins-

burg. Then it was on to Cumberland in western Maryland while selecting an evening meal from such Chesapeake Bay recipes as crab imperial, oyster pie, chicken with corn fritters, and Smithfield ham. All were served on B&O's blue china with heavy, plated silverware and yellow-gold napery. Accompaniments included the road's famous "Help Yourself Salad" and bottled water from its spring at Deer Park, Maryland.

B&O's main line to Chicago diverged at Cumberland from the original route to the Ohio River. Seasoned passengers on the *Capitol* or the *Columbian* knew now was the time to return to the Strata-Dome for the slow climb over the Alleghenies followed by a dramatic light show put on by the steel-mill furnaces of Pittsburgh. Post midnight stops at Youngstown and Akron in eastern Ohio preceded a race across rural Ohio and Indiana. Daybreak's arrival was celebrated with a "Good

Morning" demitasse—on the house—and a hearty B&O breakfast. Then Chicago's skyline came into sight, and the train eased its way across a spider web of rail lines and into B&O's Grand Central Station on the south side of the Loop.

Passengers aboard the *Cincinnatian* or *National Limited* proceeded west of Cumberland on one of the most difficult and scenic rail routes across the Alleghenies, followed by the rolling countryside of southern Ohio en route to Cincinnati. Throughout the day the *Cincinnatian*'s observation-diner offered B&O cooking southern-style, including the train's specialty—spoon bread. For the *National*, the trip across Ohio was a nocturnal one, with arrival in Cincinnati shortly after breakfast. Passengers bound for St. Louis and Western connections faced a trip of six hours across southern Indiana and Illinois.

When the *Cincinnatian* failed to attain its traffic pro-

Streamliner *Columbian*, 1949
Sporting an all-new streamlined consist, the *Columbian* poses for the B&O company photographer along the Potomac River near Harpers Ferry, West Virginia, circa 1949. In the eight-car consist is a Strata-Dome coach, the first such car to operate in the East. Because of tight clearances indigenous to Northeastern railroads, B&O domes were of low-profile design. *B&O Railroad Museum.*

Capitol Limited/Columbian, 1962

The *Capitol Limited* remained a classy operation right up to its (first) demise on May 1, 1971. (Amtrak revived the *Capitol Limited* in 1981, and it remains today one of Amtrak's best trains.) In this view recorded on the morning of February 1, 1962, the combined *Capitol/Columbian* is shown arriving Chicago and is backing down beneath the photographer's vantage point on the Roosevelt Road overpass toward Grand Central Station after having been turned at the Western Avenue wye track. Today's westbound consist includes at least two cars purchased from the C&O, including the sleeper-buffet-lounge observation car at the end of the train and a Budd dome sleeper built for C&O's still-born *Chessie* streamliner. The *Columbian*'s Strata-Dome coach can be seen near the front of the train. *Bob Johnston.*

jections, its equipment and name were transferred in 1950 to a more lucrative daylight schedule between Cincinnati and Detroit.

Declining ridership along B&O's Chicago line, especially in the first-class sleepers, prompted the consolidation of the *Capitol Limited* with the *Columbian* in 1958, and with the Baltimore-Washington-Detroit *Ambassador* in 1961. But even as other roads soured on passenger service in the early 1960s, B&O made one last attempt to attain a break-even status through innovative marketing and cost controls. While "movies-on-the train," demand-sensitive pricing, creative advertising, and more efficient food service enjoyed some success, these efforts were undermined in the late 1960s by the almost total diversion to air and truck transportation of the U.S. Mail and Railway Express Agency traffic, once major contributors to B&O's passenger train revenues.

Still, B&O's Washington-Chicago service survived until Amtrak under the *Capitol Limited* name offering coach and sleeping car accommodations with a full complement of dining and lounge amenities. After a hiatus of ten years, Amtrak reinstated the *Capitol Limited* in 1981, routing it via B&O from Washington to Pittsburgh and from there over Conrail to Chicago.

The *National Limited* suffered a different fate, In 1965, two years after the Chesapeake & Ohio had gained control of the B&O, the duplicative Washington-Cincinnati services of the *National* and C&O's *George Washington* (see next section) were restructured. The *National*'s Washington-St. Louis coaches, sleeper, and Slumbercoach were rerouted via the C&O's more densely populated route west to Cincinnati, returning to B&O rails to reach St. Louis. The train acquired the *George Washington* name. Meanwhile, the *National*'s local service along the B&O route between Washington and Cincinnati was discontinued in several phases during the late 1960's. Although Amtrak took over operation of C&O's portion of the run on May 1, 1971, the last remnant of the B&O's *National Limited*, the service between Cincinnati and St. Louis, was discontinued on that date.

East-West Streamliners of the Chesapeake & Ohio

Commemorating the 1932 bicentennial of George Washington's birth, the Chesapeake & Ohio Railway inaugurated a deluxe heavyweight train in his honor linking, overnight, the nation's capital and tidewater Virginia with Cincinnati and the bluegrass horse country of Kentucky. On the flanks of its Pullmans and dining cars were names of people, places, and events associated with the train's namesake.

The *George Washington* drew upon Georgian designs of the Colonial period for its interior decor. It employed the latest innovations in passenger comfort, including air-conditioning and spacious "Imperial Salon" coaches with 2-and-1 seating and carpeted floors, prompting C&O publicists to declare it the "Most Wonderful Train in the World." In an even more inspired promotion, C&O was soon using Viennese artist Guido Gruenewald's portrait of a dozing cat—now appropriately named Chessie—to advertise the sleep-inducing qualities of its passenger trains.

The *George* quickly eclipsed two other notable C&O trains, the *FFV* (inaugurated in 1899 as the *Fast Flying Virginian*) and the *Sportsman*, the latter being a 1930 addition to the timetable offering service between Michigan and the Virginias.

C&O provided a key link between urban centers in the East and Midwest and numerous small cities and towns in Virginia, West Virginia, and Kentucky. This was enhanced by an extensive network of interline Pullman sleeping-car operations reaching such off-line points as New York, Chicago, St. Louis, and Cleveland. Much of this first-class business was generated by on-line resort hotels, including the road's own posh Greenbrier at White Sulphur Springs, West Virginia. C&O passenger operations of the 1930s could be described as genteel and solidly conservative. The road showed little interest in the streamlining revolution gaining momentum elsewhere in the industry.

Then onto the scene came Robert R. Young. Attaining the chairmanship of C&O in 1942, Young was an outspoken advocate of rail passenger service. The road's board of directors resolved that C&O would have a postwar passenger service "second to none." There followed three major orders for lightweight, streamlined equipment:

1. A 1944 order for 14 cars from Pullman-Standard for two train sets to operate between Detroit and Grand Rapids, Mich., on affiliate Pere Marquette Railway.

2. A 1946 order for 46 cars from the Budd Company to outfit two new trains, plus feeder-line connections, linking Washington and Cincinnati by daylight. The trains were to be named the *Chessie*.

3. Another 1946 order, this time for 287 cars from P-S to re-equip all other C&O mainline trains, providing for multiple sections of many of them.

C&O, through its research department, strongly influence the design of this equipment. And the passen-

C&O's *George Washington*

At the platforms of Cincinnati Union Terminal behind the depot's domed waiting room and ticket office, Chesapeake & Ohio's *George Washington* awaits its appointed departure time on the evening of August 9, 1956. Shortly, passengers will be enjoying a "cruise" along the south bank of the majestic Ohio River as the *George*'s engine crew exchanges whistle signals with Ohio River tug boats (a tradition maintained today by Amtrak's *Cardinal,* which plies the same route). At Huntington, West Virginia, the train will begin penetrating the Appalachians as darkness prevails, and in that region it will spend most of the night negotiating scenic gorges, climbing mountains, and calling at remote resort towns. *John Dziobko.*

ger traffic department introduced a wide array of innovative amenities. Sleepers were to have the more-expensive bedrooms located in the smoother-riding center of the car—a departure from standard room positioning found on "off-the-shelf" catalog car orders. Long-distance coaches were attractively partitioned so as to relieve the feeling of being seated in a long hallway. Service features included on-board acceptance of credit cards, train hostesses and passenger representatives, and a "no tipping" policy in the diners.

The Michigan trains entered service in 1946, achieving the distinction of being the first postwar lightweight streamliners and the first C&O system trains with diesel locomotives. Named *Pere Marquette*s and used to test the market for modern rail passenger service, they proved very popular. However, it was apparent by 1948 that the planned *Chessie* would not be successful. The beautiful trains—which even featured aquariums—were delivered, but they never entered service as the *Chessie*. Rather, most of the *Chessie* cars were quickly sold to other railroads. Similarly, as the huge P-S order approached a 1950 delivery date, C&O concluded that it far exceeded its needs. Part of the order was cancelled and buyers found for many of the remaining cars.

Initial plans for a streamlined *George Washington* included a twin-unit diner, a sleeper-lounge observation car, and a consist flush with spacious, 52-seat coaches and 10-6 sleepers, all in the road's new Federal Yellow and Enchantment Blue livery. However, with only 130 of the original 351-car order actually on its 1951 roster, C&O assigned Budd-built *Chessie* diner-lounges to the *George Washington* and even resorted to heavyweight diners for some feeder-line sections of the train.

Departing Washington at the end of the workday, the "*George*" (as the train was popularly known) eased out of Union Station and beneath Capitol Hill, emerging amidst monuments and museums. After crossing the Potomac River and entering Virginia, the train's route took it over lands rich in Civil War lore. In the dining car, the evening's selections often included delicacies from tidewater Virginia. At Charlottesville the sleepers and coaches from Newport News and Richmond were switched into the Washington section.

Now swelled to 16 or more cars behind three Electro-Motive E-series passenger diesels, the *George*'s westward movement was slowed by a steep and circuitous climb over the Blue Ridge, affording grand views of the Piedmont Valley below as the train reached the summit at Afton in the final moments of daylight. Beyond, during the nighttime hours, the *George* trekked over the Alleghenies. Those who had retired to their Pullman berths were tempted to raise the window shades during brief stops at Covington and White Sulphur Springs to watch limou-

sines standing ready to accommodate guests of the Homestead and Greenbrier hotels, respectively.

The most scenic part of the route still lay ahead. Unfortunately, the *George Washington* negotiated the spectacular New River Gorge, skirted the Appalachian coal fields, and paralleled the white waters of the Great Kanawha River at night. The westbound *FFV* or eastbound *Sportsman*—now having also been partially streamlined— were best for savoring these miles in daylight. After nocturnal stops in Charleston and Huntington, West Virginia, the *George* reached Ashland, Kentucky, at a pre-dawn hour. Here through the 1960s, one long train became three of moderate length—one for Louisville, one for Detroit, and the main section for Cincinnati, each arriving at those points after breakfast. At Cincinnati, many passengers connected to trains of other lines. NYC's *James Whitcomb Riley*, in fact, carried through sleepers from the *George* to Chicago.

C&O scaled back its streamliner fleet in 1962 with the discontinuance of the eastbound *FFV* and westbound *Sportsman* and a realignment of other services. In September 1965, the Baltimore-St. Louis *National Limited* service of the B&O, a road now controlled by C&O, was integrated into the *George Washington* between Washington and Cincinnati, in effect extending the *George* to St. Louis. By December 1968, all C&O routes, other than *Pere Marquette* service, had been reduced to just one pair of trains daily—the *George*—supplemented by seasonal resort specials.

The strength of the *George Washington* made it one of the few east-west services selected to be retained by Amtrak on May 1, 1971, although Amtrak itself realigned the operation by extending the *George Washington* to Chicago (the Cincinnati-St. Louis leg was dropped at the start of Amtrak).

Although Robert R. Young's expectations and dreams for rail passenger service failed to materialize, today Amtrak's Superliner *Cardinal*—in an interesting parallel to the proposed *Chessie* streamliner of 1947— traverses by daylight the Blue Ridge, Alleghenies and New River Gorge to serve the mountain resorts of Virginia and West Virginia and cities and towns along the Greenbrier, New, Kanawha, and Ohio rivers.

East-Midwest Underdogs

NICKEL PLATE'S MODEST STREAMLINER FLEET

With so many major carriers in the East Coast-Midwest market—Pennsylvania, NYC, B&O, and C&O—competition for passengers was fierce. But some "underdog" railroads in this market made valiant attempts at capturing a slice of the already

well-cut passenger pie with streamliners worthy of note.

One of those railroads was the New York, Chicago & St. Louis—the Nickel Plate Road—a carrier better known for high-speed freight service than for streamliners. Nonetheless, in 1950 the NKP entered the world of streamliners with two handsome new trains. Since the NKP did not reach east of Buffalo, it relied on ally Delaware, Lackawanna & Western to forward the new trains to New York's doorstep at Hoboken, New Jersey.

The advent of Nickel Plate streamliners was really an upgrading of existing services with new lightweight cars and remodeled heavyweight cars. NKP's main entry in its passenger-train fleet was the *Nickel Plate Limited* between Chicago and Buffalo via Cleveland; its companion train on an alternate schedule over the same route carried two names, the *Westerner* (westbound) and the *New Yorker* (eastbound). Both trains became the recipient of NKP's order of ten new coaches, 13 sleepers, and two sleeper-lounge cars from Pullman-Stan-

dard—in reality the remnants of an over-extended order placed by C&O.

Eastbound, the *Nickel Plate Limited* exited Chicago's La Salle Street Station late in the evening and ran overnight to Cleveland making it a competitor with NYC's eastbound *Forest City* between those points as well as Buffalo. At Buffalo, the *Limited*'s through sleepers and coaches were forwarded to DL&W's *New York Mail* which handled them to Hoboken. Westbound, the *Nickel Plate Limited*'s through cars were part of Lackawanna's new regional streamliner, the Hoboken-Buffalo *Phoebe Snow* (see Chapter 6).

NKP's *New Yorker* was a mid-morning run out of Chicago with a late-evening arrival the same day at Buffalo, where cars were forwarded on Lackawanna's *New Yorker* for Hoboken. Westbound, DL&W's *Westerner* handled the NKP through cars out of Hoboken in mid-evening, transferring cars to NKP's *Westerner* at Buffalo in the wee hours for a late-afternoon Chicago arrival.

Despite a preponderance of competition from NYC, the updated trains did surprisingly well early in the 1950s. In 1952, passenger revenues were up 50 percent over 1949. In 1954, perhaps to better reflect the train's services, the *Nickel Plate Limited* was renamed *City of Cleveland* eastbound and *City of Chicago* westbound. The revenue news was too good to last, though, and by 1959 the cutbacks had started with the loss of through cars to and from Hoboken on the *City* trains. In June 1963 the *New Yorker* and the *Westerner* made their last runs. Interestingly, the *City of Cleveland/Chicago* managed to out-live the Nickel Plate, which was merged into Norfolk & Western in 1964. But on September 10, 1965, both trains followed their parent railroad into the history books.

NORFOLK & WESTERN TO CINCINNATI

With a total mileage of just over 2,000 miles in 1950, Norfolk & Western was nearly identical in size to the Nickel Plate—a railroad it would absorb in 1964. N&W was best known as a Tidewater-to-Midwest coal-hauler, but it had a fairly substantial passenger operation, some of which involved the forwarding of through trains out of the Northeast to Southeastern points (Chapter 5).

Its principal main line reached west from the tidewater coal docks at Norfolk, Virginia, to Cincinnati and it was on this route that N&W operated its flagship streamliner, the *Powhatan Arrow*. N&W wasted no time in introducing the *Arrow* following World War II, launching its new "streamliner" in 1946 when other railroads were still waiting in line for their lightweight car orders backlogged by the war. Fortunately for N&W, it had already taken delivery of streamlined coaches in

1941. Initially intended for general service throughout the N&W system, these cars together with modernized heavyweight diners and lounges allowed N&W to be among the first to introduce a streamliner after the war.

This ad hoc streamliner *Powhatan Arrow* served until 1949 when it was completely re-equipped with new smooth-side Pullman-Standard lightweight coaches, diner, and tavern-lounge observation car. Diesels were not in the picture for this new train; after all, N&W's vitality depended on coal traffic, and N&W's coal-industry customers probably would not have taken kindly diesels on the head end. Instead, *Arrow* locomotive assignments were held down by one of the most attractive streamlined steam locomotives to adorn U.S. rails: N&W's Class J 4-8-4's.

The *Arrow* was a daylight run linking Virginia's Hampton Roads area (Norfolk/Portsmouth/Newport News/Virginia Beach) with Cincinnati, 676 miles via Lynchburg and Roanoke, Virginia, and Bluefield and Kenova, West Virginia. A connecting train at Portsmouth, Ohio, served Columbus, Ohio.

Once west of the flat Dismal Swamp area of eastern Virginia, the *Arrow*'s route was anything but arrow straight: N&W's main line snaked its way through the Blue Ridge Mountains and rugged Appalachian scenery, providing *Arrow* riders with a constantly changing panoramas. Resplendent in Tuscan red, gold, and black, the *Arrow*'s daily passing no doubt flashed optimism at residents trapped in the countless impoverished coal-mining communities lining the N&W main.

The *Arrow*'s colleague train was the *Pocahontas*, providing overnight service on the same route. New sleeping cars delivered in 1949 and 1950 along with the 1941 streamlined coaches bumped by the *Arrow*'s post-war re-equipping allowed the *Pocahontas* to also achieve streamliner status. Together the pair was promoted as the "twin team" serving the Virginia seashore.

All N&W passenger trains were dieselized by the end of the 1950s, and during the 1960s its passenger trains suffered the same ailments experienced by their contemporaries on other lines. In 1967, the *Arrow*'s schedule was drastically altered by making it an overnight run between Norfolk and Roanoke and daylight running west of Roanoke in both directions to Cincinnati. The only good news coincident to this change was the addition of a former-Wabash *Blue Bird* Vista-Dome coach, inherited when N&W leased the Wabash in 1964.

By 1969, the *Arrow* was but a shadow of its former glory, offering only a couple of coaches and a diner which only operated between Roanoke and Williamson, West Virginia. In an interesting twist which ended *Arrow* service but improved the *Pocahontas*, the Interstate Commerce Commission allowed N&W to discontinue the former if it would upgrade the latter. On May 23, 1969, the *Arrow* was gone, but a "new" streamlined *Pocahontas* emerged, with upgraded cars—including the *Arrow*'s Vista-Dome—and services and a new paint scheme of blue and gold. Thus, the "Pokey" became N&W's flagship streamliner until Amtrak operations began in May 1971.

Norfolk & Western *Powhatan Arrow*
(Facing page and below) Morning sun at Cincinnati highlights the dazzle of N&W's *Powhatan Arrow*, storming out of Cincinnati Union Terminal behind Class J 4-8-4 No. 601 at the start of its all-day run to tidewater on a summer day in the 1950s. As the diner and the tavern-lounge observation car roll by, the sun glints off the cars' gold striping. A brochure from the period served both the *Arrow* and its overnight cousin, the *Pocahontas*. Both photos, Alvin Schultze; ad, Joe Welsh Collection.

Santa Fe *Chief*
Symbolizing the mystique, excitement, and allure of the American West, Santa Fe's *Chief* strikes out of Chicago for Los Angeles on a brittle-cold morning during the winter of 1964-65. Led by a trio of Electro-Motive's sleek E-series diesels sporting the railroad's classic paint scheme reminiscent of an Indian warbonnet, the *Chief* will treat its passengers to a full day of Western vistas before its late-evening arrival at California's largest city. *George Speir.*

CHAPTER 3

WESTWARD ACROSS THE CONTINENT

The Splendid Streamliners of Santa Fe
Streamliners and Domeliners of Union Pacific's Overland Route
Triumvirate Triumph: Burlington-Rio Grande-Western Pacific Vista-Dome California Zephyr
Streamliners of the Sunset and Golden State Routes
Rocky Mountain Streamliners

The American West has done more to stir the wanderlust of travelers than any other region of North America. Even before there were railroads linking both coasts of the young nation, settlers and opportunists were obsessed with getting to California and the Southwest. Western territories eventually matured into states, but the fascination with heading west never changed, just the reasons for doing it. And now getting there was half the fun.

What had once been a long, dangerous trip on horseback, in wagon train, or in stagecoach had become, by the era of the railroad streamliner, a wistful remembrance to travelers sipping champagne in the *Super Chief*'s Pleasure Dome Lounge, slicing into a steak in the dome dining car of the *City of Los Angeles*, curling up in a cozy roomette with a good book on the *Golden State*, or gazing at the wonders of Western geography from the air-conditioned Vista-Domes of the *California Zephyr*. Now the only thing travelers were likely to encounter wearing a warbonnet was the diesel on the head end of their Santa Fe streamliner.

for 1938
Santa Fe
presents

AMERICA'S LARGEST FLEET OF ULTRA-MODERN STREAMLINED TRAINS

Santa Fe

A celebration of streamliners
Streamliners abound in the train shed of Dearborn Station in Chicago on February 11 and 12, 1938, as Santa Fe proudly showcases its new transcontinental trains. Some 30,000 spectators flocked to see, from left to right, the *Super Chief*, the *Chief*, and two *El Capitans*. Gleaming Electro-Motive E1 diesels dominate the scene, but clad in streamlined shrouding, "Blue Goose" 4-6-4 No. 3460 holds its own in the limelight. *Santa Fe Railway*.

The Splendid Streamliners of Santa Fe

The Atchison, Topeka & Santa Fe was not among the cadre of railroads which boldly hopped aboard the streamliner bandwagon during 1934-36. But the Santa Fe was hardly resting on its laurels. The railroad's impeccable credentials in the realm of passenger-train operation had already been established with such flyers as the *California Limited* (1892), the *de-Luxe* (1911), and the *Chief* (1926). As new *Zephyr*s and M-10000s were being delivered, Santa Fe inaugurated a new heavyweight train that was destined straight to stardom as one of the two top streamliners in America. That train, of course, was the all-Pullman *Super Chief*, and its first run out of Chicago occurred on May 12, 1936 (only five days before IC's streamliner *Green Diamond* was launched a few blocks away). It was unusual not for its accommodations, which were the Santa Fe and Pullman could muster from the *Chief* pool, but for its motive power and speed.

The *Super Chief* represented Santa Fe's first experimentation with over-the-road diesel-electric power in the form of a 3600-hp Electro-Motive box-cab diesel set known as "Amos & Andy" that pulled the new train. As for speed, the *Super Chief* ushered in an unprecedented 39¾-hour schedule, including station stops, for the 2,227 miles separating Chicago from L.A. Until that time, the *Chief*—also an all-Pullman operation—had been the fastest Chicago-West Coast train with a running time in the 53-55-hour range, depending on direction of travel. To maintain this rigorous schedule, speeds in excess of 100 mph were at times necessary. Because there was initially only one set of *Super Chief* equipment, the train then made but one round trip per week.

The timing of the *Super*'s premiere was interesting. The first westbound *Super Chief* arrived Los Angeles on May 14. The following day, Union Pacific's streamliner *City of Los Angeles* entered service (Chapter 1), also on a 39-hour 45-minute schedule.

Despite the lure of exotic streamlined equipment on the UP, Santa Fe had no trouble keeping its *Super Chief* populated, which proved that there was still a lot to be said for speed and service in the absence of streamlining. With the *Super* firmly established as a transcontinental triumph, though, Santa Fe carefully proceeded to the next stage of its plan: a streamlined *Super Chief*.

Santa Fe management knew early on it was not interested in inflexible, diminutive articulated streamliner trainsets—"toys," as some in the industry referred to them. The lessons of such had already become well apparent but were part of the price of being a true pioneer in the streamliner field for CB&Q, UP, and others which had purchased streamliners as integral trainsets.

Nonetheless, for its streamlined *Super Chief*, Santa Fe approached two builders which had been entrenched in the very earliest streamliner projects: Electro-Motive and Budd Company. Both had proven the virtues of diesel power and lightweight, stainless-steel car construction, but both companies had also come to realize that cars and locomotives could be offered as "catalog" products—a necessary approach to production given the fact that more railroads than ever were beginning to join the race to streamline.

By the end of 1936, Electro-Motive had introduced its now-famous E-series passenger diesel in its catalog line, though none had yet been built. In June 1937 Santa Fe took delivery of an E1 model in cab-and-booster ("A&B") configuration. (Baltimore & Ohio had been the first purchaser of E-units only a month earlier for its *Royal Blue* streamliner as shown on pages 38-39.)

506—Santa Fe's "Super Chief" Traveling thru the Orange Groves, California

The 1937 *Super Chief*

The prewar postcard above idealized California orchards visited by the newly streamlined *Super Chief*. Interior appointments likewise capitalized on Western iconography, as in the Navajo-inspired fabric used in the train's sleeper-lounge observation car (below left)—which was indeed named *Navajo*. In the lounge car *Acoma*, below right, zebrawood paneling was complemented by authentic Navajo art. *Postcard, Mike Schafer Collection; two photos, Santa Fe Railway.*

Also in 1936, Budd had introduced a prototype conventional but lightweight stainless-steel coach, which it sold to Santa Fe. An initially skeptical Santa Fe was duly impressed and selected Budd to help create the first streamlined *Super Chief*.

This it did with an eight-car train: baggage car No. 3430; sleeping car *Isleta*; sleeper *Taos*; dormitory-barber shop-buffet-lounge *Acoma*; dining car *Cochiti* seating 36; two more sleepers, the *Oraibi* and the *Laguna*; and—the train's ultimate car—sleeper lounge-observation car *Navajo*.

Outside, the cars were as flashy as any of their fluted-side predecessors, but inside they represented unparalleled thematic design. For this project, Santa Fe had selected Sterling B. McDonald, a designer who worked out of a studio at Chicago's famous Merchandise Mart. Santa Fe liked the work McDonald had accomplished on UP's streamliners and assigned him the challenge of developing a conception for the *Super Chief* car interiors.

Working with Roger Birdseye, Santa Fe's advertising manager, McDonald built upon the Southwest Native American theming that Santa Fe had already been using in its promotion and decor (Birdseye was an expert in Southwest Indian culture). McDonald's and Birdseye's work was transformed into reality by Paul Cret and John Harbeson of the School of Architecture at the University of Pennsylvania; Cret and Harbeson served as architects for the Budd Company.

Each *Super Chief* car was to have its own unique interior design, going so far as to employ a different type of rare wood in each. Thus the sleeping-car rooms bore trim and panelings of zebrawood, ebonized maple, Brazilian rosewood, and other exotic woods while dining-car *Cochiti* featured bubinga wood. Navajo patterns were featured in much of the fabric work, and reproductions of Navajo sand paintings adorned pier panels between car windows.

The new *Super Chief* even had its own china pattern, developed by Mary Colter, a designer for Santa Fe and its affiliated Fred Harvey company of restaurant fame. She developed the "Mimbreno" pattern based on the ancient, geometric artwork of the Mimbres tribe. Mimbreno remained the pattern of the *Super Chief* until Santa Fe turned over its passenger operations to Amtrak in 1971. Today original and even reproduction Mimbreno china is highly sought by collectors.

Undoubtedly the crowning glory of the 1937 *Super Chief* in terms of trademark or design was its locomotive paint scheme. Electro-Motive E-series passenger diesels were considered by many students of railroad industrial technology and history to be the epitome of timeless streamliner diesel design. To render color and character to Santa Fe's new E1 locomotives, EMC called upon one of its illustrators, Leland Knickerbocker, who develop what became the most-famous railroad paint scheme in the world: Santa Fe's "warbonnet" livery. The pattern mimicked the profile of an Indian chief wearing a feather headdress. To carry this out, Knickerbocker used three basic colors—red, yellow, and black—which boldly complemented the locomotives' stainless-steel side panels. At the same time, Knickerbocker modified Santa Fe's circular logo into an oval design that served as an integral part of the overall nose treatment.

The results were stunning. The scheme, like the E1 locomotives it debuted on, had a timeless quality and instant appeal (and inherent safety qualities—there was no mistaking the approach of the *Super Chief* or any other locomotive bearing the warbonnet livery). The scheme, with slight variations through the years, was adopted for nearly all future Santa Fe passenger locomotives. It has appeared on countless model- and toy-train locomotives since World War II and, beginning in 1985, Santa Fe began applying the scheme and colors to its freight locomotives as well.

Following various exhibition runs (including a rail-burning 36-hour, 49-minute sprint from L.A. to Chicago) and displays, the new streamlined *Super Chief* rolled forth from Chicago's 1880s-era Dearborn Station on May 18, 1937, for its first regularly scheduled trip . . . powered by Santa Fe box-cab "Amos" and an EMC demonstrator box-cab. It seems the E-unit set had burned out a traction motor in the course of their record-breaking L.A.-Chicago bolt a few days earlier. Regardless, it was an altogether new era for Santa Fe.

Santa Fe was not waiting to see how the new lightweight *Super Chief* fared before continuing its streamlining program. In the infancy of the streamlined *Super*

Chief, Santa Fe was already ordering more new streamlined cars and locomotives. By the end of 1937, Budd had delivered a number of new cars to Santa Fe, which began appearing on several heavyweight trains.

As with the original heavyweight *Super,* the streamlined *Super,* even with greater load capacity, was a constant sell-out, and a long waiting list of hopeful passengers had to be maintained. More interesting was the fact that, since the birth of the *Super Chief,* patronage on the heavyweight *Chief* increased dramati-

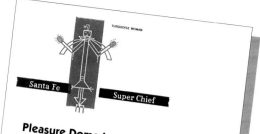

Pleasure Dome Lounge
Pausing for connecting passengers from the Denver connecting train, which is at left in the photo, the *Super Chief* gleams under the lights of the La Junta (Colorado) depot platforms on a spring evening in 1971. The *Super*'s feature car from 1950 into the 1970s was the Pleasure Dome Lounge, which can be seen just beyond the Denver train's locomotive. The car's private dining area, the Turquoise Room, featured a large, lit turquoise medallion on the wall. *Both photos, Mike Schafer.*

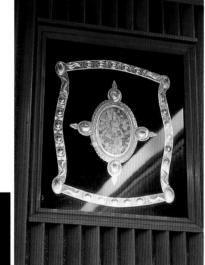

cally; Santa Fe officials had believed that the new train would draw patronage away from the *Chief*.

In 1938, Santa Fe achieved the distinction of becoming the operator of the largest fleet of streamliners in America. Another early step toward that honor was the introduction of enough new lightweight, streamlined cars from Budd and now Pullman-Standard as well to re-equip all six sets of heavyweight equipment that had been required for daily *Chief* service. This enabled the *Chief* to officially become a streamliner on January 31, 1938, albeit powered mostly by conventional steam power and one new streamlined Hudson-type (4-6-4) steam locomotive. The streamlined *Chief* offered only first-class accommodations; each consist included six Pullman-operated sleepers, baggage-barber shop-buffet-lounge, dormitory-club lounge, full dining car, and a

sleeper-lounge observation car. By this time, the *Chief*'s running time had been reduced to about 50 hours, still considerably longer than the *Super Chief* due to the greater number of stations served by the *Chief*.

Then, on February 22, Santa Fe unveiled an all-coach companion train to the *Super Chief*, running on the same fast 39³/4-hour Chicago-L.A. timing. *Economy Chief* was one of several early considerations for a name, but Santa Fe settled on the more elegant title of *El Capitan* honoring Spanish conquistadors which had influenced Southwest U.S. and Mexican culture. Consists (there were two sets of equipment) included a baggage-dormitory-coach, two 52-reclining-seat coaches, a lunch counter-diner, and a coach lounge observation car.

Four days following *El Capitan*'s debut, on February 26, a second *Super Chief* joined the fleet, allowing

Hi-Level *El Capitan*, 1956
Less than a month old, the Hi-Level *El Capitan* makes a grand entrance into Chicago's elderly Dearborn Station on August 10, 1956. Prominent in the photo is the Hi-Level "Top of the Cap" lounge car with its glassed-in roof area. Additional lounge facilities were on the lower level, an area that became known as the "Kachina Coffee Shop." *John Dziobko.*

"Top of the Cap"
HI-LEVEL LOUNGE CAR

Here's the fun car on El Capitan. Note the skylights in the roof, as well as wide picture windows. On the hi-level there are 60 seats arranged individually, as well as in pairs and in tables for a foursome of bridge. The stairway at center of car leads to the lower lounge accommodating 20 more passengers. There is a refreshment bar and attendants on both levels, also on the upper level is a completely stocked newsstand. There is plenty of room to move around in this new type lounge car and in all the other cars that make up the Hi-Level El Capitan. This roominess is just one of many features that contribute to the smooth-riding comfort of El Capitan.

twice-weekly *Super Chief* service in each direction. It used equipment drawn from the pool of cars normally reserved for the newly streamlined *Chief* until Pullman-Standard completed car deliveries later that summer.

Transcon streamliners had now become a way of life along the Santa Fe Trail. During the ensuing years, their popularity required the railroad to periodically add cars to accommodate the increase in patronage and upgrade equipment. For example, the *Super Chief* received new sleeping cars in 1939, and in 1940-41 *El Capitan* received some new rolling stock from both Budd and Pullman-Standard, enough so that a third consist was created, allowing the railroad to offer thrice-weekly *El Capitan* service in each direction.

New car and locomotive construction came to almost a complete stop during World War II as wartime restrictions greatly curtailed equipment orders. The return to peace in 1945 reopened the floodgates, and another wave of streamlining swept over U.S. railroads. Santa Fe was in the thick of it.

When the manufacturing backlog began to ease two years later, Santa Fe began taking delivery of enough new cars to, in February 1948, again re-equip the *Super Chief* and *El Capitan*. By this time, the frequency of both trains had been increased to every-other-day service; the 1948 re-equipping finally permitted both trains to go daily—an event which warranted special celebratory luncheons at Chicago and Los Angeles. At both events, Santa Fe President Fred Gurley recounted how the railroad's passenger revenues had increased 220 percent since the *Super Chief* debuted more than a decade earlier. Five Indian tribes provided songs and dances for the luncheons; comedian Bob Hope was master of ceremonies at the L.A. gathering.

The *Chief*, too, improved its credentials during the immediate postwar years. First, in 1946, the *Chief* gained New York-Los Angeles through sleeping cars. Then, new

diesels bumped steam on the *Chief* in 1947 and permitted a reduction in travel time to under 47 hours.

Streamlining continued at full throttle for numerous railroads right into the 1950s despite isolated but alarming signs which indicated the effort wasn't necessarily the panacea that would reverse the decline in patronage which resumed following the war. Because of its reputation, Santa Fe was a little less vulnerable to the problem and continued to upgrade its streamliner fleet, which now included a number regional trains as well as transcons.

In 1951, Santa Fe unveiled yet another new rendition of the *Super Chief*, one which many transportation historians believe to be its zenith. New sleeping cars from Budd and American Car & Foundry offered double bedrooms, the now-popular roomette for single travelers, compartments, and drawing rooms. Stylish 36-seat diners would feature cuisine destined to become Santa Fe hallmarks, among them Tornados of Beef and "Famous Santa Fe French Toast." Handsome sleeper-lounge observation cars continued to provide a fitting conclusion to each of the six consists required to protect daily scheduling. But the new high point of the 1951 *Super* was its stellar Pleasure Dome lounge cars.

The dome-car concept was already five years old when Santa Fe received these six remarkable cars from P-S late in 1950. The cars' main level contained an ultra-modern lounge area and a special innovation: the Turquoise Room, a private dining area for 12. The dome section featured a rarity in dome seating: single rows of individual rotating parlor chairs. A third level of the car—that beneath the dome section—contained a cocktail lounge.

The early 1950s would bring several changes to Santa Fe's Midwest-California service. For the *Chief*, it was a good news/bad news

El Capitan brochure
Santa Fe pulled out the stops in promoting its new *El Capitan*. This now-famous fold-out brochure, the portion shown at about half actual size, graphically illustrated the revolutionary new concept of a bilevel intercity train. *Joe Welsh Collection.*

situation. The bad news was that, in January 1954, the *Chief* lost its exalted all-Pullman status with the addition of reclining-seat coaches. The train also lost its New York-Los Angeles sleepers, which were shifted to the *Super Chief.* On the good news side, the *Chief's* end-to-end running time was speeded up by several hours.

In June 1954, an altogether "new" Chicago-California streamliner joined "Chico's" fleet, the *San Francisco Chief.* (Chico was Santa Fe's fictional mascot Indian lad whose caricature appeared on numerous passenger timetables and advertising through the years). The train was new in the sense that Santa Fe had never before offered through Chicago-San Francisco/Oakland service, but it was made up largely of hand-me-down streamlined cars that had been bumped by new equipment.

West of Kansas City, the *San Francisco Chief* strayed from the traditional route long used by the *Chief, Super Chief, El Capitan* and other Chicago-California trains by operating over what was the railroad's principal freight route via Amarillo, Texas, returning to the regular main line west of Albuquerque. At Barstow, California, the train again diverged from the traditional route, to head up Santa Fe's main line through the Central Valley to Oakland via Stockton.

With typical Santa Fe panache, the coach-and-sleeping-car *San Francisco Chief* was inaugurated with a unique Indian ceremony led by Hopi Chief Taptuka, who christened the train with holy water from Arizona's San Francisco Mountains. The train was a latecomer in the Chicago-San Fran market, which had no shortage of streamliners. Nonetheless, Santa Fe's golden touch rendered the *San Francisco Chief* another success.

The feature car of the daily *San Francisco Chief* was its new full-length dome. AT&SF had taken delivery of 14 of these behemoths, which Santa Fe called its "Big Dome" lounges, from the Budd Company in 1954. They were among the heaviest streamlined passenger cars ever built. *El Capitan* also received these new cars, adding yet another enhancement for that train.

But *El Capitan's* most notable upgrade was yet to come. On July 15, 1956, the train went "Hi-Level" when it was completely re-equipped with revolutionary new bilevel intercity cars—coaches, diners and

lounges— built by the Budd Company. The double-deck concept was hardly new to passenger rolling stock—bilevel cars had been in use on some Chicago suburban trains since 1950—but this was the first widespread application to over-the-road streamliners.

Their virtues were numerous. The new Hi-Levels, as they were dubbed, were more efficient in that more people could be carried in a single car with no sacrifice to space or comfort due to the fact that restrooms, restroom lounges, and baggage storage areas had been moved to the lower level. With all passenger seating located in the upper level, high above the rails, the ride was quieter and the views even better.

The same held true for the dining car, where all table seating was upstairs and the kitchen and service area was downstairs. Food was carried to the dining room via dumb waiter. In Hi-Level form, lounge facilities—often a crowded situation—were now ample. The upstairs lounge section of *El Capitan's* new Hi-Level lounge cars could accommodate 60 patrons at tables as well as individual seats. At one end of the upper level was a newsstand which sold magazines, newspapers, and travel notions; next to it was the serving bar. Downstairs was an additional lounge area with a bar.

So revolutionary was the Hi-Level *El Capitan* that the railroad spared no effort for its pre-inaugural exhibition—the likes of which hadn't been seen since the first *Super Chief.* A demonstration *El Cap* headed off line for Washington, D.C., via the B&O. Once in the nation's capital, the train made press runs out of Washington for congressmen, senators, and even members of the Interstate Commerce Commission. As many as 400 guests per run sampled the food, drink, and Hi-Level ride quality. The special *El Cap* train was also exhibited at Pittsburgh, Cleveland and Youngstown, Ohio, and Detroit before heading back to home rails where it paused at Chicago, Kansas City, Los Angeles, Pasadena, San Diego, Albuquerque and other points.

The Hi-Level cars were extraordinarily well-received by the riding public, so much so that Santa Fe even drew up plans for a Hi-Level *Super Chief* featuring bilevel sleeping cars. Under Santa Fe, the plans never materialized, but the railroad did acquire additional Hi-

San Francisco Chief

(Facing page) Santa Fe's newborn *San Francisco Chief* is stretched out against a backdrop formed by the Tehachapi Mountains of Southern California as it makes its westbound trek over Tehachapi Pass. It's June 12, 1954, and the train is less than a week old. A latecomer in the Chicago-California streamliner market, the *S.F. Chief* drew its equipment in part from a car order delivered by Budd for Santa Fe in 1953 and 1954. Among the cars of this order were eight Super Dome lounge cars—one of which is at the center of the train—intended for the *S.F. Chief, El Capitan, Kansas Cityan,* and *Chicagoan.* In 1964, the *S.F. Chief* would received Hi-Level coaches. Though the *San Francisco Chief* followed the least scenic rail route between Chicago and the Bay Area, the train was yet another successful streamliner venture for Santa Fe. *Photo, William D. Middleton; ad, Joe Welsh Collection.*

Level coaches in 1963-64 when other railroads were already exiting from the passenger market. The new cars permitted the coach portion of the *San Francisco Chief* to go Hi-Level, and occasionally the Hi-Levels showed up on secondary trains as well.

The importance of Santa Fe's venture into Hi-Level equipment can not be underestimated. After Amtrak took over selected passenger operations of most Class 1 railroads in May 1971, it acquired a large stock of Santa Fe cars, including the Hi-Levels. When it came time for Amtrak to order new equipment to upgrade its long-distance Western trains late in the 1970s, the former Santa Fe Hi-Levels were the inspiration for Amtrak's new fleet of Superliner coaches, sleepers, diners and lounge cars which prevail on most of Amtrak's long-distance trains in the late 1990s—in some cases working side-by-side with Hi-Level veterans still in service.

The Santa Fe experience in American train travel was unmatched. Few railroads operated passenger trains with the quality of Santa Fe, which did so even when U.S. passenger-train service began to unravel at an accelerated rate during the late 1960s. Although Santa Fe elected to discontinue the *Chief* in 1968, the *San Francisco Chief*, *El Capitan*, *Super Chief* and other Santa Fe liners continued to offer the best service possible right up to Amtrak's arrival in May 1971.

The Dome Dimension

Just as streamliners revolutionized rail travel, the dome car revolutionized streamliners. The idea of a glass-enclosed "observation deck" on passenger cars was the brainstorm of Cyrus R. Osborne, vice president and general manager of the Electro-Motive Division (EMD) of General Motors.

During a field trip one day in 1944, Osborne was riding in the cab of a Rio Grande F-series diesel locomotive leading a westbound freight through spectacular Glenwood Canyon in north central Colorado. He remarked to the engineer that a lot of people would pay good money to enjoy the vantage point that a locomotive crew had. Later that day, after he reached Salt Lake City, Osborne sat in his hotel room and sketched out ideas of passenger cars outfitted with a special upper-level viewing area enclosed by glass.

Eventually he showed his sketches to upper-level management at GM as well as to a friend of his, Ralph Budd, then president of the Chicago, Burlington & Quincy. Both GM and Ralph Budd were smitten with the concept, and the quest was on to transform sketches into reality. Chalk up another first for the Burlington. At its shop complex in Aurora, Illinois, 38 miles from downtown Chicago, Burlington work forces took a "straight" stainless-steel coach named *Silver Alchemy* (built in 1940 for the *Ak-Sar-Ben Zephyr*) and cut, fabricated, and welded until the world's first Vista-Dome car was born. Rechristened, appropriately, *Silver Dome*, the car was unveiled in June 1945. Burlington sent it testing on various trains of its popular *Zephyr* fleet—to the rave reviews of passengers. An ecstatic Burlington soon ordered production domes—40 of them—from its favored carbuilder, the Budd Company.

Meanwhile over at GM, officials were working with various railroad executives and with the folks at Pullman-Standard on the south side of Chicago on their dome cars. Although the GM-Pullman-Standard alliance would not be the first to create a dome car per se, GM's EMD subsidiary and P-S would jointly build a domed demonstration train that would tour the U.S. to sell other railroads on the dome-car idea. Thus was born, in the spring of 1947, the *Train of Tomorrow*.

The four-car, all-dome train featured dome coach *Star Dust*, dome sleeper *Dream Cloud*, dome diner *Sky View*, and a dome lounge-observation car *Moon Glow* pulled by a standard E7 EMD passenger diesel (standard, save for the stainless-steel fluting applied to its sides as part of the *Train of Tomorrow*'s overall design). In May 1947, the train embarked on a 65,000-mile exhibition tour and was also displayed at the Chicago Railroad Fair of 1948-49.

Undoubtedly, the *Train of Tomorrow* inspired other railroads to add the dome dimension to their streamliners, but before the first order for a dome was even placed with P-S as a result of the *Train of Tomorrow* tour, the Budd Company had out-shopped nearly 50 dome cars, most of them for the Burlington. That railroad's *Twin Cities Zephyr*s became the first regularly scheduled trains in the U.S. whose assigned equipment included dome cars, and in 1949 the Vista-Dome *California Zephyr* became the nation's first transcontinental streamliner to employ the see-all Vista-Dome car. The *CZ* operated via the Rio Grande through the Rocky Mountains, right through Glenwood Canyon where Cy Osborne conceived the dome idea, and a monument to that idea was erected along the highway in Glenwood Canyon.

Budd's domes—Burlington coined them "Vista-Domes," a name which has become almost generic—were a marked improvement over Burlington's *Silver Dome*

School children on a field trip enjoy the dome on Southern's Asheville Special *in 1975. Facing page:* Train of Tomorrow *magazine ad from the late 1940s. Both, Mike Schafer.*

in that Budd's production domes had recessed floors under the dome sections for better utilization of space. They also featured curved glass in the dome sections themselves; *Silver Dome* and the *Train of Tomorrow*'s domes employed flat panes of glass, as would all "short" domes built by P-S.

The dome-car craze was under way, and when the dust finally settled and the last dome car had been built about a decade later (for Burlington's 1956 rendition of the *Denver Zephyr*), a total of 235 dome cars, owned by 15 railroads, roamed American and Canadian rails. They were outshopped by four companies—Budd, Pullman-Standard, American Car & Foundry, and Southern Pacific Railroad—and came in a surprising variety of shapes, sizes, and configurations from dome coaches to dome lounge-sleepers. Initially, all domes were "short domes" in that the dome section comprised less than a third the length of a typical 85-foot postwar streamlined car. Then, in 1952, Pullman-Standard introduced the full-length dome wherein the dome section occupied nearly the entire length of the car, with the main lounge facilities located below. Budd followed suit in 1954 with its own full-length domes, and then in 1954-55 Southern Pacific's Sacramento (California) Shops rebuilt seven pre-war lightweight cars into "three-quarter" domes whose glassed-in area occupied about three-fourths of the cars' length and extended beyond the upper-level dome-seating section and over the main-level, providing a high glass-ceilinged lounge area.

Domes became prevalent on Western streamliners, but the tight clearances of Eastern rail routes, particularly in tunnels and large-city terminals such as New York's Grand Central restricted the use of dome cars. Thus, some prominent streamliner operators such as New York Central and Pennsylvania never owned dome cars (although PRR did lease some for *South Wind* service). Baltimore & Ohio and Chesapeake & Ohio were two notable exceptions. Both roads had P-S and Budd design "low-profile" domes that would tolerate Eastern clearances. Pullman-Standard's low-profile dome coaches first served on B&O's Chicago-Washington-Jersey City

Columbian while Budd's low-profile, stainless-steel dome coaches, dome sleepers, and dome observation cars were delivered for C&O's Cincinnati-Washington/Newport News *Chessie* streamliner. The *Chessie* was never launched, and its domes were sold to other carriers, including B&O.

After World War II, streamlining became the rule rather than the exception of most main passenger trains. Now railroads needed another attraction to entice people back to the rails, and domes undoubtedly fulfilled that goal, although they could only delay the inevitable near-collapse of the American passenger train that would occur late in the 1960s. Fortunately, dome cars were embraced by Amtrak, which kept a modest fleet of them running well into the 1990s until their age and economical considerations mandated retirement. Whether it was the postwar 1940s or auto-happy 1990s, passengers always enjoyed the unique dimension afforded by dome-car travel.

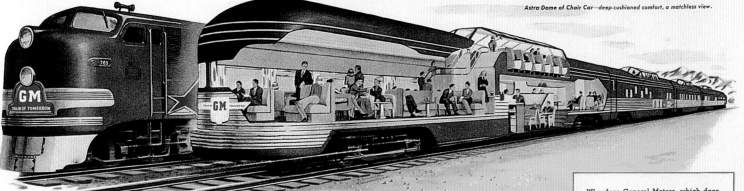

Streamliners and Domeliners of the Overland Route

The early, runaway success of the streamliner on both Burlington and Union Pacific resulted in the almost overnight proliferation of streamliner "fleets" for the two carriers. The "Q" was largely a Midwest carrier, so most of its *Zephyr* fleet was regional in nature; there would not be a transcon *Zephyr* until 1949. However, UP was different. Closely allied with Chicago & North Western, it spanned the continent west of the Great Lakes.

It was that alliance which ushered in the *City of Portland*—America's first transcontinental streamliner—and two subsequent transcons, the *City of Los Angeles* and *City of San Francisco*, with Southern Pacific being a relay player in the latter between Ogden and Oakland/San Francisco. The infancy of all three trains is covered in Chapter 1, and the ongoing history of the *City of Portland* is featured in the following chapter, "Northwest Passages."

Travel from the East and Midwest to California has always been particularly heavy, so the 1936 introduction of the first California-bound streamliners, the *City of Los Angeles* and *City of San Francisco*, was met with great enthusiasm by the traveling public. With only one trainset per route, however, streamliner service was limited to about one "sailing" per week in each direction; those who couldn't or wouldn't fit their travel plans around the streamliner departures were obliged to use standard steam-powered trains.

It soon became apparent that more streamliners were in demand, consequently late in 1937 UP, C&NW, and SP took delivery of an additional *City of Los Angeles* trainset, a new *City of San Francisco* trainset, and enough other new cars (basically five trainsets) to transform the coach-dominated *Challenger* between Chicago, Oakland, and Los Angeles into a streamliner. The new *City of Los Angeles* supplemented the existing M-10002 *City of L.A.* outlined in Chapter 1, thereby doubling *City* departures on that route to every third day. The new *City of San Francisco* replaced the M-10004 *City of S.F.* set, which was rebuilt for new assignments. Also in 1937, UP introduced the Chicago-San Francisco *Forty-Niner*, a train comprised of a mixture of new lightweight cars and modernized heavyweight pulled by

Domeliners on the Overland Route

Thirty-three miles after departing the state capital of Cheyenne, Union Pacific's combined westbound *City of Los Angeles/ City of Portland/City of Kansas City/Challenger* hastens through "cowboy country" near Dale, Wyoming, in April 1971. *Mike Schafer*

streamlined stream locomotives.

The two new lightweight *City* trains represented a departure from the M-series sets in that the motive power, rather than having been custom-built for UP, comprised locomotives from the Electro-Motive "catalog"—types that could, in effect, be purchased by any buyer. Locomotives were from EMC's new E-series line of passenger diesels, two three-unit sets of E2 models jointly owned by UP, C&NW, and SP. Similarly, the overall design of the passenger cars supplied for the two new trains by Pullman-Standard represented that manufacturer's evolution in the field. Certain traits and car components that would be found on numerous cars outshopped by P-S for the next quarter century-plus for

The NEW Streamliner

CITY OF SAN FRANCISCO

1937 *City of Los Angeles*
In the surrealistic light of a California afternoon, UP's new *City of Los Angeles* of 1937 coasts through an orange grove behind a threesome of Electro-Motive E2s, each unit lettered for the train. *Union Pacific Railroad Museum Collection, image No. 501479*

1937 *City of San Francisco* **booklet**
For its new *City of San Francisco,* UP issued a 32-page booklet carefully explaining all the train's services and equipment. *Mike Schafer Collection.*

railroads nationwide were evident on the 1937-38 *City of San Francisco* and *City of Los Angeles.* Nonetheless, UP clung to the articulated principle even on these newest trains, employing some articulated cars.

The two new *City* trains were similar. Each had 14-car consists including a veritable rolling restaurant in which one car of an articulated pair was a 64-seat dining room and the other was a combination kitchen-coffee shop. Each train also had a club-dormitory car, an observation-lounge, and a variety of sleeping accommodations—including the new "roomette" for single travelers—in several sleepers. The *City of Los Angeles* set had an articulated coach pair while the *City of San Francisco* had but a single coach. Most of the cars of both trains were named for locales in the region of their namesake cities; for example, *Rose Bowl, Santa Monica, Wilshire* (*City of Los Angeles*) and *Mission Dolores,*

Embarcadero, and *Chinatown* (*City of San Francisco*). Interior appointments of both trains were likewise similar, with one most-interesting exception: the *City of Los Angeles* dorm-lounge *Little Nugget,* done up in gaslight-era "bordello"! The observation cars of both trains featured simple but elegant "tear drop"-shaped ends that would become a hallmark of many future P-S observation cars. New cars for the *Challenger*s included coaches and articulated kitchen-dormitory/diners.

On August 12, 1939, sabotage sent the new *City of San Francisco* careening off a bridge in the Nevada desert, killing several passengers and crewmembers and destroying five cars. Substitute cars from the Pullman sleeping-car pool and from UP's own car pool shouldered *City of S. F.* service until new replacement cars were delivered. A more-optimistic note from that year was the debut of the *Treasure Island Special* between

A tale of two *Cities*' lounge cars
The overall modern decor of the 1937 *City of Los Angeles* belied its most unusual dormitory-lounge car, *Little Nugget.* In a complete departure from the rest of the train's theming, which took travelers into the future, *Little Nugget* (above) took them back to the wild West of the late nineteenth century. The bar area featured an electrically animated singing canary and electric "gaslights." The 1941 *City of Los Angeles* fulfilled the expectations some would more likely have of a futuristic train. The *Hollywood* (right) provided a swank meeting place where one might even rub elbows with the likes of Clark Gable and Vivian Leigh. Portholed windows were a trademark of early UP streamliners. *Both photos, Union Pacific Railroad Museum.*

Chicago and Oakland/San Francisco; it ran in conjunction with the *Forty-Niner* and *City of San Francisco* to provide alternate-day service to the World's Fair at San Francisco during the summers of 1939 and 1940.

Just before restrictions on new car and locomotive deliveries went into effect after the U.S. became involved in World War II, UP, C&NW, SP, and the Pullman Company took delivery of 145 new lightweight, streamlined cars from Pullman-Standard. Many of these cars were slated for "General Service," which included upgrading the *San Francisco Overland*, but enough were set aside to inaugurate yet another new *City of Los Angeles* trainset and a *City of San Francisco* consist. Six new E6-type Electro-Motive diesels supplied pulling power to *City* trains. The new cars and locomotives that were to be assigned to *City* train service represented the first use of what is still UP's standard color scheme: Armour Yellow with Harbor Mist Gray with red lettering and striping. Most of the remainder of the cars wore UP's "Overland" color scheme of two-tone gray.

These two newest *City* trainsets were the most luxurious yet, sporting barber shops, shower baths, and, for coach passengers, pillow-type radio speakers. A cafe lounge provided economy meal service aimed at coach passengers. The club-lounge, intended for Pullman passenger, of this newest *City of Los Angeles* was a particular standout, from the inside out. Named *Hollywood*, it featured porthole windows outfitted with Polaroid glass which could be rotated to reduce sun glare. This latest trainset allowed the *City of Los Angeles* to go to an every-third-day departure from home terminals.

All this new equipment permitted UP-C&NW-SP to ride out the war with grace and style, for it allowed the railroads to run the *City* trains in sections to meet wartime travel demands—and do it largely with lightweight equipment. The war created casualties on the railroad too, one of which was the M-10000—the world's first true streamliner. Its aluminum body was apparently more important to the war effort than to hauling passengers between Kansas City and Salina, and a few days after Pearl Harbor, "Little Zip"—as the train had become known to UP employees—was retired and scrapped. A similar fate had already befallen the M-10001, the original *City of Portland*. Another casualty in 1941 was the *Forty-Niner*, which was discontinued and its assigned equipment dispersed to other UP trains.

Even before the War had formally ceased, UP began planning postwar passenger strategies which included additional new cars, daily Streamliner service between Chicago and Los Angeles and San Francisco, and a new *City* train serving St. Louis. Part of this was prompted by rumors that a Burlington-Rio Grande-Western Pacific consortium were planning new transcontinental streamliner service. By the spring of 1946, the first group of cars were on order from American Car & Foundry, and by the end of 1950 ACF and Pullman-Standard had delivered more than 200 new lightweight cars to UP, SP, C&NW, and the Wabash for *City* and other UP streamliner services.

On June 2, 1946, the new *City of St. Louis* went into service between St. Louis and Cheyenne, Wyo., on a daily basis via Kansas City and Denver. Wabash handled the train between St. Louis and Kansas City. The train carried through cars destined to Portland, San Francisco (Oakland), and Los Angeles that were forward to and from connecting trains at Cheyenne. In 1951, the *City of St. Louis* became its own train all the way through to L.A.

The flood of new cars and the refurbishing of older cars allowed UP and partners C&NW and SP to establish daily service of the entire *City* fleet during 1947, albeit at the expense of the *Challenger*, which was discontinued. Despite the number of new cars, the rolling stock fleet was stretched pretty thin and car dispersement was monitored by detailed planning sheets. Consequently, heavyweight car substitutions were not unheard of, and some *City* trains had to be cleaned, turned, and restocked to be doubled back out of the home terminals the same day they arrived.

This equipment crunch did not ease up until the delivery of another major batch of equipment—one that would propel the *City* and Streamliner fleet to its pinnacle—during the mid-1950s. By this time, some railroads that had embarked on postwar streamliner projects were beginning to lose hope in the future of the passenger train, but UP passenger trains—the *City* trains in particular—continued to enjoy a strong passenger allegiance. Part of this, perhaps, was due to the postwar popularity of travel to the West. With more discretionary income in the euphoric Fifties, more people were taking bigger vacations, and the American West was full of popular destinations served by the UP: the new Disneyland on the outskirts of Los Angeles; the ski haven, Sun Valley, Idaho; and the new neon mecca Las Vegas. Union Pacific, like rival Santa Fe, had established a sterling reputation for quality transportation.

Winged Streamliner dinner plate
UP carried the Streamliner theming into many aspects of train operation. In 1936 the road introduced the handsome "Winged Streamliner" china pattern, which featured a likeness of a later M-series-powered train—with wings to denote speed. UP continued to order this pattern for its dining service into 1955. *Mike Schafer Collection.*

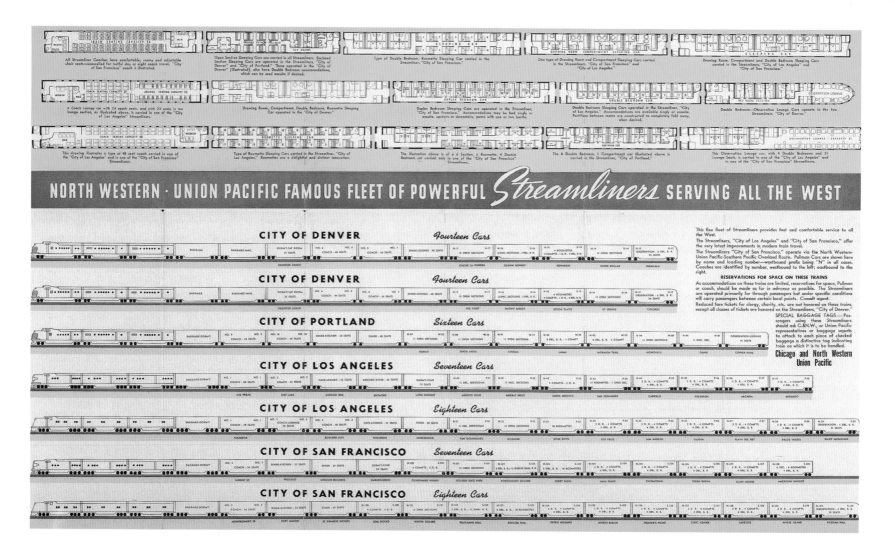

Streamliner guide, 1943

During the first few years of UP's growing Streamliner fleet, the railroad periodically issued brochures that detailed train "sailing dates" and equipment assignments. This was in the days, of course, when train consists were largely kept intact. Eventually this treatment of streamliners was dispensed with in lieu of equipment pools—necessary for daily train operation—from which cars might be drawn for service on any given train. In this brochure issued in November 1943, the diagrams go so far as to provide specific car names and floor plans. Even the locomotive sketches correctly define the type of motive power normally assigned. *Mike Schafer Collection.*

The goal of maintaining this reputation was clearly evident in the mid-1950s car order, as UP finally joined the ranks of transcontinental dome operators with the delivery of ten dome coaches, 15 dome lounge-observation cars, and ten stunning dome dining cars in addition to more than 140 other new cars including sleepers, regular diners, and coaches (some belonging to C&NW). No doubt, the decision purchase domes was prompted by the competition. The CB&Q-D&RGW-WP Vista-Dome *California Zephyr* had been competing with the *City of San Francisco* since 1949, while Santa Fe's *Chiefs* had begun sporting domes as early as 1951.

The ACF-built domes—called Astra Domes by UP— initially went to work on the *City of Portland*, *City of Los Angeles*, and the Los Angeles *Challenger*, which had been revived in 1954. All UP trains carrying domes became known as "Domeliners," a name invented by the Wabash in 1954. In 1958, the *City of St. Louis* also received domes, built by Pullman-Standard but to the same specs as the earlier ACF domes. Its

highly scenic route notwithstanding, the *City of San Francisco* was domed only on the SP between Ogden and Oakland, SP supplying its own homebuilt domes for that segment. East of Ogden, the *City of San Francisco* remained domeless until combined with the *City of Los Angeles* in 1960.

UP's dome diners were the star attraction on those trains which carried them, and they, along with the dome diner on the *Train of Tomorrow* that UP had purchased in 1950 (see dome sidebar on pages 58-59), were the only such cars to operate on regularly scheduled pre-Amtrak passenger-train routes. As the authors of this book will testify, the dining-on-rails experience was unparalleled on a dome diner. The main level of these beautiful conveyances featured restaurant-style round tables—almost unheard of in railroad dining cars. Below the dome was a reserved dining area—the Gold Room—for groups of up to ten. The dome dining section featured divan-type seats accommodating 18 in groups of two and four under the curved glass of the dome section. Dumb waiters carried food from the kitchen on the main level up to the dome area, which had its own staff of waiters.

The dome lounge-observation cars had little to apologize for either. The main lounge section, toward the rear of the car, seated 19 in living-room-style furniture. Under the dome section was the cocktail lounge and bar, and the dome section seated 24 in divan-type seats that were angled outward for better viewing. A unique feature of these cars was the card-playing room, for five, at the forward end—a good way to warm up en route to Las Vegas.

UP was a master at publicizing its Domeliners, particularly the *City of Los Angeles* which, arguably, had become its pre-eminent train. The railroad published lavishly illustrated brochures for each train, drawing particular attention to the domes. UP also capitalized on its reputation for exemplary dining service, running "Meal-of-the-Month" ads in national magazines detailing the special gourmet dinners being served on feature trains that month.

In perhaps its finest moment of mass-advertising, Union Pacific played prominent in several episodes of

the immensely popular "I Love Lucy" TV series, which was in its peak years when the Domeliners were born. Best-remembered is Lucy and Ricky Ricardo's return to New York following an extended stay in Hollywood. UP was featured in the two consecutive episodes which dealt with the trip. In the first, Ricky makes a call to the UP and, in his trademark Cuban-accented English, asks specifically about the new dome cars on the *City of Los Angeles*. The segment includes a scene at the UP ticket office, prominent with UP advertising. When Ricky finally announces to Lucy that they're going to be taking the train home, she exclaims in front of cohorts Fred & Ethel Mertz,

C&NW car for Streamliner service
Though jointly operated by UP and Chicago & North Western, the *City* and Streamliner transcons were still primarily UP trains, and UP called the shots on their operation. For uniformity, this meant that *City* train cars owned by C&NW had to wear UP colors, as in the above view of diner 6956, four of which were built for *City* train service for C&NW by American Car & Foundry in 1949. *ACF Collection, St. Louis Mercantile Library.*

1941 *City of San Francisco*
The Western Avenue wye track west of downtown Chicago made for a nice location for C&NW to pose the new 1941 *City of San Francisco*, which the railroad jointly owned with UP and Southern Pacific—hence the three owners' logos on the nose of the lead Electro-Motive E6A. *C&NW.*

THE MILWAUKEE ROAD
UNION PACIFIC RAILROAD

Domeliner
CITY OF LOS ANGELES

Enroute

Pleasant under glass

One of the ultimate dining experiences of the streamliner era was an elegant dinner in the dome section of a UP dome dining car on the *City of Los Angeles* or *City of Portland*. Amidst soft background music and ever-changing scenery right outside the curved glass windows (including an interesting view of the forward and aft ends of the train as it sped through towns, around curves and past signals), UP chefs in the kitchen below prepared such tantalizing fare as Nebraska Corn Fed Charcoal Broiled Steak ($5.75 in 1969) or Broiled Lake Michigan Trout, Maitre d'Hotel ($4.40). With such dinners UP offered its own California red or white wine ($1.25 per bottle), bottled expressly for UP by J. Filippi Vintage Company of Mira Loma. And dessert? Wild Oregon Blackberry Sundae, with wafers. *ACF, St. Louis Mercantile Library.*

"We're taking the *City of Los Angeles* home!" to which Ricky retorts as he attempts to lift her bag, "So that's what's in your suitcase!" The following hilarious episode takes place on board the train, and is interspersed with several movie clips of the *City of Los Angeles* in action. All in all, it was a media coup for the Union Pacific Railroad.

The numbers began to catch up with UP, however, late in the 1950s and through the Sixties—a dismal decade for the American passenger train as a whole. As early as 1956, the *Challenger* and the *City of Los Angeles* were combined during the off seasons, and that same year the Streamliner *San Francisco Overland* started being phased out. By this time, Streamliner and Domeliner operations between Chicago and Omaha had been shifted from the C&NW to the parallel Milwaukee Road, reportedly due to disputes

between UP and C&NW. More train consolidations occurred in the 1960s, such as the *City of St. Louis* being combined with the *City of Los Angeles* west of Ogden. Yet, there were some bright spots. As late as 1964 UP was still taking delivery of new passenger cars.

In 1969, the *City of St. Louis* was cut back from St. Louis to Kansas City and renamed *City of Kansas City*. In 1970, the dome diners were pulled from service, and the *City of San Francisco* reduced to tri-weekly operation. By this time, the *City of Los Angeles*, *San Francisco*, *Portland*, *Denver*, and the *Challenger* had been combined into one giant train into and out of Chicago, with split-up/combining done at various points along the way. Thus an L.A.-bound passenger having dinner out of Chicago might be seated with others destined to, say, Portland. This "City of Everywhere" arrangement was maintained until Amtrak started on May 1, 1971. After this the *City of San Francisco* became the sole survivor of a once-grand fleet whose heritage drew upon a spunky little yellow-and-brown train that had introduced the world to streamliners 37 years earlier.

Triumvirate triumph: The California Zephyr

THE CALIFORNIA Zephyr

Out of the hubbub generated by a multitude of travelers milling about the cavernous waiting room of Chicago Union Station comes a singularly resonant announcement echoing over the public address system:

"May I have your attention . . . please . . . Burlington-Rio Grande-Western Pacific Vista-Dome *California Zephyr* . . . train number 17 . . . scheduled to depart at 3:30 p.m. for Omaha, Denver, Salt Lake City, San Francisco, and scheduled intermediate points . . . is ready for boarding at track 28 . . . Welcome aboard!"

For 21 years, from 1949 to 1970, this announcement signaled the daily sailing of one of the most cherished streamliners the U.S. The *California Zephyr* was a triumph in a market where the *CZ*'s operators—Burlington, Rio Grande, and Western Pacific—had previously played second fiddle to the world-class *City of San Francisco*, operated by SP-UP-C&NW.

Preceding page

Night has fallen over Salt Lake City, Utah, on a warm July day in 1969 as the *California Zephyr* goes through its ritual Rio Grande-to-Western Pacific locomotive change in the Mormon capital. Since early morning, the train has climbed mountains, burrowed through countless tunnels (including the six-mile Moffat), negotiated precipitous canyons, and visited the Rocky Mountain towns that cling to the Denver & Rio Grande Western's 570-mile main line between Denver and Salt Lake. *Photo, Mike Schafer/Jim Boyd; CZ brochure, Joe Welsh Collection.*

CZ Zephyrette

Zephyrettes were a fixture on the *CZ* right to the last day of service on March 22, 1970. They were the train's social director, tour guide, nurse, babysitter, conductor's assistant—just about anything required to ensure a safe, memorable trip for the millions of men, women, and children who were lucky enough to experience "America's Most Talked-About Train." Zephyrette Beaulah Ecklund, of Kirkland, Illinois, was a Zephyrette from 1964 to 1970, one of a pool of about a dozen Zephyrette women assigned to the CZ. When Amtrak revived the *CZ* in 1983, the carrier invited Beaulah (having become Mrs. James Bauman since the first CZ was discontinued) to host the first trip. *Mike Schafer.*

CZ in the Feather River Canyon

The *California Zephyr* brought notoriety to what had been a relatively unknown but stunningly beautiful canyon in northeastern California—that of the Feather River. For more than 100 miles, Western Pacific's Salt Lake City-Oakland main line wound its way through the quiet splendor that still makes the Feather River Canyon—though today void of regularly scheduled passenger trains—an almost spiritual place. This westbound CZ is at Pulga, California, in the heart of the canyon in July 1969. *Mike Schafer.*

The *CZ* story has a double beginning dating from 1934. As is well documented in this volume's first chapter, this was the year Chicago, Burlington & Quincy unveiled the world's first diesel-powered streamliner, the *Burlington Zephyr*. Also that year, on June 16, the little *Zephyr*—during its 1934 exhibition tour—made a special guest appearance at an event which would be key to the *CZ* 15 years hence: the opening of Rio Grande's Dotsero Cutoff in central northwest Colorado.

Until this 40-mile line opened, all trains heading west from Denver to Salt Lake City on the Rio Grande faced a circuitous routing via Pueblo and the Royal Gorge—a routing far too long to make the Rio Grande competitive transcontinental passenger service via Denver. The 1928 opening of the Moffat Tunnel and the 1934 completion of the Dotsero Cutoff, which shortened Rio Grande's route through the mountains by 175 miles—changed all that.

The first Chicago-San Francisco train to take advantage of the new route was the *Exposition Flyer*, introduced in 1939 for folks traveling to the Golden Gate International Exposition at San Francisco Bay. Running time for the steam-powered, heavyweight train initially was around 60 hours—more than 20 hours longer than the *City of San Francisco*. Nonetheless, the *Flyer* was well-received, in no small part owing to the spectacular scenery it traversed.

At the close of World War II, another event occurred that would be key in the life of the *CZ* and at the same time radically change the face of streamliners everywhere: the unveiling of the first true Vista-Dome car. With the war over, the Vista-Dome invented, and streamliner fever at high pitch, the stage was set for the *California Zephyr*. In December 1945, Burlington, Rio Grande, and Western Pacific officials agreed on an overall construction and operating strategy for the new *CZ*—the name already having been singled out two years earlier. Orders were soon placed with Budd for six ten-car trainsets, with four owned by Burlington, two by Rio Grande, and one by WP.

The concept of the *CZ* was somewhat unconventional for the period: it was designed, built, and scheduled for sightseeing. As such, Vista-Domes would be the train's hallmark, with five such cars normally assigned to each train—a record number of domes for a transcontinental train. In fact, at the time of its introduction, the

CZ was the only long-distance train to feature domes.

Each trainset was normally assigned a baggage car, three reclining-seat Vista-Dome coaches, a Vista-Dome dormitory-buffet-lounge, diner, four sleepers, and, concluding the consist, the train's preeminent car—a Vista-Dome sleeper-lounge observation. For a time, one sleeper operated through to and from New York. All cars carried the train's name on their letterboards. Car names reflected Western theming, and all had CB&Q's trademark "Silver" prefix; e.g., *Silver Rifle, Silver Aspen*.

As a diesel-powered lightweight train, the *CZ* enabled the three carriers to speed up overall Chicago-Oakland running times to under 51 hours. This had a positive effect of putting the train right where the railroads wanted it in daylight hours: in the Rocky Mountains on one day and in California's Feather River Canyon the next (or vice versa if traveling eastbound).

When enough new cars had arrived from Budd, the date of the first *CZ*s to depart from Oakland and Chicago was set at March 20, 1949. Three exhibition consists were assembled for each carrier to parade over its system. The exhibition *CZ*s visited nearly all on-route cities and a few off-beat places as well. For example, on March 19 WP brought its train to the Embarcadero in downtown San Francisco via a down-the-middle-of-the-street industrial spur. (Because San Francisco sits on a peninsula then accessible only by Southern Pacific rails from the south, in actual operation the *CZ* terminated at Oakland where passengers transferred to ferries and/or buses for the final leg of travel across San Francisco Bay to San Francisco proper.)

Presiding over the ceremonies at the Embarcadero were San Fran Mayor Leland Cutler, WP President H. A. Mitchell, and California Lieutenant Governor Goodwin Knight. The train was christened by Warner Brothers actress Eleanor Parker who, with a swing of the champagne bottle, launched an era. The following day, the first *CZ*s departed Oakland and Chicago. First-run passengers, many of whom were adorned with orchid corsages flown in from Hawaii, included Edward G. Budd Jr., president of the train's manufacturer.

One particularly well-remembered feature of the *CZ* were its "Zephyrettes" or train hostesses. Hostesses were not a new innovation, especially on the Burlington, which had employed hostesses on its *Denver* and *Twin Cities Zephyr*s in the mid-1930's.

The *California Zephyr* was very much a people's train. It was marketed—particularly to families—as a vacation unto itself. The train's overall relaxed yet sometimes partylike atmosphere, markedly enhanced by the ever-present Zephyrettes, made it user friendly, a contrast to the air of eliteness that surrounded the *City of San Francisco*. Christmastime meant a Christmas tree in the observation lounge and holly on the dining-car tables. On some runs, Santa Claus rode for part of the trip, visiting children in each of the cars.

Typifying the *CZ* operators' abilities to make the best of what could be a tenuous moment was the unscheduled "arrival" of one Reed Zars on March 1, 1955. With a porter and the Zephyrette acting as midwives, baby Reed was delivered as the train snaked through Colorado's Gore Canyon. Seven years later, the railroads invited young Reed and his classmates to ride the *CZ* on March 1, 1962, with a birthday party held in a balloon-bedecked dining car. Such events generated reams of good p.r. for the *CZ*.

Not that it needed it. The *CZ* was immensely successful, at least in terms of popularity if not the ledger books. For all of the 1950s and into the early 1960s, the *CZ* packed them in. Ridership hovered at an 80 percent average load factor for entire years—a remarkably high figure in the transportation industry; summer often saw the train sold out. Ridership was so strong that additional cars had been purchased in 1952.

But good things do come to an end. Despite the train having having enjoyed periods of complete sell-out as late as 1965, and even boasting at least a modest profit up to that time, all was not well. By the mid-1960s, rising costs, especially labor, required WP accountants to refill their pens with red ink when working on *CZ* ledgers. Although Rio Grande and Burlington had experienced similar alarming cost increases, WP was the smallest and least financially stable of the three *CZ* operators. Thus, any loss sustained was greatly magnified within the scope of WP's operations.

In September 1966, WP filed with the Interstate Commerce Commission to discontinue its portion of the train. The public outcry was vocal and widespread, so much so that the ICC was stymied. It finally ordered WP to continue running the train, calling the *CZ* a "unique national asset." Then in 1969, D&RGW filed to discontinue its portion of *CZ* operations while mounting losses caused one of the train's staunchest supporters—the Burlington—to have second thoughts. Still, the ICC ordered all three to continue *CZ* service.

The death knell sounded on Friday the 13th in February 1970, when the ICC gave its final ruling: The WP could discontinue *CZ* operations, but Rio Grande and Burlington had to continue some semblance of *CZ* ser-

vice on a tri-weekly basis between Chicago and Ogden, Utah, where the truncated *CZ* would turn its passengers over to SP's *City of San Francisco* to continue to the West Coast—and vice versa.

The final departures of the "real" *CZ*s left Oakland and Chicago on March 20, 1970 . . . 21 years to the day after the trains had been inaugurated. Those final trains arrived at their destinations on March 22, 1970, having paraded past thousands of spectators who lined the trackside for a last glimpse of one of America's greatest streamliners.

The surviving operation was a ghost of the *CZ* that Americans everywhere had come to love, if not by traveling on the train, then vicariously through the publicity that had been generated by its demise. On the Burlington, the tri-weekly replacement operation, only a few cars long, became known variously as the *California Zephyr Service* or just "California Service." On the

Rio Grande portion of the run, the train became known as the *Rio Grande Zephyr*, itself a popular train.

For the purposes of this book, which deals largely with pre-Amtrak liners, this is the end of the *CZ* story. But we can't resist this happy postscript: As it turned out, little grieving was necessary for the *California Zephyr*. The *CZ* did something that few other departed streamliners of yore can claim. Like the proverbial phoenix that arose from ashes to reclaim life, the *CZ* was reinstated in 1983 by Amtrak. And as this volume goes to press in 1997, one can still board the *CZ* in Chicago Union Station, awake to vistas of the Front Range of the Rockies the following morning, marvel at the precipitous walls of Glenwood and Gore canyons, have Rocky Mountain trout in the dining car while watching a Utah sunset, and detrain at the doorstep of the "City by the Bay." In this day and age of hyperspeed and cyberspace, it is a refreshing change of pace.

CZ in twilight
The westbound *California Zephyr* races toward an icy sunset, both literally and figuratively in this scene on the Chicago, Burlington & Quincy at Earlville, Illinois, in January 1970. Within two months, the CB&Q will be gone, swallowed into the Burlington Northern merger on March 2, 1970. BN will operate the *CZ* only for 20 days beyond that. On March 22, the original *California Zephyr* will arrive at Oakland and Chicago for the final time. *Mike Schafer*

Streamliners of the Sunset and the Golden State Routes

SUNSET—THE WESTERN STREAMLINER WITH THE SOUTHERN ACCENT

Established in 1894, Southern Pacific's *Sunset Limited* was (and is) the oldest name train in America. It operated over the last transcontinental route developed in the U.S., traveling a southerly course between New Orleans, Los Angeles and, for a time, San Francisco. A classic heavyweight operation through most of its career, the *Sunset* underwent a dramatic and complete makeover in the immediate post-World War II period. On August 20,1950, thanks to the arrival of five new sets of equipment delivered by the Budd Company, the *Sunset* was re-equipped as a dedicated extra-fare streamliner on a fast 42-hour schedule between New Orleans and Los Angeles.

The new stainless-steel cars with red letterboards were attractive on the inside as well as the outside. Passengers could enjoy fine southern cooking inside the "Audubon Diner," a modern car which featured famous paintings of birds by noted naturalist James

Audubon. In the "Pride of Texas" Coffee Shop car a bevy of Texas livestock brands were on display to amuse patrons while they enjoyed an excellent economy meal. If you were in the mood for a drink, The "French Quarter Lounge," featuring typical old New Orleans decor including the distinctive iron grillwork found on so many homes in the Quarter, was a fine place to slake your thirst.

Back in the sleeping cars, modern roomettes and double bedrooms offered all the comforts of home, while up front in the coaches, Heywood-Wakefield's famous Sleepy Hollow reclining seats helped economy-minded passengers put the miles behind them in complete comfort. There was even valet service available to first-class passengers.

The scenery from the *Sunset* was not the high point of the service. In contrast to competitors Union Pacific and Santa Fe whose own routes between Los Angeles and the Midwest were more scenic, the Sunset Route traversed the flat bayous of Louisiana and the desert

Sunset, 1950 rendition

Save for the locomotives that head up this evening's *Sunset* westbound at Phoenix, Arizona, around the time of Amtrak's start-up in 1971, the equipment is much the same as when delivered two decades earlier—a long consist of Budd stainless-steel cars. Originally, Electro-Motive E-series locomotives clad in SP's red-and-orange *Daylight* scheme pulled the *Sunset*; in later years, EMD F-series units, as shown here, did the job, clad in SP's later gray-and-red livery. In the late 1960s, the *Sunset* was almost a goner, but the Interstate Commerce Commission goaded SP into restoring the sleeping cars, diner, and other amenties. *Jim Boyd.*

Audubon diner on the *Sunset*

In a departure from the usual theming of a diner or lounge—which often played on a geographical highpoint of the train's route—Southern Pacific chose to honor naturalist James Audubon, whose realistic paintings of birds adorned the walls of *Sunset* diners. (*Kerplunk!* What dropped into my soup?!) *Southern Pacific Lines.*

country of the southwest, leaving the public relations people to claim the vague advantages of the *Sunset*'s low altitude crossing of the Continental divide. But New Orleans did possess a powerful allure of its own and there were connections available there to the East Coast via the Louisville & Nashville's *Crescent* or Southern Railway's *Southerner*. For a time the *Sunset* even carried a through a sleeping car to and from New York which was exchanged with the L&N at New Orleans. A through sleeper to Dallas via El Paso and the Texas & Pacific Railroad was also available for awhile.

For much of the 1950's the *Sunset Limited* operated as the SP had intended, but as the decade wore on and the railroad's perspective on the long-distance train changed, a period of long decline set in. In 1958 the train lost the "Limited" portion of its title. In 1964 it was combined between Los Angeles and El Paso, Texas, with the joint SP-Rock Island *Golden State* running between Los Angeles and Chicago. By the late 1960's, with the demise of the *Golden State*, the *Sunset* was reduced to a shadow of its former glory offering only coaches and an "automat" buffet car between New Orleans and Los Angeles. Some respectability was

regained on October 1, 1970, when, thanks to the urging of the Interstate Commerce Commission, SP agreed to reinstate sleeping and dining lounge service on the train in exchange for being allowed to operate the train tri-weekly instead of daily. The through sleeping car between Los Angeles and New York was also restored. The *Sunset* survived until the advent of Amtrak at which point it became a key component in the national intercity network. Today's Amtrak *Sunset Limited* (the "Limited" having been restored to its title) is the only true transcontinental train in the U.S. now that it has been extended east of New Orleans to Florida.

THE *ARIZONA LIMITED*

Despite its lonely routing and healthy competition from giants Santa Fe and Union Pacific, the Golden State Route alignment between Chicago, Kansas City, Phoenix, and Los Angeles hosted some respectable streamliners, including the West's first all-room streamliner and a "ghost" train that, although highly touted, never ran an inch in revenue service.

The first streamliner on the route was also the West's first all-room (no coach seating or sections) train, the *Arizona Limited*. Designed to attract winter-weary Midwesterners to the warm climes of southern Arizona, the streamliner operated for two seasons from December 15, 1940, to April 3, 1941, and for an identical time period in 1941-42. Comprised largely of lightweight sleepers from the Pullman pool, the *Arizona Limited* was one of the most interesting trains assembled in the prewar period. Unique streamlined observation cars *American Milemaster* displayed at the 1939 World's Fair and *Muskingum River* a one-of-a-kind stainless-steel sister to the *Milemaster* operated on the train during its first season. For the second season, the *Milemaster* was replaced by a two-car articulated set comprised of observation *California Republic* and duplex sleeper *Bear Flag* which previously had operated on Union Pacific's *Forty Niner*.

Lightweight all room sleeping cars, *Imperial Banner*, *Imperial Clipper*, *Imperial Guard*, and *Imperial Throne* offered four compartments, four double bedrooms and two drawing rooms. *Cascade Banks* and *Cascade Basin* containing ten roomettes and five double bedrooms operated for both seasons while sisters *Cascade Boulders* and *Cascade Gully* operated only for the first season before being permanently assigned to Baltimore & Ohio's *Capitol Limited*.

Supplementing these Pullman-operated cars, the Rock Island provided four modernized heavyweight cars —baggage dormitories (6014 and 6015) and dining cars (8028 and 8031). Power for the train consisted of diesels on the Rock Island from Chicago to Tucumcari, New Mexico. West of there on the SP, GS type steam locomotives often hauled the train. The train was dressed in Pullman's pool colors of two-tone gray with black roofs. The exception was the *Muskingum River* which retained its natural stainless-steel exterior.

A victim of government restrictions abolishing seasonal operations as a result of World War II, the *Arizona Limited* left Phoenix for the last time on April 1, 1942, ending a brief but fascinating career as the West's first all-room streamliner.

THE *GOLDEN ROCKET*

Although the 1940s were famous as a time when dozens of new streamliners were being introduced, an interesting footnote to the period was the fact that at least two trains, both meticulously planned and constructed, never ran an inch in revenue service. C&O's *Chessie*, projected to run on a day schedule between Cincinnati and Washington with a Hampton Roads (Virginia) leg, featured exotic equipment, including the first dome cars in the East. Lesser known was the Rock Island-SP's *Golden Rocket*.

Intended to be introduced on a fast tri-weekly schedule between Chicago and Los Angeles, two 11-car trains were originally planned, one to be owned by SP and the other by Rock Island. The cars would be cloaked in an eye-popping scheme of silver and vermilion and feature festive Mexican-themed interiors. While Pullman-Stan-

The *Arizona Limited*
Because of its short life span—two seasons early in the 1940s—color views of the *Arizona Limited* are extremely rare. In this view near Phoenix, the train is cruising along behind an SP GS-series steam locomotive. Two heavyweight cars are at the head of the train while the observation car on this day is the *Muskingum River*, an experimental all-stainless-steel car built by Pullman-Standard in 1940. Following the demise of the *Arizona Limited*, this and sister car *American Milemaster* went to work on SP's Los Angeles-San Francisco *Lark*. Southern Pacific Lines, Joe Welsh Collection.

dard was well along in completing the Rock Island trainset in 1947, partner Southern Pacific abruptly changed its mind about the service, leaving the Rock Island high and dry. Rock Island's *Golden Rocket* set of equipment (one baggage-dorm car, three coaches, a coffee shop-bar-lounge, diner, four sleepers, and a sleeper-lounge-observation car, with barber shop) was delivered anyway—in *Golden Rocket* colors and lettering—but without the sibling it needed to help protect a tri-weekly schedule, the train's future looked mighty dim, despite the aggressive ad campaign already under way. Rock Island instead immediately placed the cars in service on the *Golden State* enriching that train's consist and, undoubtedly, confusing a few passengers. The cars never turned a wheel as the *Golden Rocket*.

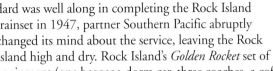

Streamliners on parade
Same departure times; same destinations: SP's eastbound *Golden State* eases away from Los Angeles Union Passenger Terminal simultaneous with Santa Fe's *Chief*. The date is July 24, 1949, and at the time both Chicago-bound trains departed LAUPT at 12:30 p.m. The photographer is enjoying this dramatic scene of streamliner action from his vantage point up in famous Mission Tower, which controls the approaches to the LAUPT complex. *William D. Middleton.*

THE *GOLDEN STATE*

Originally established as a seasonal train in 1902, the *Golden State Limited* had an erratic early career of an on-again, off-again nature. By the mid 1930s, however, the train had long since settled down as deluxe operation offering a valet, a barber shop, showers and even air conditioning. During World War II, the train received its first lightweight cars as new Pullman 4-compartment 4-double bedroom 2-drawing (4-4-2s) and 6-section 6-roomette 4-double bedroom sleepers (6-6-4s) were added. Rock Island also added three Budd lightweight dining cars to the largely heavyweight train.

In an effort to remain competitive on the Chicago-Los Angeles run, the *Golden State* (the "Limited" portion of the name had been dropped in May 1947) was fully re-equipped as a streamliner by early 1948. Now diesel powered and operating on a 45-hour schedule, the streamliner featured the stunning red-and-silver color scheme created in 1947 for—and inherited from—the stillborn *Golden Rocket*. Consists included a

fascinating array of equipment as the *Golden State* incorporated pre- and postwar cars from the Southern Pacific and various Rock Island orders.

Transcontinental daily sleeping-car service between New York and Los Angeles was added for a short time in the immediate post-World War II period with the cars being carried on a regular alternating basis by the New York Central or the Pennsylvania Railroad.

This would prove to be the highwater mark of the train's streamlined career and soon the *Golden State* would begin a slide into obscurity. Hemmed in by the competition—SP and Rock Island could not boast of the scenery and dome cars enjoyed by competing trains—and impacted by shrinking patronage, the *Golden State* died a slow death. On April 8, 1968, down to a few cars, the train departed on its last runs leaving a legacy deluxe service on the Golden State Route dating to the turn of the century.

The *Golden State*

Eastbound SP train 4 is at Alhambra, California, making the first stop on its 1,996-mile journey to Chicago via SP's line to Tucumcari, New Mexico, and the Rock Island beyond. The date is July 25, 1953, and the train still wears the vermilion colors adopted from the *Golden Rocket*—the train that never was. *Donald Duke, collection of Robert P. Schmidt.*

Golden Rocket ad

SP and Rock Island came awfully close to launching the planned *Golden Rocket*, and cars lettered for the train were even delivered. This ad promised it to be "America's Newest, Most Beautiful Streamliner." *Mike Schafer Collection.*

Rocky Mountain Streamliners

Burlington's big new

VISTA-DOME DENVER ZEPHYR

CHICAGO—DENVER—COLORADO SPRINGS

Left: The Colorado Springs section of Rock Island's Rocky Mountain Rocket at Colorado Springs, Colorado, in 1959. Blunt-nose Electro-Motive diesel No. 750 was in essence a regular E-series locomotive but designed so that it would blend as the middle of the three-unit set that would result from mating at Limon, Colorado, with the A-unit from the Denver section of the train. W. A. Gibson Sr. Above: This famous view of the Denver Zephyr appearing on the cover of a handsome Burlington-issued brochure for the new (1956) train was photographed on location in . . . suburban Chicago! Darkroom trickery added the mountain backdrop, which is not at all the Rocky Mountains but the Grand Tetons. Joe Welsh Collection.

For decades, beautiful, mystique-filled Colorado has been a lure for travelers. The state's capital, Denver, poised at the foot of the Front Range, serves as a gateway to the vacation paradise that is the Rocky Mountains. Small wonder, then, that Colorado in general and Denver in particular were targets for several new trains introduced during the era of the streamliner. Steam-powered heavyweight trains in service between the Midwest and Colorado often held to a leisurely carding of 24 hours en route. High-speed streamliners would change that, making the 1,000-plus-mile trip on schedules of about 16 hours that put Denver just an overnight jaunt from the gritty concrete canyons of Chicago.

Burlington's *Zephyr* 9900 was the first streamliner to set wheels in Denver, in May 1934, and it would also be Denver's first regularly scheduled streamliner—indeed, Colorado's first too. Elated with the success of its first *Zephyr*s, Burlington placed orders with Electro-Motive and Budd to build two ten-car *Denver Zephyr*s. When Burlington realized that those new trains would not be ready in time to joust with Union Pacific's new *City of Denver*, set to begin service on July 1, 1936, Burlington did the next best thing: it pressed *Zephyr*s 9900 and 9903 into interim Chicago-Denver streamliner service as the *Advance Denver Zephyr*s on June 1, 1936, operating via Burlington, Iowa, Omaha and Lincoln, Nebraska, and Fort Morgan, Colorado. The short, coach-only trains were hardly up to the task of accommodating Chicago-Denver overnight traffic, but they got Burlington's foot in the door in that market.

UP's *City of Denver* was one of several new trains rushed into operation in the mid-1930s by Union Pacific and Chicago & North Western (see Chapter 1). Two sets of equipment provided daily service in each direction between Chicago and Denver via Cedar Rapids, Iowa, and Omaha and Grand Island, Nebraska, and Sterling, Colorado. The first trains rolled out of Chicago and Denver on June 18, 1936.

This original *City of Denver* was comprised of a full baggage car, baggage-RPO, a baggage-bar car, two coaches, a diner, three sleepers, and a sleeper-lounge observation car. The train was partially articulated. The social center of the train was the "Frontier Shack" lounge in rear half of the baggage car, made to look like a wild West saloon, complete with rough-hewn wood paneling and WANTED desperado posters. Although perhaps hokey by today's standards, Depression-weary travelers of the 1930s found the Frontier Shack to be quite a novelty.

Burlington's new regular *Denver Zephyr*s relieved the 9900 and 9903 on November 8, 1936, after being christened by the granddaughter of Buffalo Bill Cody. They carried on the overall *Zephyr* theme established by their earlier kin. Among the innovations featured in the new 10-car semi-articulated trains (each with an RPO-baggage, baggage-dormitory-lounge, two coaches, diner, four sleepers, parlor-observation) was a soda fountain, 110-volt outlets, and a phonograph.

The *City of Denver* and *Denver Zephyr* were highly successful, which perhaps prompted a third railroad to enter the Chicago-Denver race: Chicago, Rock Island & Pacific. Having already entered the streamliner arena with its fleet of *Rocket*s, including the *Denver Rocket* of 1937 between Kansas City and Denver, the Rock Island streamlined its *Rocky Mountain Limited* on November 12, 1939, renaming it the *Rocky Mountain Rocket*. The all-stainless-steel train, built by Pullman-Standard and Budd and powered by Electro-Motive diesels, operated west from Chicago via Rock Island, Illinois, Des Moines, Iowa, and Omaha to Limon, Colorado. Here, the train was split into two sections, the main leg heading over UP tracks to Denver and the other to Colorado Springs. Though slower than its UP and CB&Q rivals by over three hours, the *Rocky Mountain Rocket* thrived on a greater population base.

World War II was already underway when Missouri Pacific, working jointly with

Denver & Rio Grande Western, became the last to enter the Midwest-Colorado streamliner market. Inspired by its successful new (1940) *Eagle* streamliner between St. Louis, Kansas City, and Omaha, MP launched the St. Louis-Denver *Colorado Eagle* on June 21, 1942, operating by way of Kansas City and Pueblo, Colorado. The new streamliner operated over the Rio Grande between Pueblo and Denver, skirting the Front Range of the Rockies before its arrival in the Mile High City.

Clad in blue and gray with yellow trim, the *Colorado Eagle* featured Budd-built stainless-steel coaches, diner-lounges, baggage, baggage-mail and coach-dormitory cars. From Pullman came the first streamlined sleeping cars ever to be operated on the Missouri Pacific, four 6-6-4-type sleepers named for Colorado rivers.

The *Colorado Eagle* closed out the Midwest-Denver streamliner fraternity. All four trains were upgraded following World War II, starting with the *Rocky Mountain Rocket* and the *Colorado Eagle* in 1948. That year, the *Rocket* received new stainless-steel coaches from Pullman-Standard while the *Colorado Eagle* became the first Denver train to receive dome service with three new Budd-built Vista-Dome coaches.

In 1954 UP totally re-equipped the *City of Denver* with new cars from American Car & Foundry and Pullman-Standard, although the carrier had yet to join the growing legions of railroads embracing the dome concept. Also in 1954, the *Rocky Mountain Rocket* received new sleeping cars.

As popular as its *Denver Zephyr* was—and it's safe to say it was probably the most popular of the four Midwest-Denver trains—CB&Q held back on any major re-equipping of its *DZ*s until 1956. Then it did so in a big way.

For the new *Denver Zephyr*, the "Q" returned to the Budd Company with an order for 28 new cars, more than enough to replace the two 1936 *DZ*s which for twenty years had held down the daily service, dashing back and forth across the 1,034 miles of plains separating Chicago and Denver (that's over 7.5 million miles per trainset). Budd delivered one of the most striking streamliners ever to hit the rail.

Each new *DZ* featured two "flattop" coaches, a Vista-Dome coach, a Vista-Dome

lunch counter-lounge known as the "Chuck Wagon" (which also included a crew dormitory), a full dining car, five sleepers, two Slumbercoaches, and a Vista-Dome observation car which featured parlor-car seats, a drawing room, a buffet-lounge and a sub-dome lounge called the "Colorado Room." The new *DZ* went into service on October 28, 1956, with a new twist: through-car service to Colorado Springs, home of the new Air Force Academy. For this new service at least one *DZ* coach, the Chuck Wagon dome, and one *DZ* sleeper were forwarded from Denver 75 miles south to the Springs in Rio Grande's *Royal Gorge* train.

Although UP began adding domes to its transcon streamliners in 1955, the *City of Denver* was a late recipient of the revolutionary cars—possibly because the Chicago-Denver trip in itself was not particularly scenic and took place mostly overnight. But dome service did finally come about in 1959 when the *City of Denver* was consolidated with the Domeliner *City of Portland*, the latter having been rerouted to operate between Chicago and Portland via Denver rather than Cheyenne, Wyoming.

Not even the popularity of Midwest-Colorado service could stave off the decline. On January 31, 1964, Pullman and dining-car service on the *Colorado Eagle* was discontinued west of Kansas City, and the trains lost their names altogether by March of the same year. The *Colorado Eagle* remnants made their final runs on April 2, 1966, leaving the Mopac a freight-only railroad west of K.C. Also in 1966, Rock Island took its *Rocky Mountain Rocket* out of orbit.

In 1968, UP downgraded Chicago-Denver service by re-rerouting the *City of Portland* through Cheyenne and making the *City of Denver* merely a split-off coach-and-Pullman connection to the *City of Portland* at North Platte, Nebraska. Through all this, the Burlington soldiered on, keeping its revered *Denver Zephyr* a spit-and-polish operation. The *DZ* remained largely intact into the Amtrak era—carrying on the legacy of Midwest-Colorado streamliner service that had started with *Zephyr*s 9900 and 9903 in 1936.

Evening light reveals Missouri Pacific's Colorado Eagle *in full splendor in this 1954 scene at the joint MP-Rio Grande depot in Pueblo, Colorado. The train is eastbound behind an Electro-Motive E-unit and an Alco PA, and the train includes its Budd "Planetarium Dome." During the noon hour the following day, the* Eagle *will arrive at St. Louis. The colorful train inspired the A. C. Gilbert Company of New Haven, Connecticut, to offer an American Flyer S gauge version of the train in its electric toy train line in 1958 and again in 1963-64, a set of which today commands well over $1,000. Donald Duke.*

CHAPTER 4

NORTHWEST PASSAGES

The Great Trains of Great Northern
A Northwest Adventure on the Northern Pacific
Milwaukee Road's **Olympian Hiawatha**
Southern Pacific's **Shasta Daylight** *and* **Cascade**
Union Pacific/Chicago & North Western's **City of Portland**

What makes the Pacific Northwest so alluring? Perhaps it's because it is a world of its own. From the volcanic peaks that loom above the vibrant cities of Portland and Seattle to the awe-inspiring grandeur of the Columbia River; from the misty splendor of the North Coast and its Olympic Peninsula to the surrealistic beauty of the semi-arid Palouse country, this is a region quite different from all the rest. Oregon, Washington, and Idaho beckon travelers with a change of pace and attitude.

The passenger department of the Great Northern Railway knew this; so did Northern Pacific's. . . as did that of NP and GN affiliate Spokane, Portland & Seattle Railway. Even the California Kids—Union Pacific and Southern Pacific—and granger line Milwaukee Road were aware of the appeal exuded by the Pacific Northwest. All six carriers capitalized on the magnetism of the region with some of the finest streamliners ever to roll: the *North Coast Limited*, the *City of Portland*, the *Shasta Daylight*, the *Cascade*, the *Olympian Hiawatha*, the *Western Star*, and (perhaps the king of them all) the *Empire Builder*. For readers who never had the opportunity to travel on one of these great streamliners to the Pacific Northwest, the following pages will provide at least a taste of what it was like to venture to this serene corner of America that is a world unto itself.

Great Dome *Empire Builder*
Jointly operated by Great Northern, Burlington, and Spokane, Portland & Seattle, the *Empire Builder* has been an American institution since its inaugural in 1929. Nearly thirty years after that date, the "Great Dome" version of the *Builder* is shown getting a scrubdown during the extended station stop at Havre, Montana, on September 19, 1957. *Scene, John Dziobko; lighted sign at Great Northern Station, Minneapolis, Jim Heuer.*

In 1929 the Great Northern Railway chose to honor its late founder James J. Hill by renaming its crack Chicago-St. Paul-Seattle passenger train, the *Oriental Limited*, in his honor. In perhaps the greatest tribute of all, the railroad named the train not for Hill himself but for his accomplishments: the *Empire Builder*.

It was no exaggeration. Hill's achievements had shaped not only the future of American transportation and trade but its geography. Rising from the lowly rank of Mississippi River shipping clerk to respectability, Hill had purchased and rehabilitated the St. Paul & Pacific Railroad—in the process extending the line all the way to the shores of Puget Sound at Everett, Washington,

opening a new trade route to the Orient. Along the way his growing transportation empire, consolidated in 1889 as the Great Northern Railway Company, had also proved pivotal in developing much of the northern plains where dozens of towns had literally sprung up overnight along the new line.

The formidable Montana Rockies were another Hill conquest. Locating the lowest crossing of the Continental Divide north of New Mexico, the railroad drove through Montana's Marias Pass (and established Glacier Park—a national treasure). The rugged Cascade Mountains of Washington State were crested at Stevens Pass.

The railroad's passenger services would prove

dependable and, in the case of the heavyweight *Empire Builder*, even opulent. Like many of its peers, GN took steps to modernize despite the Depression. For example, new Electro-Motive FT freight diesels arrived in 1941.

Improvements to GN passenger trains were announced in November 1943 when GN and partners Chicago, Burlington & Quincy and Spokane, Portland & Seattle announced in November 1943 that they would be ordering new streamlined cars to completely re-equip the *Empire Builder*. On February 23, 1947, five sparkling new streamlined *Empire Builder* trainsets hauled by ten new EMD E7 passenger diesels entered service between Chicago, Spokane, Portland and Seattle, making GN the first to completely streamline its top train in the Midwest-Pacific Northwest market.

The lightweight *Builder*'s new 45-hour Chicago-Seattle schedule bested by 13 1/2 hours the schedule of the heavyweight train it replaced. On board the amenities were top notch, too. The new train's sleeping cars were the first delivered in the postwar period. Its long-distance coaches featured legrest seats. Decor in the *Empire Builder*'s coffee shop car, diner, and lounge observation car was influenced by the colors and images of Glacier Park and Montana's Blackfeet Indian. Irish table linens and "Mountains and Flowers" china were part of the culinary experience in the diner.

This popular new train helped cement GN's position as a leader in the Northwest market. Demand increased and within four years the railroad re-equipped the train again, at a cost of $12 million. The all new "Mid Century" *Empire Builder* comprised five brand-new 15-car

Mountain-series lounge observation car, 1951 *Empire Builder*
In 1951, American Car & Foundry built six lounge observation cars for the "Mid-Century" *Empire Builder*. All honored mountains along the train's route with names like *Going-to-the-Sun Mountain*, *Cathedral Mountain*, and *Appekunny Mountain*. Car interiors were smartly appointed and colorful. *ACF, St. Louis Mercantile Library.*

Empire Builder, 1951 rendition
On its way out of Seattle, the eastbound *Empire Builder* skims the banks of Puget Sound at Richmond Beach, Washington, in March 1953. This was the "Mid-Century" version of the train, as re-equipped in 1951. Although delivered in 1947 for the first streamlined edition of the *Builder*, the Electro-Motive E7 diesels shown here were eventually reassigned to flatland duties, their inherent drawback being that they weren't well-suited to mountain-climbing. They were replaced by "passengerized" versions of Electro-Motive freight units. *David W. Salter.*

Safe from grizzlies
Graphically illustrating how dome cars opened up new vistas in rail travel is this view looking forward from one of the *Builder*'s dome cars as the train snaked through Glacier National Park behind a quartet of Electro-Motive F7s. Don't let the snow in this scene fool you—it's the *summer* of 1957. *John Dziobko.*

Empire Builder on the Burlington
CB&Q handled the *Empire Builder* for 427 of its 1,783- mile Chicago-Seattle trip, from Chicago to St. Paul Union Depot where it was handed over to GN. In August 1965, back-to-back Burlington E-units boil out of Chicago Union Station just after 2 p.m. with the departing *Builder* as Gulf, Mobile & Ohio's streamliner *Abraham Lincoln*, due in at 2:08 p.m., coasts toward the station for an on-time arrival. *George Speir.*

train sets was inaugurated on June 3, 1951. The displaced 1947 train sets (bolstered by one new additional consist) became GN's second new streamliner on the route—the *Western Star,* inaugurated at the same time.

This train operated on a different carding than the *Builder* and covered a variety of intermediate traffic requirements (portions of its intermediate route were occasionally changed). But by far the *Star*'s most important job was playing tour-guide to the numerous groups who visited Glacier National Park in sleepers and coaches chartered for the purpose by companies such as Thomas Cook. At the peak of its popularity in the summer of 1959, the tour business routinely added five to six extra cars to each consist of the *Western Star.*

Business continued to grow through the early 1950s and the progressive Great Northern took note of passenger car developments on both partner CB&Q and rivals Milwaukee Road and Northern Pacific—notably that of the dome car. Milwaukee Road introduced full-length "Super Domes" on its *Olympian Hiawatha* in January 1953, and in 1954 NP's *North Coast Limited* also received domes. GN countered with its own "Great Dome" *Empire Builder.* Dome coaches were introduced on May 29, 1955, and full-length dome lounges arrived in October of the same year. There was no finer way to see the sights along GN's right of way than from these cars. And what sights they were.

Eastbound departing Seattle the *Builder* skirted Puget Sound as far as Everett, affording glimpses of ocean-going vessels, ferries, and a host of marine life including hordes of irrepressible sea lions. At Everett, the *Builder* left the coast and turned east, entering the rugged North Cascades and Stevens Pass. There was nothing subtle about the North Cascades, and passengers gazed in awe as the saw-toothed silhouette of some of the roughest peaks in North America came into full view. In its assault on the Cascades the railroad followed western Washington's Skykomish River for several miles. A sweeping, white-water marvel laced with numerous Class 5 rapids, the Skykomish was a natural amusement ride run amok. Bald eagles loved the waterway and at the right time of year passengers could, with little effort, see dozens of the majestic birds doing what they did best—scavenging for food along the banks.

Dizzying pinnacles reminiscent of the Swiss Alps overhung the railroad, and just as it seemed there was no way out, the *Builder* ducked into Cascade Tunnel— at 7.79 miles one of the longest bores in the Western Hemisphere. The train's next stop was Wenatchee, Washington. From 1929 to 1956, GN hauled its trains from Skykomish to Wenatchee over the pass and through the tunnel using electric locomotives. In 1956, diesels began operating straight through.

After a fast ride through the Columbia basin of eastern Washington, the *Builder* arrived in late evening at Spokane where it picked up cars forwarded from Portland to Spokane by the Spokane, Portland & Seattle. Passengers on the Portland cars had been given an eyeful of the awe-inspiring Columbia River Gorge and Mount Hood on their afternoon/evening run to Spokane. With the Portland cars meshed into the consist, the *Builder* hurried eastward.

The next day, breakfast's main course was Glacier National Park. Its proximity to the GN was no accident. Much of the credit for establishing and popularizing the park went to the railroad and James Hill's son, Louis, who coined the phrase, "See America First." In Glacier there was plenty to see. Aside from numerous majestic peaks, there were glimpses of wildlife galore including a spot where GN's trademark mountain goats flocked to a natural salt lick—passenger representatives on the *Builder* never failing to point out "Rocky the Goat" to enthralled passengers.

As it skirted the southern border of the park, the train ducked in and out of numerous snowsheds while offering sweeping vistas of mountain valleys and alpine meadows. At East Glacier Park, the Glacier Park Lodge, built by the GN, stood ready to welcome guests as it had since 1913. Cresting Marias Pass at 5,216 feet, the train rolled eastward—and switched hats. Now the *Builder* was in the business of linking the small communities of the northern plains—places like Shelby and Wolf Point, Montana, or Minot and Fargo, North Dakota—all of which depended on GN as a lifeline to the outside world and each other.

Through the afternoon as the train roared across the flat plains, it was time to explore inside. The *Builder*'s unique "Ranch Car" lunch counter-lounge offered an ideal setting in which to unwind. Not surprisingly, the car's decor emulated a Western ranch with rough-hewn "logs" trimming the room and seats covered with pinto leather. The "G-bar-N brand on display was, of course, properly registered with the Montana Livestock Association. Dinner in the *Builder*'s more formal dining car offered regional specialties like Walleye Pike or fresh (Washington) baked apple and cream. Soon it was time to turn in for a second night's sound sleep.

The following day, after an early morning call at the Twin Cities, the train headed for Chicago over the CB&Q, showing passengers the wonders of the Mississippi River valley. At Chicago the *Builder* arrived in time to make connections with East Coast-bound streamliners such as NYC's *20th Century Limited* or B&O's *Capitol Limited*.

GN's top trains remained popular throughout most of the 1960's, undergoing changes along the way

***Western Star* brochure, 1956**
Showing that the *Western Star* was itself worthy of consideration for travel to the Pacific Northwest, GN issued this lavish brochure for the train, which served as the alternate schedule on the Chicago-Seattle/Portland route. Oddly enough, the *Star*, which never had regularly assigned dome cars, passed through more of the route's scenery in daylight than did its more-famous counterpart. *Mike Schafer Collection.*

Empire Builder in the Cascades
A streamlined GE electric locomotive—360 tons worth—hums along through the Cascades east of Skykomish, Washington, with the eastbound *Empire Builder* during the spring of 1954. At one time, 43 miles of the *Builder*'s route were electrified, mainly because of the grades and the seven-plus-mile Cascade Tunnel. *David W. Salter.*

including the abandonment of the trademark green and orange paint scheme for a simplified "Big Sky Blue livery." With the arrival of Amtrak in 1971, the *Western Star* disappeared from the timecard for good.

The *Empire Builder,* fortunately, was one of the few classic streamliners to survive, and under the Amtrak banner it still offers lifeline transportation between the Midwest, the northern plains and the Pacific Northwest. New generations can experience awesome views of Glacier Park from the comfort of one of Amtrak's finest long-distance trains. Glacier Park Lodge, 84 years young, is still a fashionable destination, and there's no finer way to reach it than by train. As you leave the *Empire Builder* and walk across fields of flowers toward the lodge, the majestic Rockies forming a backdrop, you can't help but be grateful to those who, while building their empire, had the vision to forge the way here by rail—and yet preserve the beauty they saw.

A Northwest Adventure on the Northern Pacific

Heir to an impressive history of service dating to 1900, the Northern Pacific Railway's *North Coast Limited* was first streamlined in the immediate post World War II period. Concerned about competition from rivals Great Northern and Milwaukee Road, the railroad's board ordered new equipment—over $65 million worth—from Pullman-Standard in October 1944. Wartime restrictions prevented prompt delivery, and the new equipment arrived piecemeal between June 1946 and the summer of 1948. Not until then was NP able to field six complete streamlined train sets with the 78 cars it had ordered, the ten cars received by partner CB&Q, and the two cars purchased by ally Spokane Portland & Seattle which operated the train's Portland section west of Pasco, Washington.

North Coast Limited, final rendition
A 300-mile cruise along the Father of Waters was just one scenic treat in store for cross-country passengers on this westbound *North Coast Limited* just out of Savanna, Illinois, on Chicago, Burlington & Quincy's Aurora (Illinois)-Twin Cities main line. It's 1961, and the train is in its peak years in terms of deluxe equipment, the last of which had been delivered in 1959. *Al Schultze.*

Attired in a sedate scheme of dark and medium green, the streamliner featured modern interiors and state-of-the-art accommodations. Somehow, though, the train's decor seemed less spectacular than that of the rival *Olympian Hiawatha* which featured Milwaukee Road's unique Skytop sleeper-lounge observation cars or the GN's *Empire Builder* with its customized interior artwork reflecting the natural beauty of Glacier Park.

The new *North Coast* also lacked one improvement essential to meeting the competition—a faster schedule. The train operated on a three-night-out carding and covered a variety of local service requirements on NP's more populous route in contrast to that of the *Olympian Hiawatha* and the *Empire Builder* whose faster schedules also belied the lack of major intermediate population centers on their routes.

That was to change beginning in November 1952 when NP slashed the schedule of the *North Coast Limited* by up to 12 hours, permitting a two-night-out carding, and inaugurated a running mate, the *Mainstreeter*, to cover the local-traffic requirements and handle head-end (mail and express) business. The *North Coast* also got a face lift with all of its streamlined equipment being refurbished and the railroad and partners ordering 20 Vista-Dome coaches and sleepers from Budd and assorted other equipment from Pullman-Standard. The *North Coast* was about to come of age.

In addition to a schedule and equipment change, the *North Coast*'s appearance improved with the hiring of industrial designer Raymond Loewy who cloaked the train in a beautiful new two-tone green scheme. The color scheme reflected the train's personality—classy but not overstated. The Vista-Domes arrived in the summer and fall of 1954 giving the NP the only dome sleeping cars in the Midwest-to-Northwest market and beating contestant GN in the dome race by a year. NP didn't stop there. New diners were added in 1958 and thrifty Slumbercoaches arrived from Budd in November 1959

North Coast ad from 1956
Right after the Traveller's Rest car was added to the *North Coast Limited*, NP ran this full-page ad in *Time* and other periodicals. *Mike Schafer Collection.*

North Coast Limited: Hello, Butte
Morning sunshine promises a good day of scenic views for passengers aboard the Chicago-bound *North Coast Limited* (right), arriving Butte, Montana, on a July morning in 1969. The train will spend most of the day crossing the scenic southern tier of Montana. *Mike Schafer.*

Traveller's Rest lounge car
The addition of stewardess-nurses and the popular Traveller's Rest buffet-lounge car (above) to the *NCL* in 1955 completed the mid-1950s revitalization of the train. Named for a favorite western Montana campsite of Lewis and Clark and decorated to commemorate the legendary explorers, the Traveller's Rest featured a full wall mural showing areas of the Pacific Northwest explored by Lewis and Clark. *Robert P. Schmidt.*

Dining, *NCL* style
NP dining cars were best known for their "Great Big Baked Potato," several of which (right) are being pulled from the oven in the kitchen of a *North Coast* diner. The *North Coast*'s steward (upper right) stands at his post in the dining car in August 1969. Note the *North Coast Limited* souvenir duffel bags for sale. *Kitchen photo, Collection of William F. Howes Jr.; steward, Robert P. Schmidt.*

offering budget sleeping-car accommodations.

Few Western streamliners offered a better view of the amazing geographic variety of the Pacific Northwest. On its trek, the *North Coast* crossed 28 individual mountain ranges and traced over 1,400 miles of river. Between Butte and Bozeman, Montana, the train passed through some of the most scenic country in America. Crossing the Continental Divide at Homestake Pass, the *NCL* weaved through fabulous rock formations, affording breathtaking views of the Jefferson Valley and the Tobacco Root Mountains. The train also offered access to spectacular Yellowstone Park via NP's station at Livingston, Montana.

While the industry on average was experiencing a decline in the late 1950s, the NP's passenger fortunes were on the rise. Passenger revenues remained amazingly stable from 1947 to 1966. After 1958 and into the early 1960s NP's passenger earnings actually rose. Much of the credit for the success can be attributed to the NP's corporate attitude that anything still worth doing was worth doing well, and the *North Coast* had earned a reputation for being one of the best trains around.

Nonetheless, cost control became a big issue, and in the late 1960s the train was combined with its chief competitor, the *Empire Builder*, east of St. Paul. In 1970 GN, NP, and SP&S merged to form Burlington Northern, a railroad with little interest in running fine passenger trains.

One year later Amtrak relieved the railroads of their passenger burden, and for a short time most of the *North Coast*'s route was served by the new carrier's *North Coast Hiawatha*. Eventually, despite its populous routing and spectacular scenery, the *North Coast Hi* was discontinued due to funding constraints. The *North Coast Limited* route passed into the history books, leaving a fond memory of a classy, passenger friendly railroad which offered wide-eyed tourists their first look at the diversity of America along the "Mainstreet of the Northwest."

Milwaukee Road's Olympian Hiawatha

THE *Olympian Hiawathas*
NEWEST MILWAUKEE ROAD SPEEDLINERS

"A Train Fit for the Gods"
Milwaukee Road's *Olympian Hiawatha* offered a variety of equipment and accommodations and a route that featured a wide range of scenic splendor. The photographer captured the train's hallmark car—the Skytop Lounge sleeper-observation—at speed along the Milwaukee Road main line in south central Wisconsin in 1957. To the rear of the car's private rooms was a glass-ceiling observation lounge, a great place to sip a drink while Montana scenery drifted by outside. The colorful cover of the brochure that accompanied the train's unveiling featured Fairbanks-Morse diesels which initially handled the train all the way through to the West Coast. *Photo, William D. Middleton; brochure, Bob Wayner Collection.*

The progressive Chicago, Milwaukee & St. Paul—later popularly known as the Milwaukee Road—was a latecomer to the Pacific Northwest, opening its Pacific Extension between Mobridge, South Dakota, and Puget Sound in 1909 well after Northern Pacific and Great Northern had built their lines west from Minneapolis and St. Paul across the northern tier of the U.S. to Seattle and Tacoma.

In May 1911, the Milwaukee established through passenger service between Chicago, the Twin Cities, and Seattle/Tacoma, at the doorstep of Washington state's beautiful Olympic Peninsula. The premier conveyance on the route was the *Olympian,* a deluxe heavyweight train that initially was entirely steam powered.

Between 1911 and 1927, Milwaukee completed the electrification of much of its Pacific Extension—the only U.S. railroad to apply mainline electrification over a major portion of a transcontinental route—and afterward was (appropriately) reorganized as the Chicago, Milwaukee, St. Paul & Pacific. Also in 1927, Milwaukee upgraded its *Olympian* with new cars. That together with the smooth, fast, clean electric operation of the *Olympian* provided Milwaukee Road with even more reason to extol its "Queen of Transcontinental Trains."

Milwaukee Road was an aggressive proponent of streamlining, being one of the pioneers in the field with its 1935 *Hiawatha* (Chapter 1). At first, however, Milwaukee's streamlining endeavors were regional in nature,

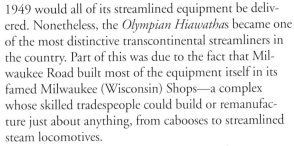

Olympian Hi "under wire"

A trip across the country on the *Olympian Hiawatha* meant nearly a full day of soaking in Montana's Big Sky Country. The eastbound *Hi* is at Eagles Nest Tunnel near Sixteen-Mile Canyon (Montana) in 1954 behind a "Little Joe" electric locomotive. Electric locomotives handled the train between Harlowton, Montana, and Avery, Idaho, on the railroad's Rocky Mountain Division and again in the Cascade region between Othello, Washington, and Seattle and Tacoma. *Sandy Goodrick.*

but following World War II, the *Olympian* became an obvious candidate for a transcontinental streamlining project—a decision no doubt prompted by Great Northern/Burlington's 1947 streamlining of their Chicago-Seattle/Portland *Empire Builder*. Accordingly, Milwaukee Road in 1946 placed extensive car orders with its own shops as well as Pullman-Standard

To vie with the introduction of the *Builder*, Milwaukee Road had to rush its "streamliner" *Olympian Hiawatha* into operation with a mixture of heavyweight and streamlined equipment on June 29, 1947, including earlier pre-war streamlined equipment. Six sets of equipment were required to protect daily departures in each direction from Chicago and Seattle. Not until

1949 would all of its streamlined equipment be delivered. Nonetheless, the *Olympian Hiawatha*s became one of the most distinctive transcontinental streamliners in the country. Part of this was due to the fact that Milwaukee Road built most of the equipment itself in its famed Milwaukee (Wisconsin) Shops—a complex whose skilled tradespeople could build or remanufacture just about anything, from cabooses to streamlined steam locomotives.

The *Olympian Hi*'s styling was another factor. Its exterior and interior design was the work of Milwaukee industrial designer Brook Stevens, who was perhaps best known in mainstream public conscious as the designer of the Harley-Davidson Heritage Classic bike and the Oscar Meyer Weinermobile. Stevens' expertise touched just about every aspect of the *Olympian Hiawatha*, from nose to tail. For example, powering the transcon were handsome new Fairbanks-Morse passenger diesels, which Stevens enhanced with chrome nose trim and lettering. Initially the FMs handled the *Olympian Hiawatha*s for their entire runs, but a change in motive-power procedures in 1949 put electric locomotives on the *Hi* over the Rocky Mountains and the Cascades.

When the *Olympian Hi* was inaugurated, its regular consist included an RPO-express car, baggage-dormitory, three coaches, what Milwaukee called a "tap-grill" car for light food service, a "Touralux" coach for women and children, two Touralux sleepers (for intermediate or "tourist" accommodations), a 40-seat dining car, and two heavyweight sleepers. Car interiors utilized generous amounts of wood trim—a Milwaukee Road hallmark in general—and distinct modern styling features such as angled tables in the diner (affording patrons a better view out the windows) and recessed lighting, much of it fluorescent.

Delivery of the train's signature car from Pullman-Standard—the Skytop Lounge bedroom-observation cars—was not completed until January 1949. Based on the radical new design of Milwaukee's Skytop parlor observation cars homebuilt in 1948 for *Twin Cities Hiawatha* service, the *Olympian Hi*'s Skytops featured a rakish observation end that was almost entirely comprised of glass panels—a feature so radical that the cars made the pages of *Popular Mechanics*. The Skytop concept was yet another creation of Brook Stevens, and it provided one of the most sensational lounging areas ever devised for rail travel.

The train received an additional upgrade in 1952 when Milwaukee Road took delivery of ten Super Dome buffet-lounge cars from Pullman-Standard. Six of the massive cars—among the heaviest streamlined cars ever built—were assigned to the *Olympian Hi* with the rest being relegated to *Twin Cities Hiawatha* service.

The full-dome cars were a natural for the *Olympian Hiawatha*, which traversed a route that was arguably more scenic than those traveled by the esteemed *Empire Builder* and *North Coast Limited*.

Between Lake Michigan and the Twin Cities, the *Olympian Hi*'s route passed through Wisconsin's driftless area between Milwaukee and La Crosse, including famous Wisconsin Dells, and then skirted the Mississippi River for well over 100 miles as a finale to its evening arrival in St. Paul/Minneapolis. On the second day out, while GN's *Empire Builder* was skimming the endless flatlands of northern Montana, the *Olympian Hi* was touring the Dakota Badlands and the Yellowstone River region of scenic southern Montana via Miles City and Three Forks—gateway to Yellowstone Park. By mid-afternoon, the train was well into the railroad's Rocky Mountain Division and travelers were enjoying the vistas afforded by Sixteen-Mile Canyon and the crossing of the Continental Divide at Pipestone Pass, with late

afternoon and evening stops at Butte and Missoula. On the second morning out and prior to the mid-day arrival at Puget Sound, passengers were treated to a spectacular trip over the Cascade Mountains—something which *Empire Builder* passengers missed due to that train's early morning arrival at Seattle. The train was also unusual in that it served two terminals at its west end, Tacoma and Seattle—the latter in effect being at the end of a branch—and because of track arrangements the train had to be hauled backward between Tacoma Union Station and Seattle's Union Station.

Despite its sterling reputation, though, the *Olympian Hi* could not hold out against the heavy promotion and excellent services offered by contestants *Empire Builder* and *North Coast Limited*. High costs and fading patronage forced even pro-passenger Milwaukee Road to pull the plug, and on May 22, 1961, the final *Olympian Hiawatha*s—one of the most exotic transcons ever to run—departed Tacoma and Chicago for the final time.

Rocky Mountain high
With Tacoma some 690 miles behind and Chicago some 1,515 miles ahead, the *Olympian Hiawatha* is near Newcomb, Montana, and climbing Pipestone Pass in the west central part of the state. Too bad those new Super Domes are still a year or so off—Big Sky Country is Super Dome country! *Sandy Goodrick.*

Southern Pacific's Shasta Daylight and Cascade

Shasta Daylight

Southern Pacific's streamliner service to the Pacific Northwest included overnight and day schedules north of the San Francisco Bay Area to Portland, Oregon. The day train—a wonderful conveyance known as the *Shasta Daylight*—is well-remembered by long-time residents of Northern California and western Oregon. The train is shown northbound at the Pit River Bridge on Shasta Lake above Redding, California, in 1955. This man-made lake was formed by damming the Sacramento River, which required the relocation of the SP main line away from the river for some 25 miles north of Redding to Tunnel No. 10. *Sandy Goodrick.*

The 1937 unveiling of Southern Pacific's remarkable *Daylight* streamliner between Los Angeles and San Francisco propelled the carrier to stardom. The popularity of that train inevitably spawned a whole fleet of *Daylight* trains. Many *Daylight* trains were considered to be regional to Los Angeles and Oakland/San Francisco and are therefore also presented in Chapter 6, but one long-distance *Daylight* and a companion train, the *Cascade*, linked California with the Pacific Northwest.

Introduced between Oakland and Portland, Oregon, in April 1949, the new *Shasta Daylight* was perhaps the most glorious of the *Daylight* fleet. By the time the *Shasta* was introduced, SP had refined the art of equipment design to near perfection. The red-and-orange *Shasta* was state-of-the art. Built new for the service by Pullman-Standard were 29 cars, almost enough to equip two trains so that daily service could be provided over the 714-mile route. Two parlor-observation cars built

several years earlier for regional *Daylight* service completed the new *Shasta Daylight* consists.

Each of the train's nine chair cars featured restful Oregon-inspired colors like "Crater Lake Blue," "Cedar Red," and "Summit green." The train's showcase piece of rolling stock was an articulated triple-unit diner/kitchen/coffee shop car. *Shasta* patrons could enjoy famous SP meals after which a trip to the train's lounge car—known as the Timberline Tavern—might be in order. Inspired by Mount Hood's Timberline Lodge, the Timberline Tavern was furnished in a decor reminiscent of the famous Oregon resort.

One of the most distinctive features of the new *Shasta Daylight* were its oversized picture windows, designed to give passengers an unobstructed view of the splendors of the Shasta Route. Enhancing this feature was the 1955 addition of one of SP's homebuilt dome-lounge cars. The view through *any* of the train's windows was worth the ride.

Leaving Oakland Pier early in the morning after passengers from San Francisco transferred from the ferries, the *Shasta* began its race up the Sacramento Valley. After stops at Gerber and Davis (Sacramento), California, Lassen Peak, an active volcano, could be seen from the *Shasta*'s windows. Beyond Redding, California, the scenery began in earnest. Crossing Shasta Lake (formed by Shasta Dam) on the Pit River Bridge, the *Daylight* began a winding climb through the spectacular Sacramento River Canyon to Dunsmuir as Mount Shasta (14,161 feet tall) came looming into view. This majestic snow-capped peak, one of the tallest and most-dramatic

mountains in the Cascade Range, would dominate the scenery for hours as the train skirted its shoulders. Arrival at Klamath Falls, Oregon, at the base of the Cascades and the gateway to Crater Lake, preceded a spectacular climb to the summit of the line at Cascade Summit, 4,844 feet above sea level. Dropping downgrade from there, the *Shasta* skirted the south shore of beautiful Odell Lake and then followed the Willamette River all the way to Eugene. After stops at Albany and Salem, the state capital of Oregon, it was on to the Rose City—Portland—in the shadow of Mount Hood and the northernmost terminal of the SP. Arrival was shortly

Shasta in the Cascades

High point—literally—of the *Shasta*'s scenic daytime sashay between Portland and Oakland was the climb over Cascade Summit. The Oakland-bound *Shasta Daylight* is in the heart of the Cascades at Oakridge, Oregon, in the spring of 1955. A triple-unit set of Alco PAs heads up the eye-catching train, whose "*Daylight*" colors complement the subdued greens and tans of the Cascade Range. *Sandy Goodrick.*

"Cascade Club" DINER & LOUNGE

before midnight at handsome Portland Union Station.

Given the nature of the scenery on the Shasta Route, it was unfortunate that SP's new overnight streamliner, the *Cascade*, which replaced a heavyweight train by the same name in August 1950, traversed most of the same Oakland-Portland route in darkness on its $16^{1}/_{2}$-hour run. The two-tone gray streamliner was, consequently, best known for its accommodations. The all-room train offered modern roomettes, bedrooms, compartments, and drawing rooms, but the train's greatest feature was its triple-unit articulated kitchen/diner/lounge, the Cascade Club. After a nightcap in the Club it was off to bed for a good night's rest before arrival the next morning. In addition to offering reliable overnight service between Portland and the Bay Area, the *Cascade* served Seattle as well via a through sleeping-car connection, and the *Cascade* also connected at Martinez, California, with the *San Joaquin Daylight* to and from Los Angeles.

Despite the scenery and the dome cars, in 1959 the beautiful *Shasta Daylight* was reduced to a tri-weekly operation, except in summer when it continued to run daily. In 1964 the train was reduced to summer-only operation, and in 1967 it was discontinued altogether. The *Cascade* was reduced to tri-weekly service in 1970, but survived into Amtrak, evolving into that carrier's very popular *Coast Starlight*.

The Dining Car is Two Cars Back

Since before the turn of the century, one of the defining experiences of travel by rail was a meal in the dining car. Once populating even the lowliest of trains which moved at meal time, the dining car offered the passenger a welcome break from the tedium of the journey—but it was much more than that. As the centerpiece of their passenger service, the railroads placed a great deal of emphasis on making the diner an encounter the customer would remember and one which would reflect positively on the railroad. To quote Atlantic Coast Line president Champion McDowell Davis, "Good passenger service is the railroad's best . . . . advertisement. With good dining-car service as a collateral, passenger service offers evidence of the character of those many unforeseen factors and services that enter into a railroad operation."

The railroads invested heavily in the cars, the food and the presentation itself. Reflecting the diversity that abounded in the days of private railroad operation, it seemed that no two railroads' dining cars, menus, or services were exactly the same. While most roads provided dining service in a car of standard design seating as few as 30 and as many as 48 patrons, Southern Pacific often hosted its streamliner passengers in articulated triple-unit dining cars which contained a kitchen, crew dormitory, and offered over 100 feet of dining and lounge space. Twin-unit diners, which could cater to over 60 patrons at once, were common on fast overnighters such as the NYC's *20th Century Limited* and Illinois Central's *Panama Limited*. Santa Fe offered private dining to groups in the Turquoise Room in the dome car adjacent to the diner aboard the *Super Chief* while Union Pacific provided perhaps the greatest dining-car experience, operating dome diners on its *City of Los Angeles* and *City of Portland* where passengers could feast at rooftop level while watching the West pass by outside.

Dinnerware was as unique as the cars themselves. Santa Fe meals were served on dishes featuring the ancient, distinctive artwork of the Mimbres Indians of the American Southwest. Baltimore & Ohio's classic blue Centenary china held the road's homey meals and *20th Century Limited* patrons supped on dinnerware bearing the classic art deco logo of the "world's most famous train."

The cuisine was equally and wonderfully diverse. This was an era when much of the food was prepared right on the cars. Each railroad, it seemed, was determined to be famous for a culinary specialty. Diners never went wrong ordering Rocky Mountain trout on the Rio Grande. Those in the mood for a feast chose the King's Dinner on IC's *Panama Limited*, a multi-course repast reflecting the Creole penchant for excess at the table. B&O, underdog in the East Coast-Midwest market, carved out a niche for itself offering what many agreed were the finest meals on rails with outstanding recipes such as Crab Imperial.

Side dishes, too, distinguished a railroad or an individual train. Northern Pacific was famous for its mammoth "Big Baked Potato," a tuber the size of a man's forearm. Deep South Seaboard Air Line Railroad offered peanut soup, and if you rode the Wabash you never failed to order the pie, which the experienced traveler knew was baked from scratch right on board.

But there was something special about eating aboard the cars that extended beyond the dinnerware and the food. The distinctive and delicious smells originating from an impossibly small kitchen, snappy table linens, cut flowers, the tinkling of silver as the train canted to a curve, and the expert service of a polished staff were just part of the ambiance. Put this whole scene in motion with America rolling by outside the window and the result was magic. SP dining patrons could linger over a second cup of coffee while watching migrating whales spout in the blue Pacific. *Broadway Limited* patrons tucked into a sizzling hot beef dish, the train's specialty, as long evening shadows painted the tree-lined streets of Philadelphia's distinguished Main Line suburbs, and passengers on the Southern Railway's *Crescent* could contemplate a plateful of the best fried chicken in the world as the train rolled through the rural charm of the deep South.

It was a way of life disappearing fast by the 1950's. Drive-in fast-food restaurants were much better suited to patrons in a hurry on the new Interstate Highway System—coming soon to a town near you. Airline passengers still found themselves eating off of real china, but it was practically balanced on their knees as their Lockheed Constellation provided a nearly useless, high-altitude view of America below.

While some railroads sought to economize in the 1960s, cutting corners and even offering automat-style service in lieu of diners, others continued to place an emphasis on high-quality dining right up until the end of private railroad operation. The *Super Chief* was still one of the finest restaurant addresses in America in 1971. Seaboard Coast Line's *Florida Special* offered a Candlelight Dinner that was second to none in ambiance and the Southern kept serving that fried chicken right up to 1979.

While today many intercity passengers cruising along at 30,000 feet contemplate just how small a bag of peanuts can really get, a growing cadre of travelers are rediscovering an alternate travel adventure once taken for granted. Amtrak has managed to preserve the experience of dining on rails. Passengers aboard the *Coast Starlight* linger at tables as whales spout in the sparkling Pacific. Eastbound breakfast guests on board the *Empire Builder* are reminded by crews to look for elusive mountain goats in Glacier Park as did GN passenger representatives a generation ago. America's geography is a welcome part of the travel experience, again. And a meal in the dining car is one of the highlights of the adventure.

LUNCHEON

Table Flowers are Colorado Carnations

"As you travel over this bountiful land of ours, may you be ever reminded of the grace Almighty God has bestowed upon us. Let us acknowledge our debt to Him with prayers of thanksgiving."

Please Write Each Item on Meal Check. WAITERS ARE NOT PERMITTED TO TAKE ORAL ORDERS.

A la Carte

Appetizers Tomato, Grapefruit or Orange Juice, 40 — Chilled Fruit Cup, 50

Soups Hot or Jellied Consomme, 35 — French Onion Soup, Aux Croutons, 35
Spring Vegetable Soup, Cup, 40; Tureen, 65

Sandwiches (Double-Deck) Sliced Chicken, 1.65 — Chicken Salad 1.45
Baked Ham, 1.65 — American Cheese, 1.10
Hamburger Sandwich on Toasted Bun, Grilled Onion Slice-Garni, Potato Chips, 1.40

Entrees Sugar Cured Ham and Eggs, Country Style, Hash Brown Potatoes,
Sliced Combination Salad Plate — French Dressing, Hot Rolls 2.50
Hamburger Steak, Brown Onion Gravy, Whipped Potatoes,
Sliced Combination Salad Plate — French Dressing, Hot Rolls 2.75
Chilled Red Salmon, Garni, Potato Salad, Saltines, Melba Toast 2.25
Hot Roast Beef Sandwich, Whipped Potatoes,
Sliced Combination Salad Plate — French Dressing 2.65

Salads Head Lettuce, Half Portion, Choice of Dressing, 45
Chicken Salad, Mayonnaise, 1.75 — Potato Salad, 50
Chilled Fruit Salad Plate, Cottage Cheese, 1.85
(Includes Saltines and Melba Toast)

Desserts Chocolate Sundae, 55 — Freshly Baked Apple Pie, 45; A la Mode, 70
Chilled Melon, 50 — Fresh Peach Shortcake, 75

Beverages Coffee, Tea or Hot Chocolate, Per Pot, 35 — Individual Milk, 25
Selection of Soft Beverages, 25

It will be a pleasure to serve any dish not listed that you may wish if it is available.
Additional charge will be made for service outside the dining car. This service is subject to delay when dining car is busy.

Employee in charge of this car is ....

P. S. COBEL, Supervisor, Dining Car Service, Dallas 2, Texas
Y. E. JUGE, Regional Manager, Sales and Rates, Fort Worth and Denver Railway Co., Fort Worth 2, Texas
MARK MODGLIN, General Passenger Agent, Colorado and Southern Railway Co., Denver 2, Colorado

TZ

Way of the Zephyrs

Burlington Route

City of Portland on the C&NW
With three brand-new dome cars in its 12-car consist, C&NW train 106, the eastbound *City of Portland*, pauses for passengers at Union Station (towered building behind first baggage car) in Cedar Rapids, Iowa, on April 10, 1955. C&NW E-series locomotives for a time were the normal motive power on some *City* trains east of Omaha. *William D. Middleton.*

The last train featured in this chapter was the first streamliner to serve residents of the great Pacific Northwest—in fact, the *City of Portland* was the first transcontinental streamliner ever (see Chapter 1), as well as the first streamliner to offer sleeper and complete dining service.

The *City of Portland* made its first trip between Chicago and its namesake on May 5, 1935, and like most other UP-based transcons, the train was a joint effort with Chicago & North Western, over whose tracks the *City* trains sped between Omaha and Chicago. The *City of Portland* was unlike the Chicago-Pacific Northwest streamliners of other carriers, all of which headed northwest from Chicago to serve Minneapolis and St. Paul before turning west. Rather, the *City* for most of its life operated via the famed C&NW-UP "Overland Route" due west out of Chicago as far as Granger, Wyoming, where the train diverged northwesterly onto the Portland main line.

The *City of Portland's* traditional schedule put it on an overnight timing between Chicago and Cheyenne, Wyoming. West of there, passengers enjoyed daylight views of classic cowboy country as the train sped through southern Wyoming over one of the more subtle crossings of the Rocky Mountains. By evening the train called at Pocatello, Idaho—gateway to Yellowstone Park and the Grand Tetons—and at Shoshone, Idaho, the stop for the famous Sun Valley ski resort owned by UP. By late evening the train was at Boise, Idaho's state capital. From there, it was overnight to Portland with a breakfast-hour arrival following a cruise along the spectacular Columbia River Gorge. Eastbound, the timings

were similar—overnight between Portland and Boise, daylight through southern Wyoming, and so forth.

Direct connections at Portland with the Portland-Seattle Pool Train services of UP, Northern Pacific, and Great Northern linked Seattle and Tacoma, Washington, with the *City of Portland*.

The arrival of new locomotives and rolling stock (and some upgraded older cars) before and after World War II allowed UP to make the *City of Portland* its first transcontinental streamliner to expand to daily service, which it did on February 15, 1947. UP always treated the *City of Portland* as one of its top two streamliners, the other being the *City of Los Angeles*. Those two trains, along with the *Challenger*, were the first UP trains to receive dome cars in 1955. At this time, the *City of Portland* featured a marvelous array of fine equipment; a typical consist included a baggage-dormitory, a dome coach, three reclining-seat legrest coaches, a cafe-lounge car expressly for coach travelers, dome diner, four Pullman sleeping cars, and the dome lounge-observation car.

The year 1955 represented another fairly radical change for the *City of Portland* and its Overland Route kin when all of UP's Chicago-anchored trains were permanently rerouted east of Omaha on the Milwaukee Road due to disagreements between UP and C&NW. *City of Portland* operations remained constant for another four years when, in 1959, it was rerouted west of Julesburg, Colorado, to operate via Denver, at the same time being "combined" with the *City of Denver* all the way between Chicago and Denver in both directions. In essence the *City of Denver* had simply been dropped and its passengers accommodated by the

rerouted *City of Portland*. UP's passenger revenues had seen a modest decline since 1952, and train consolidations were one way to reduce costs.

This was not entirely bad news, as this consolidation provided Chicago-Denver passengers with the better-equipped *City of Portland* trains, including the famous dome diners. Until this consolidation, dome cars were never a regular feature of the *City of Denver*. Westbound from Denver, the *City of Portland* rejoined the Overland Route not far west of Cheyenne. The more-roundabout Denver routing only cost a couple of extra hours in overall *City of Portland* timings and it gave the train Denver's strong traffic base. This routing lasted for nearly a decade when, in 1968, the *City of Portland* returned

to its Cheyenne routing and the *City of Denver* became a meager split-off connection to and from the *City of Portland* at North Platte, Nebraska.

By the end of 1969, the *City of Portland* had been combined with all other *City* trains in and out of Chicago with its cars being split off from the *City of Los Angeles/ Challenger* at Green River, Wyoming. The dome diners disappeared not long before Amtrak assumed operation of a skeletal network of nationwide train services on May 1, 1971. Unfortunately, the *City of Portland* was not among the chosen few trains that the underfunded Amtrak could afford to operate, and direct Chicago-Portland service ended once the final *City of Portland*s arrived at their terminals on May 2, 1971.

Classic *City of Portland*
In this memorable publicity view choreographed by the UP, the *City of Portland* shows off its classic 1955 consist when the dome observation car was still being carried at the end of the train. Eventually, these handsome cars would be converted for mid-train operation. The train is eastbound along the Oregon side of the Columbia River Gorge. *Union Pacific Railroad Museum Collection.*

CHAPTER 5

STREAMLINERS TO THE SOUTHLAND

By Streamliner, New York to Florida
By Streamliner, New York to Dixie
Streamlining the Way From Midwest to Florida
Streamliners Uniting the North and the South
Lone Star Streamliners

Take a look at those breeze-swept palms in Leslie Ragan's dreamlike portrait of the Florida East

Coast's *Champion* and you'll understand instantly the allure of Florida and the sunbelt. Long before the

proliferation of interstates and airlines, railroads carried the bulk of passengers to this paradise, in turn,

helping to develop the region. Fun streamliners such as the *Silver Meteor*, the *Champion*, and the *South*

Wind helped establish the Florida rail travel market as perhaps the strongest in the nation.

Streamliners also linked the North to the red-earth country of the Deep South—trains as varied

in their personalities as their destinations and passengers. Aristocrats like the all-Pullman *Panama Lim-*

ited and the *Crescent* linked Chicago and New York, respectively, to New Orleans. Northern families

bound for grandma's house in Mississippi ate fried chicken and hummed gospel tunes to their sleepy

children in the coaches of the *City of New Orleans* or the *Southerner.* Those traveling to and from Texas

and the South Central states had a number of wonderful trains to choose from including the seduc-

tively named *Southern Belle* and the flashy red-and-silver *Texas Special.*

Southland streamliners tied two distinct regions together, encouraging us to learn more about each

other in the process. The little boy standing on the station platform in the heat of a Georgia afternoon

watching a streamliner roll in was just as fascinated as his counterpart looking out the window. It was a

valuable lesson in geography and sociology, and the passenger train was the best teacher in the world.

By Streamliner, New York to Florida

"Streamlining through Wonderful Florida"

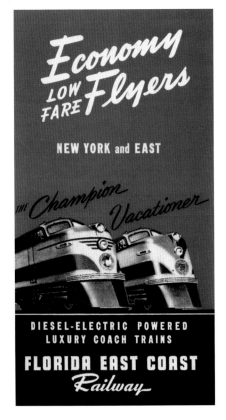

The Florida Three

Three Southeastern railroads can be credited with pioneering the Florida streamliner movement: Seaboard Air Line, Atlantic Coast Line, and Florida East Coast. All three issued a wealth of promotional material including folders, postcards, and advertising for their streamliner fleets. The wonderful prewar ACL postcard above shows the as-delivered *Champion* streamliner of 1939, complete with its purple-and-silver Electro-Motive E3 diesel; the Seaboard ad coincided with the arrival of the first Florida streamliner, the *Silver Meteor*; the Florida East Coast folder informed travelers of newer trains such as the *Vacationer*. All, *Joe Welsh Collection.*

Given the allure of the destination, one would have expected Florida-bound trains to be immensely popular, even in the worst of times. But with the country in the teeth of the Depression early in the 1930's, railroad passenger traffic—even to exotic Florida—had declined precipitously.

Realizing that the ultimate challenge lay in the need to attract passengers back to the rails rather than to save money moving those who had remained, the railroads which linked the North to Florida followed the examples set by pioneers like Union Pacific, Burlington, and Milwaukee Road that had made bold, positive steps to streamline starting in the mid-1930s. Marketing research showed that the newfangled trains were indeed attracting a healthy number of new riders—not only to the new streamliners themselves, but to heavyweight trains that shared routes with streamliners.

Mindful of this and prodded by the formidable Florida tourism industry, the Seaboard Air Line Railroad—a maverick north-south railroad linking Richmond, Virginia, with the Carolinas, Georgia, and Florida—contracted with the Edward G. Budd Manufacturing Company of Philadelphia to construct a seven-car, non-articulated, lightweight, stainless-steel all-coach streamliner for service between New York and Miami and Tampa/St. Petersburg.

The new *Silver Meteor* would operate over the Pennsylvania Railroad from New York to Washington, D.C., and from Washington to the SAL at Richmond via the

Richmond, Fredericksburg & Potomac Railroad. Because there was initially only one set of equipment, the *Meteor* could only provide a tri-weekly departure from New York. Furthermore, Miami alternated with Tampa/St. Petersburg as a destination.

Launched on February 2, 1939, the *Silver Meteor* initiated one of the most successful rail passenger renaissances in the country—the Florida streamliner. Within months, the new train had helped perennial underdog Seaboard eclipse its formidable competitor, Atlantic Coast Line, in monthly passenger earnings. Coast Line and ally Florida East Coast Railway, sensing the threat, quickly ordered their own streamliners—four sets worth—in June 1939. On December 1, 1939, ACL-FEC introduced a daily lightweight coach streamliner between New York and Miami, the *Champion*. Similar to the *Meteor*, the *Champion* was handled north of

Richmond by RF&P and PRR. At the same time, FEC introduced a companion intrastate streamliner. A veritable twin to *Champion*, the *Henry M. Flagler* operated between Jacksonville and Miami with measurably less success than its long-distance cousin. Within a year, the train would be reintroduced as the *Dixie Flagler* between Chicago and Miami.

SAL countered the daily *Champion* by adding additional *Meteor* trainsets so that it could offer daily service as well, to both Miami and St. Petersburg. Both the *Meteor* and the *Champion* were patterned after Santa Fe's all-coach *El Capitan* streamliner, which had been introduced in 1938 between Chicago and Los Angeles.

Perhaps the most amazing thing about the new New York-Florida streamliners was the public's reaction to them. Despite the addition of more trains, demand for travel continued to rise—and even on non-streamlined trains operated by SAL and ACL between New York and Florida. Trade periodical *Railway Age* reported that some Florida hotel employees had even developed a healthy side business scalping tickets for the new streamliners.

By 1940 the *Silver Meteor* and *Champion* consists had been doubled in size. In the spring of 1941 both trains had Pullman heavyweight sleeping cars added to their consists with the intention of boosting the popularity of sleeper service by operating it on the faster schedules of the streamliners. The *Champion* also received a new name—*Tamiami Champion*—and ran in sections, one for the east coast of Florida and one for the west coast.

Throughout World War II the new streamliners' high capacity and high speeds made them a particularly valuable asset as the Florida roads were called upon to move substantial passenger loads. The streamliners often ran in multiple sections, their consists diluted with older heavyweight cars. In 1944, its highest revenue year ever, the *Silver Meteor* grossed over $8 million—more money than the SAL itself had lost in 1933 while in the throes of receivership.

With the war but a memory, both the Seaboard and Coast Line began re-equipping their streamliners and introducing new ones. New coaches, diners, lounge, observation and baggage-dormitory-coaches were received from Budd Company by the railroads in 1946 and 1947. Beginning in the 1946-47 winter season, ACL and partners PRR, RF&P, and PRR were able to introduce for the first time an all-streamlined *Champion* between New York and the west coast of Florida. The all-coach train was quickly changed to a lightweight coach/heavyweight sleeper operation in the summer of 1947.

SAL too had some improvements up its stainless-steel sleeves. In December 1947, it and partners PRR and RF&P christened the *Silver Star* as a running mate to the *Silver Meteor*. Operating on the former *Advance Silver Meteor*'s schedule, the *Star* mixed hand-me-down streamlined equipment from the prewar *Silver Meteor* with heavyweight sleepers. Originally a winter-only train to both coasts of Florida, the *Star* returned in August 1948 as a year-round New York-Miami train.

Despite the fact that they carried heavyweight cars and technically operated as partial streamliners, the New York-Florida trains continued to be immensely popular. While ridership dropped off somewhat in the immediate postwar period, it was still much higher than in the pre-World War II era. SAL, for example estimate

The train that started it all
Underdog in a north-south transportation corridor dominated by Atlantic Coast Line, the Seaboard Air Line Railroad was first with a streamliner, the *Silver Meteor*. Very early in the *Meteor*'s long career (the train was still running in the final years of the twentieth century), the southbound run departs Savannah, Georgia, in March 1939. The locomotive sported Seaboard's eye-appealing "citrus scheme" of dark green, yellow, and orange with silver pilot and trucks. *Hugh M. Comer, Joe Welsh Collection.*

that it carried 200 percent more passengers in 1948 than in 1940.

Streamlined sleeping cars were the only thing missing. Both ACL and SAL and their partners ordered new sleepers and sleeper-lounges in the immediate postwar period. Delays at the carbuilders meant that the roads would have to wait until 1948-49 to introduce the new cars. The arrival of the new sleepers allowed ACL to announce that its swank winter-season-only all-Pullman *Florida Special* was now the streamlined all-Pullman *Florida Special*. The train's principal rival, Seaboard's seasonal all-Pullman heavyweight *Orange Blossom Special*, was never re-equipped. The difference was decisive and by 1953 the *Blossom*—a fixture since 1925—would be gone, leaving behind only a song of the same name. Perhaps to counter the loss, SAL would add still more new sleeping cars to its *Silver* fleet in 1955-56 including a sleeper-lounge of unique style. With sunshine streaming through oversized windows (including those on the ceiling), lounges decorated in a tropical theme, and complementary orange juice available in the afternoons, Seaboard's new "Sun

Lounge" cars were some of the most attractive on rails.

Although not blessed with the scenery enjoyed by Western streamliners, the Florida trains had a unique charm of their own. Winter-weary southbound passengers seemed to undergo a metamorphosis as soon as they stepped on board. Hanging up coats they'd no longer need, Florida-bound riders settled in for the fast overnight run to tropical paradise. On board there was the wonderful experience of dinner in the diner (both ACL and SAL trains got high marks for their dining-car cuisine) while passengers stared out at the frigid winterscape they were leaving behind. The cozy confines of a sleeping-car room with starched, clean linens turned down for the night invited sleep as the Carolinas slid by in darkness. The next morning one awoke to sunshine streaming through the window as his or her train rocketed along through Florida orange groves. Following a breakfast of fresh-brewed coffee and ham and scrambled eggs highlighted by such exotica as orange or grapefruit marmalade, passengers began arriving at their various destinations—West Palm Beach, Fort Lauderdale and such. Delighting in the unaccustomed warmth, passen-

Still a Champ
What began as a svelte seven-car streamliner in 1939 grew to a magnitude that caught even the railroads off guard. The date is June 1968—a time when other streamliners had withered into short local trains—and a Penn Central GG1, still in Pennsylvania paint, flies high above the Susquehanna River at Perryville, Maryland, with a long *Champion* bound for New York City. And this was the off season for Florida travel, no less! *Herbert. H. Harwood Jr., Joe Welsh Collection.*

Silver Meteor in the 1960s

Seemingly strung out across half of Jacksonville (top), an impressive *Silver Meteor* backs into Union Station on August 5, 1965, enroute to New York. For ten years now, the Sun Lounge sleeper (postcard inset, above) had been a fixture Seaboard's most-notable streamliner. At left, the train's lounge observation car, bearing the train's celestial drumhead, is Florida-bound at Washington in 1968. *Jacksonville scene, David W. Salter; postcard, Mike Schafer Collection; observation scene, Bob Johnston.*

gers were rested and ready to start their vacation.

In part because of the popularity of their destination and in part due to the devotion of the operating railroads, the Florida trains continued to draw high ridership and remained well-run trains through the 1960's—a time when many other American long-distance trains were being downgraded or eliminated. As late as 1962, Atlantic Coast Line pulled out all of the stops in upgrading its *Florida Special* for its 75th anniversary. A 24-hour New York-Miami schedule was reintroduced. Train hostesses, movies, fashion shows, and games were available in the train's new recreation car, and the primarily first-class train offered reserved seat dining and radio telephone service. For the privilege of riding, passengers had to pay an extra fare of $5/sleeping car or $ 2.50/coach. Passengers flocked to the train and throughout the 1960s the *Special* continued to be well patronized.

In July 1967, the ACL and the SAL merged to form Seaboard Coast Line. By this time, FEC was out of the picture—a vicious strike in 1963 had caused the railroad to withdraw its participation in through Northeast-Florida passenger service.

Despite their popularity, the cost of operating the Florida trains continued to mount, and the SCL moved to address some of the redundancies in the newly combined system. The *East Coast Champion* was discontinued in December 1967; its west coast counterpart continued to run, now redubbed simply as the *Champion*. To the east coast, the former SAL *Silver Meteor* was the flagship and by April 1968, the *Meteor* had stopped carrying cars for the west coast of Florida, leaving that job to the *Champion*. The *Silver Star* now carried cars to both coasts.

Although patronage was healthy relative to the trains of many other contemporaries, operating costs continued to mount, exceeding revenues. Likewise, capital replacement costs to re-equip the aging fleet of cars were becoming prohibitive. SCL made the hard choice to join the fledgling National Railroad Passenger Corporation—Amtrak. On May 1, 1971, the SCL Florida fleet became Amtrak's fleet. Fortunately, the popularity of the New York-Florida trains continued, and the route was the only original Amtrak route which supported two separate long-distance trains daily as well as seasonal operations like the *Florida Special*, which returned for one season under Amtrak. Today's Florida fleet boast four daily trains in each direction, the *Silver Meteor, Silver Star, Silver Palm,* and *Auto Train*, keeping alive a tradition that began back in February 1939 with a lone seven-car coach streamliner.

The *Florida Special*
(Right) One of the top-ranking trains of the impressive armada of streamliners that streaked back and forth between the Northeast and Florida was Atlantic Coast Line's seasonal *Florida Special*, right, streaming out of Jacksonville, Florida for New York City in the 1960s. *Jim Boyd.*

***Florida Special* hostess, 1962**
(Above) A *Florida Special* hostess conducts a sing-a-long in the recreation car during the train's 75th anniversary in 1962. *ACL, Joe Welsh Collection.*

By Streamliner, New York to Dixie

SOUTHERN RAILWAY'S *SOUTHERNER*, *TENNESSEAN*, AND *CRESCENT*

Unlike many of its contemporaries, the Southern Railway embraced streamlining grudgingly. Unconvinced of the merits of lightweight construction, conservative Southern watched warily as streamliners flourished on other roads like the Burlington, the Union Pacific, and even in the conservative deep South on the Seaboard Air Line. Although the railroad took steps to attract passengers and lower costs, implementing lower coach fares, air-conditioning its heavyweight cars, and introducing diesels in local short-haul trains, the Southern at first refused to take the plunge on what would prove to be the single most successful improvement in attracting passengers to the rails—streamlining.

Courted unsuccessfully at first by manufacturers Pullman-Standard and Budd who attempted to convince the railroad to streamline its *Florida Sunbeam*, Southern resisted the siren's call of modernization in the face of mounting evidence elsewhere that the concept was successfully attracting passengers back to the rails. That is, until the community of Atlanta took notice.

Railroad and industrial center of the South, served by over 100 passenger trains daily, but no streamliners, Atlanta was a proud city unwilling to take a back seat in anything. Thanks to an *Atlanta Journal* editorial one Sunday in March 1940, residents discovered over toast and coffee that their city was somehow not reaching its potential, in part because it was unserved by lightweight trains. A series of other well-researched articles followed, detailing the good, the bad, and the ugly of the city's current rail passenger situation. Before long local civic groups had stirred from their slumber and began asking tough questions of both the Southern and the L&N who, at first, held firm on the issue—streamliners were not under consideration. Later, while Southern sulked, L&N had a change of heart. Joining a consortium of nine railroads which was actively planning a coach streamliner service between Chicago and Miami, L&N would operate a Florida streamliner, the *Dixie Flagler*, through Atlanta every third day beginning in December 1940. Atlanta had its first lightweight train.

Other events were conspiring to move the Southern inexorably toward streamlining. Competitor Seaboard was, by now, visibly reaping the benefits of streamlining with its New York-Miami *Silver Meteor* introduced back in February 1939. Impressed enough with the Seaboard's earnings, conservative Atlantic Coast Line, a

Southern timetable, 1950
Although at first resistant to streamlining, SR eventually played host to a respectable stable of streamliners. The *Crescent* got cover honors on Southern's timetables in 1950.

The *Southerner*
In contrast to the obsolete technology of horse-powered agriculture, Southern Railway's new *Southerner* races toward Washington, D.C., at 80 mph circa 1941 near the end of its overnight trip from Atlanta. *SR, Southern Railway Historical Association Collection.*

The *Tennessean*
The engineer of Southern's southbound *Tennessean* pours on the coal as the train marches out of Alexandria shortly after the train's 1941 introduction. While new Electro-Motive E6 diesels supplied power for the *Tennessean*'s cousin, the *Southerner,* the *Tennessean* itself was initially in the charge of streamlined steam at the eastern end of the run. SR 4-6-2 No. 1380 need not apologize, though. The work of noted industrial designer Otto Kuhler, the Pacific represents streamstyling at its best, and with a green-and-silver paint scheme that neatly segues into the all-stainless consist of the train. *David W. Salter Collection.*

Southern ally, had reversed its position, implementing its own New York-Miami streamliner, the *Champion,* in December of the same year. While freight revenues were up considerably in 1940, Southern's passenger revenues rose at a much lower rate. Not surprisingly, an internal study conducted by the railroad concluded that, indeed, the Southern should streamline.

When it finally introduced streamliners, Southern did so on its strongest corridors. In October 1940 the railroad announced the purchase of 44 streamlined cars and five diesel locomotives with which it introduced two distinct trains. Between New York and New Orleans via Atlanta and Birmingham, the railroad implemented the *Southerner,* a fast, all-coach streamliner, on March 31, 1941.

The *Southerner* provided luxury reclining-seat coaches, dining and lounge facilities, and offered connections to and from New England at New York as well as connections to the West at New Orleans. Slant-nosed Electro-Motive E6 diesels wearing green and imitation aluminum provided the power. While the *Southerner* was breaking new ground and testing the all-coach luxury train concept, its new counterpart, the *Tennessean,* targeted an existing market. Designed to replace the *Memphis Special* as the top train on the Washington-Memphis, Tennessee, alignment, one of the *Tennessean*'s most important

assignments was carrying the mail. Because the local sleeping-car business on the route was promising, the *Tennessean* also carried a Chattanooga-Memphis sleeper, a New York-Memphis sleeper, and a Bristol (Tennessee)-Nashville sleeper. These heavyweight cars were painted silver to match the train's stainless-steel head-end cars, coaches, diners, and observation.

Unlike its *Southerner* cousin, which operated exclusively over Southern rails south of Washington, the *Tennessean* operated via the SR from Washington to Lynchburg, Virginia, then on the Norfolk & Western from Lynchburg to Bristol; it rode SR rails again between Bristol and Memphis. Between Washington and Bristol, the train was hauled by streamlined steam on the Southern and the N&W, and SR's new E6 diesels handled the train between Bristol and Memphis.

The *Southerner* and the *Tennessean* enjoyed early success. This coupled with the increased passenger traffic experienced by the railroad during World War II resulted in the Southern re-equipping both trains in the postwar period and creating a third streamliner, the *Crescent.* Historically Southern's top heavyweight train on the New York-Washington-New Orleans route, the *Crescent Limited* received new lightweight sleeping cars, sleeper-lounges, diners, head-end cars, and distinctive high-windowed sleeper-observations by early 1950; new coaches operated between Atlanta and New Orleans. The *Crescent* ran over a collection of railroads on its route including the Pennsylvania (New York-Washington), the Southern (Washington-Atlanta), the Atlanta & West Point (Atlanta-West Point, Georgia), the Western Railway of Alabama (West Point-Montgomery, Alabama), and the Louisville & Nashville (Montgomery-New Orleans). A through New York-Los Angeles sleeper was added in 1954 operating west of New Orleans on Southern Pacific's *Sunset Limited* (Chapter 3).

Southern's passenger operations became something of a legend in the early Amtrak era. Southern was one of the few railroads eligible to join Amtrak which chose not to, instead being obligated (by the Amtrak law) to continue to operate its *Southern Crescent* (essentially a renamed *Southerner*, the skeletal remains of the once-proud *Crescent* having ridden into oblivion during 1970) as a private railroad operation.

While the *Tennessean* and the original *Crescent* had long since vanished from its timetables, the SR maintained its *Southern Crescent* in the grand manner. Up front, the train's E-unit diesels re-emerged from years of somber black paint with a fresh coat of Southern's historic green which years earlier had been applied to its crack passenger steam locomotives and early diesel fleet. Sleeping-car accommodations still included the expansive master room complete with a shower. Meals in the diner meant muffins baked fresh on the car for breakfast and Southern's savory fried chicken for dinner. Ultimately, SR did join Amtrak, in 1979, and this last example of a great, privately operated, overnight American passenger train became but a pleasant memory of the wide array of individualistic railroad streamliners which once spanned the U.S.

SEABOARD'S *SILVER COMET*

The Seaboard Air Line Railroad was a latecomer in a market which itself was a bit of a late bloomer for streamliner service: New York to Dixie. As early as 1939, though, SAL had contemplated a New York-Atlanta-Birmingham streamliner, but found itself concentrating on its lucrative New York-Florida route instead.

Part of this could be attributed to the powerful Pennsylvania Railroad, a key connection for railroads from the South wanting access to the nation's largest city, New York. Shortly following the 1939 debut of its *Silver Meteor* between New York and Miami/St. Pete, SAL approached the PRR about operating the *Meteor* to Atlanta and Birmingham on selected days. PRR nixed the idea, apparently not wanting to alienate one of its most-important connections to the South, the Southern, which at the time was still staunchly opposed to streamlining. SAL let the matter drop—for the meantime.

Comings and goings of the *Crescent*
(Top) Handsome in their apple green and off-white attire, a pair of Southern E-units wheel the New York-bound *Crescent* through the S-curve at Lennox Road in suburban Atlanta in 1957. The *Crescent* featured a high-windowed five-bedroom buffet-lounge observation car, shown above on the eastbound *Crescent* detouring over the Piedmont & Northern Railway between Greenville and Spartanburg, South Carolina, on June 26, 1950, due to a wreck on the nearby SR main line. P&N was an electric interurban railroad, hence the overhead catenary wires. *Top photo, David W. Salter; above, Sandy Goodrick.*

Seaboard's *Silver Comet*

Sparkling in the ambient light of the Emory University station in Atlanta in December 1962 is the *Silver Comet*, taking on passengers before continuing its through-the-night sweep up the Seaboard Air Line to Virginia and points north. SAL was never strong in the Atlanta and Birmingham market, and by the late 1960s it was not uncommon for the *Comet* to arrive Birmingham with but a single coach, diner-lounge, and sleeper. *David W. Salter.*

After World War II, Seaboard's plan for a New York-Birmingham streamliner bloomed. On May 18, 1947, the *Silver Comet*—SAL's response to SR's *Southerner*—was christened by actress Eleanor Parker. Though considered a streamliner, the *Comet*'s streamlined consist was at the onset diluted with heavyweight sleepers until newly ordered cars finally arrived. As with Seaboard's Florida trains, PRR and Richmond, Fredericksburg & Potomac contributed cars to *Comet* operation.

Departing southbound in mid day, the train followed the route used by its more-famous sister, the *Silver Meteor*, from New York to Hamlet, North Carolina, where the *Comet* cut west from the Florida main line to

Birmingham via Greenwood, South Carolina, and Atlanta. Atlanta and Birmingham were reached in the morning. For a time, the *Comet* tapped the Hampton Roads area of northeast Virginia (Norfolk/Newport News/Portsmouth) market by carrying a through Portsmouth-Atlanta coach and sleeper west of Hamlet.

The *Silver Comet* enjoyed a modicum of success, though not quite to the extent of its Florida sisters; SR proved a worthy competitor and eventually tied up the New York-Atlanta-Birmingham market with its *Southerner*, which was an impressive train even at the end of the 1960s. Such was not the case for the *Comet*, and in 1969 the train was discontinued.

Streamlining the Way From Midwest to Florida

THE *CITY OF MIAMI, SOUTH WIND,* AND *DIXIE FLAGLER*

The Northeast did not have a monopoly on Florida-bound streamliners. When winter winds began their sweep in from Canada across the Upper Midwest and Great Lakes, Mid-Americans knew it was time time to call WAbash 2-2575, ANDover 5570, or WEbster 9-4343.

WAbash 2-2575 got you through to the Illinois Central Railroad and, if the train wasn't sold out, passage on IC's streamliner *City of Miami*; a perfectly acceptable alternative was Pennsylvania Railroad's *South Wind* (call ANDover 5570). As for WEbster 9-4343, that got you a passenger agent of the Chicago & Eastern Illinois who could put you aboard the *Dixie Flagler*—a train named in honor of Henry M. Flagler who in the late nine-

teenth century was key to transforming Florida into "America's Riviera."

These three Florida-liners represented a coordinated effort to provide Midwesterners with daily streamliner service to Florida's Gold Coast; each train departed Chicago and Miami every third day. For example, the *City of Miami* would depart Chicago on Monday, the *South Wind* on Tuesday, the *Dixie Flagler* on Wednesday, and so forth. Advertising and ticketing was a joint effort.

When the triumvirate streamliners began service in 1940, no fewer than nine railroads were involved in their operation. All three trains operated on a stringent one-night-out schedule, southbound departing Chicago in the morning and arriving Miami late afternoon the following day. On-time performance southbound was paramount, for the trains had to be promptly cleaned,

Dazzling dieseliner
Illinois Central's all-coach *City of Miami* streamliner of 1940 wore blazing tropical colors that helped dispell the mid-winter blues of Midwesterners. Color photos of the actual train are extremely rare, but this publicity artwork issued by the railroad aptly illustrates the one-of-a-kind livery that barely lasted through World War II. The original *City of Miami's* seven cars were built by Pullman-Standard and the train was powered by a single 2000-hp Electro-Motive E6 passenger diesel. *Collection of Mike Schafer.*

restocked, and turned at Miami for a same-day early evening departure back to Chicago, which was reached late the following night.

The most spectacular of the threesome was the *City of Miami*, dispatched on its first trip December 18, 1940, after being christened with water from Florida's Biscayne Bay. As delivered, the seven-car train wore one of the most radical paint schemes that ever canvassed a streamliner: bright yellow-orange with green roofs and and a green bow wave that swooped up from the locomotive nose. Red separation stripes completed the treatment, which evoked images of

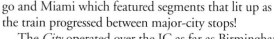

The *Dixie Flagler*
Steam ruled on some portions of the routes of the three new Chicago-Miami streamliners inaugurated in 1940. Pacific 1008 (above) of the Chicago & Eastern Illinois followed a dress code of early streamliners that called for shrouded steam locomotives where streamliner diesels might not be assigned. The 4-6-2 seems to be doing an admirable job of wheeling the *Dixie Flagler* out of Chicago on March 29, 1944. All three of the new Chicago-Miami trains rode Florida East Coast rails south of Jacksonville, and FEC issued its own little brochures promoting the new trains. *Photo, R. H. Kennedy, William A. Raia Collection; brochure, Joe Welsh Collection.*

citrus groves, palm trees, ocean waves—*very* Florida.

The *City* included a baggage-dormitory-coach named *Bougainvillea*, coach *Camellia* with a nurse's station, regular coaches *Japonica*, *Hibiscus*, and *Poinsettia*; diner *Palm Garden,* and tavern-lounge observation car *Bamboo Grove*. The Florida theming was, of course, carried out in the train's interior appointments (possibly to excess). Photo murals on car bulkheads—*de rigeur* on mid-century streamliners— displayed Florida scenes and between-window draperies featured palm designs.

Lounge-observation car *Bamboo Grove* was a panoply of tropical motifs and other intrigues. Pier panels (that between windows) were of zebrawood, and some of the cocktail-lounge seating was upholstered in coral-colored leather. The bar area had a canopy supported by—yes—bamboo poles, a fake palm tree, and wall-mounted masks carved from coconut shells. On the wall behind the bar was (aside from the obligatory photo mural of a Florida scene) a map of the train's route between Chica-

go and Miami which featured segments that lit up as the train progressed between major-city stops!

The *City* operated over the IC as far as Birmingham, Alabama. The Central of Georgia forwarded the train from Birmingham to Albany, Georgia, where Atlantic Coast Line took over for the run into Jacksonville. The last leg of the trip, to Miami, was under the jurisdiction of Florida East Coast, which tapped just about every important Atlantic coastal resort city down to Miami. Total distance: 1,493 miles.

Also a seven-car all-coach streamliner, the *South Wind* was a product of the Budd Company, and car types were similar to the *City of Miami*. Pennsy was a bit more restrained in terms of decor, however, largely dispensing with the Florida motif. Although the train was built of stainless steel, it was one of the few Budd fluted-stainless-steel streamliners that was entirely painted, wearing PRR's conservative Tuscan Red rather than exhibiting the natural luster of stainless steel—reportedly to the consternation of Budd which felt its products looked best *au naturale*.

The PRR handled the train for a relatively short distance, from Chicago to Louisville, Kentucky, about 313 miles. From there, L&N sped it to Montgomery, Alabama, via Nashville, and Birmingham, 490 miles; ACL took it beyond Birmingham to Jacksonville, 389 miles, where FEC took over for the remaining 366 miles to Miami. Total mileage was close to 1,560 miles.

This was its second assignment for the seven-car streamlined trainset protecting *Dixie Flagler* schedules. The *Dixie Flagler* equipment—also of Budd manufacturer (but not painted)—had originally been delivered to Florida East Coast in 1939 to serve as a regional train, the *Henry M. Flagler* between Jacksonville and Miami. As delivered, this train was similar to the *South Wind* with a baggage-dormitory-coach, four coaches, diner, and tavern-observation car, all named for Florida locales—perfect for the new Chicago-Florida operations. The *Dixie Flagler* departed Chicago's Dearborn Station (after having been christened with a bottle of orange juice) on December 17, 1940.

Chicago & Eastern Illinois rails provided a raceway for the *Dixie Flagler* between Chicago's Dearborn Station and Evansville, Indiana (287 miles), where L&N took over for the 159-mile trip to Nashville. L&N affiliate Nashville, Chattanooga & St. Louis handled the train from Nashville to Atlanta (285 miles), and ACL affiliate Atlanta, Birmingham & Coast took over for the 355-mile cross-Georgia run to the FEC at Jacksonville. Total mileage: 1,452 miles.

From the start, the *City of Miami*'s own E6 diesel operated all the way through the Miami, but the *South*

Wind and *Dixie Flagler* initially were steam-powered between Chicago and Jacksonville, from which an FEC Electro-Motive E6 handled the *Flagler* and *South Wind* to and from Miami. In keeping with the spirit of streamlining, the steam locomotives supplied by the operating railroads featured streamlined shrouding.

As was the case with most new streamliners of the period, the three sunliners were well-received by the traveling public, so much so that their operation was made year-round; initially they were to have been winter-season operations only. The new streamliners complemented three all-Pullman heavyweight trains, the *Sunchaser*, *Dixieland*, and *Jacksonian*, that ran on schedules similar to the streamliners, as well as other heavyweight coach-and-Pullman trains operating on two-night-out schedules.

World War II temporarily ended much of the heavyweight seasonal Midwest-Florida trains as railroads were called upon to supply cars for troop movements. The three Chicago-Florida streamliners remained, though, carrying more than their fair share of war traffic during the period.

In 1949, the trio received sleeping cars—albeit heavyweight—about the time some of the heavyweight

The *South Wind*
(Top) The faint haze of hot diesel exhaust suggests that the northbound *South Wind* is ripping along at maximum permissible speed on FEC's main line near Eau Gallie, Florida. It's April 1960, and the *South Wind* has grown to be a streamliner of impressive girth. The consist includes a Vista-Dome sleeper-lounge which has been leased from Northern Pacific for the winter season. The original *South Wind* of 1940 depicted above in a rendering by Leslie Ragan—an artist who did a number of railroad commissions—was built by Budd and painted in PRR's omnipresent Tuscan Red. *Photo, David W. Salter; artwork, Joe Welsh Collection.*

The postwar *City of Miami*

During the World War II years, the vivid colors of the original *City of Miami* gave way to the livery that Illinois Central ultimately would adopt for all its trains, heavyweight as well as streamlined: brown and orange. On Chicago's south side, the southbound City glistens in morning sunlight as it sweeps around the curve near 57th Street on June 5, 1968. Four cars up from the club-lounge observation car is a former Missouri Pacific dome coach, one of several IC purchased from MP to upgrade *City of Miami* and *City of New Orleans* service. Like PRR, IC also leased NP dome sleepers during the winter season. *Mike Schafer.*

seasonal trains were dropped. Then in 1950, the *City of Miami* and the *South Wind* were upgraded with additional new lightweight coaches and sleepers, which allowed an increase in frequency of service as well as the addition of a through St. Louis-Miami sleeping car switched in and out of the *City* at Carbondale, Illinois. By this time the *City of Miami* had lost its remarkable, one-of-a-kind exterior paint scheme and been converted to the brown-and-orange scheme that IC had adopted as its official passenger colors after it streamlined its Chicago-New Orleans *Panama Limited* in 1941. In the postwar years, railroads were leaning more toward the practice of "pooling" their fleets of rolling stock for added operating flexibility, so paint schemes that were unique to a given train began to be phased out.

In 1954, the *Dixie Flagler* finally got new additional cars—coaches and sleepers—and assumed the new name *Dixieland*, perhaps because by this time few remembered who Henry Flagler was. Alas, the *Dixieland* did not fare well. In 1957 a freight train ran a stop signal and broadsided the *Dixieland*'s dining car,

killing a number of passengers. Later that same year, the train was discontinued, probably a victim of the severe recession of that period, leaving Chicago-Florida streamliner service to the *City of Miami* and the *South Wind.* At about that same time, the *City* and the *South Wind* began handling through cars to St. Petersburg and other locations on Florida's west coast. Fortunately, those two trains, now running on an every-other-day schedule and maintaining daily year-round streamliner service between Chicago and Florida, enjoyed relatively healthy lives, even during the 1960s.

In 1963, a bitter strike on the Florida East Coast Railway forever rerouted the *City* and *South Wind* on the ACL and SAL south of Jacksonville. Both trains survived to Amtrak, although the *South Wind* had by that time been truncated, and its northernmost terminal was now Louisville rather than Chicago. When Amtrak began operations in 1971, it chose the *South Wind* over the *City* to be its daily Chicago-Miami/St. Petersburg flagship, primarily because its route served greater population centers.

THE *ROYAL PALM*

Another Midwest-Florida streamliner of note, one that catered primarily to major Upper Midwest cities east of Chicago, was the *Royal Palm*. The history of this elegantly named Cincinnati-Florida train dates from the 1920s; a winter-only streamlined version of the train, known as the *New Royal Palm*, came on line on December 17, 1949, working shoulder to shoulder with the all-year-round heavyweight *Royal Palm*, which ran on a similar schedule but about an hour and a half apart from the streamliner.

The *New Royal Palm* was primarily a Cincinnati-Miami train operated by the Southern Railway, but it was largely comprised of through sleeping cars out of Chicago, Detroit, Buffalo, and Cleveland to Cincinnati by overnight New York Central trains. Following the early morning arrival of those trains at Cincinnati, the through sleepers were marshalled into the main consist of the *New Royal Palm*, which included Cincinnati-Miami coaches, diner-lounge, a Cincinnati-originating sleeper, and a sleeper-buffet-lounge observation car.

The breakfast-time departure southbound from Cincinnati meant that the *New Royal Palm* spent most of the day strolling along Southern's highly scenic Rathole Division (so-named because of the route's numerous tunnels) to Chattanooga, thence to Atlanta and Jacksonville where, in the small hours of the morn-ing, the train was handed over to Florida East Coast for a near-noon arrival at Miami. Northbound, the train's evening departure from Miami put it back into Cincinnati late evening the following day, just in time to forward the through sleepers into NYC's overnight trains out of Cincinnati to Chicago, Detroit, and Cleveland.

After 1955, the *New Royal Palm* was discontinued and much of its equipment used to upgrade the regular *Royal Palm*. Unfortunately, the positive effects of this move were short-lived, for by the end of the decade the through sleeping cars off the NYC had been dropped, and the south end of the *Royal Palm* truncated at Jacksonville where passengers continuing south had to change to connecting trains. By the fall of 1967, the *Palm* had shrunk to a coach-only Cincinnati-Atlanta train. The dining experience on the *Royal Palm* had gone from real meals prepared by skilled chefs aboard a stainless-steel dining car to a dash-into-the-lunch counter at Chattanooga depot and box suppers put aboard the train en route. On January 31, 1970, the last remnant of the *Palm* withered into history.

The *Royal Palm* at CUT
A Cincinnati Union Terminal switcher is in the final steps of adding the through sleeping cars to the *Royal Palm* that have arrived on overnight New York Central trains from Chicago, Detroit, and Cleveland on the morning of August 8, 1956. Today's sleeper-buffet-lounge observation car in fact is the *Royal Palm*, built for Southern Railway subsidiary Cincinnati, New Orleans & Texas Pacific Railway. The car was one of four (the other three being the *Royal Arch*, *Royal Crest*, and *Azalea*) built in 1950 for service on the streamliner *New Royal Palm*. The sleeper ahead of the observation car belongs to Atlanta & West Point—the West Point Route—and has strayed from its normal assignment, which is the New York-New Orleans *Crescent*. *John Dziobko.*

Are You Planning a Trip?

TAKE THE **NEW ROYAL PALM** TO
LUXURIOUS, WINTER-SEASON, STREAMLINED TRAIN

ATLANTA
CHATTANOOGA
CINCINNATI
INDIANAPOLIS
CHICAGO
TOLEDO
DETROIT
COLUMBUS
CLEVELAND
BUFFALO
TORONTO
AND INTERMEDIATE CITIES

Consult your Railroad Representative
for information and reservations

GO DIRECT OR VIA ASHEVILLE, N. C., AT NO EXTRA COST

It's Safe to Travel by Train - it's Smart to go by **SOUTHERN RAILWAY SYSTEM**

Streamliners Uniting the North and South

Mysterious and alluring, New Orleans was and remains a magnet for the travel-prone—not to mention its role as a port of paramount importance for export and import activity along with its sister city Mobile, Alabama, both on the Gulf of Mexico.

A prime carrier in the Midwest-to-the-Gulf corridor since the 1870s has been the Illinois Central—the "Main Line of Mid-America." Of several Chicago-Memphis-New Orleans runs fielded by IC, the *Panama Limited* was by far the most prestigious. Inaugurated in 1911, the swift, all-Pullman train—whose name honored the then-under-construction Panama Canal, poised to boost the importance of New Orleans—made the Gulf but an overnight journey from Chicago.

As IC's leading lady, the *Panama* was a natural for streamlining. IC ordered new diesel locomotives from Electro-Motive and lightweight cars from Pullman-Standard (plus two heavyweight cars rebuilt at IC's own shops)—enough to create two *Panama* trainsets—before the December 7, 1941, attack on Pearl Harbor,

and in fact the train's diesels were delivered that year. In the spring of 1942 the War Production Board attempted to halt construction of the cars, but IC argued that delivery of the new equipment would free up older cars that could be used in the war effort. IC won its point. The new, streamlined *Panama Limited* debuted on May 3, 1942, with one train leaving Chicago and one from New Orleans that afternoon, including through St. Louis-New Orleans sleepers operating on a St. Louis-Carbondale (Ill.) connecting train.

The *Panama*—IC's third streamliner following its *Green Diamond* of 1936 and *City of Miami* of 1940—was easily the finest of all IC streamliners. Indeed, the *Panama* has been ranked by rail historians among the top ten U.S. streamliners, a list which usually includes such esteemed contemporaries as Santa Fe's *Super Chief* and New York Central's *20th Century Limited*.

Such accolades were well-deserved. The streamlined *Panama* was all-Pullman and very posh—a far cry from its work-a-day heavyweight companion train, the overnight-and-then-some *Louisiane*. Four-thousand horses worth of diesel power drew each 12-car *Panama*

Um convite para visitar

O CORAÇÃO DA AMÉRICA DO NORTE A BORDO DO

The Panama Limited

Panama Limited brochure, Latin American version
IC apparently anticipated that the *Panama Limited* would play host to South American business clientele when it issued this Latin American version *Panama* brochure for the new streamliner. *Don Sarno Collection.*

(two trains were necessary to provide daily service in each direction), each comprised of a baggage-dorm, eight sleepers offering private rooms and sections, a sleeper-bar-lounge, 48-seat dining car, and a stunning round-end sleeper-lounge-observation car which carried the train's name, in pseudo-neon, on its sides and in a diamond-shaped tail sign. The *Panama* represented the first appearance of what became IC's revered chocolate brown-and-orange livery, highlighted with yellow striping and Art Deco lettering.

In keeping with industry custom, the cars carried names associated with the territory to be served by the new *Panama*; e.g., diner *Vieux Carre* (French for town square), sleeper-lounge *General Beauregard*, observation car *Memphis*, sleepers *Banana Road* and *Volunteer State* (Tennessee). Not surprisingly, lounge interiors played on French Quarter styling and had copious quantities of Venetian blinds—another design ploy to make passengers feel at home aboard the train.

In rush to get streamliners on the road, railroads of the period were always quick to be on top with innovations and conveniences, and IC was no exception with

the *Panama*. The sleepers contained dial telephones directly linked to lounge and dining areas. Train speedometers reminded passengers that the smooth, quiet roll of the *Panama* did not mean it was merely strolling through Illinois—IC's passenger speed limit through Lincolnland was as high as 100 mph. Though not unique to the *Panama*, it also featured public-address system and radios.

When first streamlined, the lightweight equipment and diesel power allowed IC to speed up the *Panama*'s Chicago-New Orleans schedule by two hours, making the 921-mile trip in 18 instead of 20 hours. Departure from both terminals was in mid afternoon, with breakfast-hour arrivals at the other end of the run. Following World War II, the *Panama*'s running times were again reduced until early in the 1950s it achieved its fastest end-to-end schedule ever, 16½ hours.

Other postwar improvements brought additional new cars, including parlor cars offering first-class seating for short-haul travelers. New cars also included twin-unit diners (with kitchen facilities in one car paired with a 66-seat dining-room car and connected via a double door). In 1959, when other streamliners were beginning to be downsized and downgraded, the *Panama* received Vista-Dome sleeper-lounges leased from Northern Pacific during the winter season.

The *Panama* was best known for two things: punctuality and the King's Dinner. The train's precise time-keeping was legendary. Wayne Johnston, IC president from 1945 to 1966, was so insistent about the *Panama's* on-time performance that, if he could still see the train's observation car from his office high above the platform tracks at Chicago's Central Station at 5:01 p.m. (departure was scheduled for 5 o'clock sharp), he would immediately be on the phone questioning station personnel about the delay.

The legendary King's Dinner was actually a late addition to the train's repertoire, in the mid-1960s. For $9.85—in those days an eye-opening sum to spend on a single dinner—a diner patron received a cocktail, appetizer, a shrimp cocktail, a fish course, a main entree of charcoal-broiled steak with potato and vegetable, a post-entree salad, bread, sliced apple and cheese, coffee

and wine, an after-dinner liqueur, and a special King's Dinner lapel pin to prove the undertaking.

The *Panama* managed to maintain more of a semblance of dignity to the end than some some of its contemporaries. In the fall of 1967, coaches were added to the train albeit disguised as a "separate" all-coach streamliner known as the *Magnolia Star*. "Maggie," as the train was known among IC crews, had its own set of cars, but the "two" trains always ran "combined" as a single train. It really boiled down to semantics, although most rail historians felt that the *Magnolia Star* was a ruse—the *Panama* had really lost its all-Pullman status, briefly leaving Pennsylvania's *Broadway Limited* as the last surviving all-Pullman streamliner in the U.S.

The *Panama* made its final departures from Chicago and New Orleans on the late afternoon of April 30, 1971. At Central Station at 12th and Michigan near Chicago's lakefront, a special ceremony in the public waiting room toasted the end of one of the country's greatest rolling hotels.

Panama Limited/Magnolia Star
When photographed while accelerating away from its suburban Chicago stop at Homewood in June 1968, the *Panama Limited*—at the time combined with the all-coach streamliner *Magnolia Star*—was still a spit-and-polish operation. Electro-Motive E6 No. 4001 leading the train on this day was originally delivered in 1941 for *Panama* service and was lettered for the train. Tonight, its companion locomotives are two later series E-units built for general service in the 1950s. *Mike Schafer.*

IC'S STORIED *CITY OF NEW ORLEANS*

With Mid-America's traveling elite having been accommodated by the new *Panama Limited*, it was time for IC to introduce a "people's" streamliner on the Chicago-Memphis-New Orleans route. With World War II thankfully a fading memory, IC did just that. In 1947, a legend was born: the storied *City of New Orleans*.

In terms of both rolling stock and scheduling, the *City* was a radical upgrading of IC's *Creole*, a heavyweight, steam-powered express departing Chicago southbound in the morning as train No. 1 for a 24-hour-plus, 921-mile run to the Crescent City. The northbound *Creole*, train 2, left New Orleans mid-evening for a next-day late-evening arrival at Chicago.

The new streamliner *City of New Orleans* took on the *Creole*'s train numbers, 1 and 2, and its southbound breakfast-hour time slot out of Chicago's Central Station. There, the similarities ended. The *City* arrived at New Orleans not the following day but the *same day*, covering the 921 miles in just shy of 16 hours! Northbound No. 2 left New Orleans in the morning and arrived Chicago late that same evening. Like its *Creole* predecessor, the *City* had a St. Louis section which was combined with the main-stem train at Carbondale, Illinois, as well as a Louisville section combined with the main section at Fulton, Kentucky.

The *City*'s Chicago-New Orleans running times represented an end-to-end average speed of nearly a mile a minute—remarkable considering that this included some 25 scheduled intermediate station stops. Such impressive running times were made possible by all-diesel-electric power, the new lightweight equipment, an almost-arrow-straight route for most of the way to the Gulf, and 90- and 100-mph speed limits.

For locomotives, IC once again went to Electro-Motive, this time ordering 18 E7-type passenger diesels, enough to power the *City of New Orleans* as well as new IC regional streamliners being introduced at about the same time. The *City*'s rolling stock was a combination of new cars from Pullman-Standard and heavyweight cars rebuilt into streamlined equipment at IC's Burnside Shops in Chicago. The orders for *City* equipment totaled 28 cars, enough for two main trainsets and Louisville and St. Louis sections. All equipment followed IC's eye-pleasing brown-and-orange dress code.

Whereas the *Panama Limited* catered primarily to rich Chicagoans and New Orleanians account of its

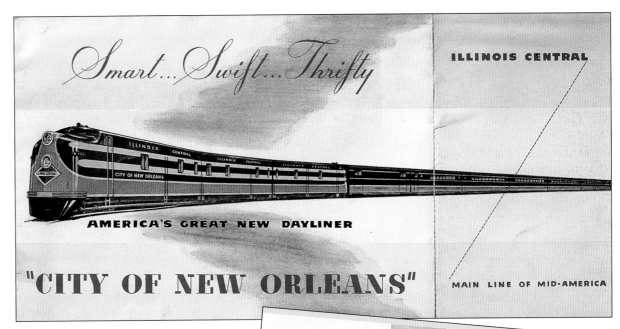

overnight schedule and Pullman-only accommodations, the *City of New Orleans*—referred to by IC as "The Great Dayliner"—served numerous cities and backwater towns all up and down the Main Line of Mid-America throughout the day. This and its coach-only status made the train immensely popular with mainstream Americans, even in the 1960s. In 1967, IC added dome coaches purchased secondhand from Missouri Pacific.

Amtrak assumed operation of the *City of New Orleans* on May 1, 1971, but later in the year discontinued the *City* and revived the *Panama Limited* and its overnight schedule. Deteriorating IC track conditions had prevented the *City* from maintaining its tight, high-speed all-day schedule. At about this same time, songwriter Steve Goodman eulogized the *City of New Orleans* with his song of the same name.

The *City of New Orleans* refused to die, though. On February 1, 1981, Amtrak rechristened its *Panama Limited* as the *City of New Orleans*—a name which by then had more meaning to Americans, thanks in part to the song. The *City* kept with the overnight schedule, but today's version of the *City of New Orleans* remains a popular run utilizing new stainless-steel, double-deck Superliner coaches, sleepers, lounge, and diner, complete with Cajun and Creole cooking.

GAY COMPANIONS

Travel time will always be pleasure time aboard the "City of New Orleans." And those who choose will find gaiety and companionship in the modern lounge with its decorations of chromium and quilted leather. Note the varied accommodations for individuals and for groups. One of the features of this car is a decorative wall map locating the major points of interest in New Orleans.

City of New Orleans brochure, 1947
Simultaneous with the introduction of its "Great New Dayliner," IC published a colorful brochure that detailed each of the cars on the train and even the locomotives' workings. Although the artist's rendering of the train itself made it look as though it were double-deck, the *City* was of course very much the traditional single-level streamliner. Its lounge, illustrated on page 5 of the 10-page booklet, was done in chrome and quilted leather and featured a wall map of New Orleans that located major points of interest. *Mike Schafer Collection.*

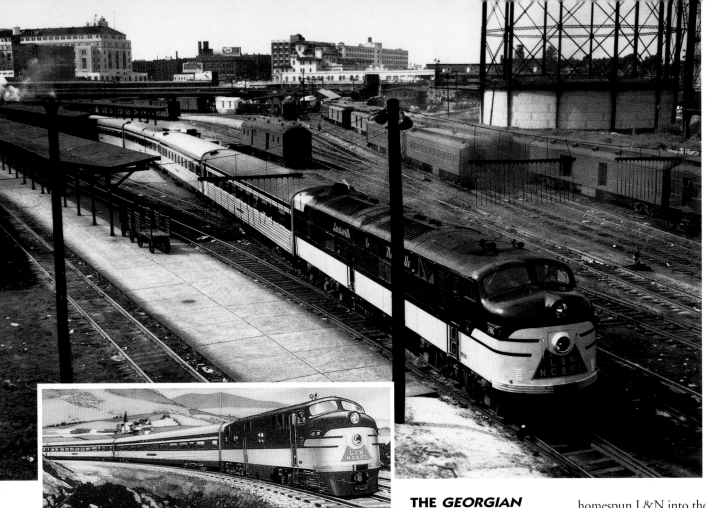

The Humming Bird had a close cousin, the Georgian, another streamliner which L&N and affiliate Nashville, Chattanooga & St. Louis instituted at the same time. The Georgian linked Atlanta with St. Louis via Chattanooga, Nashville (where it crossed the Humming Bird's path), and Evansville, Ind., and it operated on an all-day schedule between Atlanta and St. Louis.

Rolling stock for the Humming Bird and the Georgian was manufactured in 1946 by American Car & Foundry, that company's first postwar passenger cars. As built, both trains were basic, no-frills streamliners, with coaches, diner, and a tavern-lounge. There were no sleepers, no observation cars, no stewardess-nurses, or other trendy enticements, but the pair propelled homespun L&N into the streamliner era, delivering modern, basic transportation to the masses. (Although the railroad had been a partner in Chicago-Florida streamliner service since 1940, the two new trains were L&N's first own streamliners.) The lower halves of the cars were sheathed in stainless steel; the upper halves were dark blue with aluminum striping above the windows. L&N purchased Electro-Motive E7 diesels to power the trains.

Enter the Chicago & Eastern Illinois, long-time feeder line to the L&N at Evansville in southern Indiana. C&EI and L&N had been operating various coordinated through passenger services for decades, and in 1948 the pair apparently decided that Atlanta-Chicago was perhaps a better streamliner market than Atlanta-St. Louis—the net result being that the Georgian became an overnight Atlanta-Chicago train (a St. Louis-Evansville connection was retained, however). Applying similar logic, the Humming Bird gained a Chicago leg and a St. Louis connection in 1951. Those two sections combined at Evansville, then traveled to Nashville where they were combined into the original Cincinnati-New Orleans Humming Bird run—and vice versa, northbound. By this time, sleepers had been added to both trains. Also added during

The Georgian, 1947
The brand-new Georgian, top, eases out of Atlanta Union Station shortly after its 1947 debut. Note that the Electro-Motive E7 powering the train carries the initials of both Louisville & Nashville and Nashville, Chattanooga & St. Louis on its nose. Photo, George B. Mock Jr., David W. Salter Collection; promotional brochure, Don Sarno Collection.

THE GEORGIAN AND THE HUMMING BIRD—L&N, NC&STL, C&EI

With its straight, fast north-and-south spine, Illinois Central had the Midwest-to-the-Gulf passenger market pretty well sewed up. For this reason, another Chicago/St. Louis-New Orleans streamliner, the joint Chicago & Eastern Illinois-Louisville & Nashville Humming Bird, dwelled in relative obscurity, though reasonably well-patronized into the 1960s.

The Humming Bird was born in 1947 as an L&N-only train, an all-coach streamliner running between Cincinnati and New Orleans via Louisville, Nashville, Birmingham, Montgomery, and Mobile. Southbound, the train left Cincinnati in early afternoon for a late evening arrival in Birmingham and an overnight run from there to New Orleans. Northbound, a late-morning departure from New Orleans put the "Bird" at Nashville by midnight and Cincinnati at daybreak.

the 1950s was a Memphis leg, which split from the main train at Bowling Green, Kentucky, thereby providing through Cincinnati-Memphis service.

The expanded territories of the twin streamliners required additional cars, but with so many railroads having placed so many orders for new rolling stock, there was a backlog for new-car deliveries. L&N's interim solution was to have its South Louisville (Ky.) Shops create semi-streamlined cars from 1920s-era heavyweight rolling stock. These and regular heavyweight cars augmented the original ACF streamlined cars until L&N could purchase some secondhand streamlined cars in 1951 and take delivery of additional new lightweight cars, including sleepers, in 1953 and 1955. In addition, C&EI, which had taken

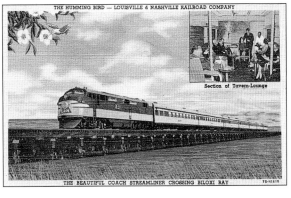

THE HUMMING BIRD — LOUISVILLE & NASHVILLE RAILROAD COMPANY

Section of Tavern-Lounge

THE BEAUTIFUL COACH STREAMLINER CROSSING BILOXI BAY

delivery of new streamlined cars from P-S in 1946 for two of its own streamliners, contributed cars to the *Georgian* pool by discontinuing one of those streamliners, the Chicago-Evansville *Whippoorwill*, which became superfluous when the *Georgian* was extended to Chicago.

Once anchored in Chicago, St. Louis, and New Orleans, the *Humming Bird* took off. But with a Chicago-New Orleans running time of about 23 hours—some seven hours longer than IC's *Panama Limited*—and a route nearly 150 miles longer than IC, it's doubtful that many travelers originating at Chicago, St. Louis, or New Orleans opted to ride the *Humming Bird* all the way through. Rather, the *Bird* worked best for travelers destined to and from interme-

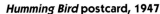

Humming Bird postcard, 1947
As delivered, the *Humming Bird* was a virtual twin to the *Georgian* as illustrated in the vintage postcard at left of the *Bird* crossing Biloxi Bay, Mississippi. *Mike Schafer Collection.*

Humming Bird/Georgian in 1966
Eventually the Chicago legs of both the *Humming Bird* and the *Georgian* were combined, making for an impressive train. The two-for-one train stands at Chicago's Dearborn Station in 1966, ready to depart over the C&EI for points south. Its streamlined consist has been interrupted by head-end mail and express traffic being carried in heavyweight cars. *Mike Schafer.*

diate points, such as Chicago to Birmingham, St. Louis to Montgomery, or New Orleans to Nashville. The story was a little different for the *Georgian*, which provided the only direct, fast, daily, streamliner service between Chicago/St. Louis and Atlanta. Consequently, the *Georgian* was often the first choice for Chicago-Atlanta rail travel well into the 1960s.

As the decline in rail travel increased markedly during the recession of the late 1950s, though, some rationalization in operations became inevitable. Because the *Humming Bird* and the *Georgian* had similar schedules at the Chicago end of their operations, the two were combined in 1958 between Chicago and Evansville, an arrangement that lasted until their demise north of Evansville ten years later. Because of the drawn-out and varied equipment purchases made by the three railroads that operated the *Humming Bird* and *Georgian*, the combined operation into Chicago between 1958 and 1968 was a monster of a train featuring an eclectic array of rolling stock and locomotives.

In 1968, the Evansville-Chicago leg of both trains were discontinued, and in 1969 the L&N, long since disillusioned with passenger trains in general, abruptly terminated the *Humming Bird* in mid run at Birmingham, stranding passengers and making national news. The *Georgian*, ironically now trimmed back to its original Atlanta-St. Louis operation, and the *Bird*'s Cincinnati-New Orleans partly heavyweight companion train, the *Pan-American*, remained until Amtrak commenced two years later.

Humming Bird in twilight
The *Humming Bird* of 1968 has changed markedly from that featured in the postcard on the previous page. The scene is of the northbound train out of New Orleans, again at Biloxi Bay, but the *Bird*'s cars wear a more somber attire of solid dark blue, and heavyweight cars—including an elegant diner-lounge from the 1920s—have crept into the consist. *Jim Boyd*

MISS BELLE AND THE CROW

Running through the scarcely populated regions separating Kansas City from the Gulf of Mexico, the Kansas City Southern Railroad was hardly a bastion of passenger traffic. In fact, in 1938, KCS's entire passenger-car roster numbered only 51 cars, most of them heavyweight, of which 20 were solely for moving mail and express. What scant passenger traffic existed at the time contributed a disturbingly low 3.65 percent of the road's yearly revenues for 1938. The future didn't hold much hope for KCS passenger trains.

That all changed on September 2, 1940, when KCS unveiled its new *Southern Belle* streamliner. KCS must have been confident of its venture into streamlining, for it plunked down nearly $1 million for new locomotives (three Electro-Motive diesels) and rolling stock (three baggage-RPOs, five coaches, and three diner-parlor observation cars from Pullman-Standard)—a respectable sum of money back then for a modest-size railroad. The equipment was delivered in an unusual but handsome scheme of nearly solid dark green offset by yellow and red stripes and silver roofs.

The first run of the *Belle* was preceded by a publicity campaign which invited women from on-line cities and towns to vie for selection as "Miss Southern Belle," the personification of KCS's new flyer. Margaret Landry was the winner and, dressed in stylized and feminized railroad garb, went on to partake in a number of KCS promotions. Meanwhile, the *Belle* equipment went on a 10-day publicity tour.

The new *Southern Belle* plied KCS's 868-mile K.C.-New Orleans route on a leisurely 21 1/2-hour schedule. Southbound, the train departed Kansas City Union Station in the morning and arrived New Orleans the following morning. Northbound, the *Belle* departed New Orleans late in the evening and arrived K.C. the next evening. A companion train that long pre-dated the *Belle*, the Kansas City-Port Arthur (Texas) *Flying Crow*, operated on a schedule nearly opposite the *Belle* north of Shreveport, Louisiana.

The Pullman Company provided sleepers for the *Belle*, initially only between Shreveport and New Orleans, the overnight portion of the train's trip, but sleeper service was soon extended north of Shreveport. The *Belle* was quickly embraced by the traveling public, not only for its modernity, but also its convenience. KCS had a captive market, as roads between K.C. and Shreveport were poor, and no other railroads offered direct K.C.-New Orleans trains. World War II sent ridership into orbit (KCS served a number of army bases), and by the end of the war, passenger revenues were contributing 12 percent of KCS's gross revenues.

Overnight Sensation
Kansas City Southern passenger service went from rags to riches in 1940 when the *Southern Belle* was delivered. Twenty-eight years later (top) the *Belle*—canting through a curve south of Kansas City—still looked good. *Jim Boyd.*

When Billboards were billboards
The billboard above for the new *Belle* stood at Canal and Gayoso streets in New Orleans about the time of the *Belle*'s introduction into New Orleans-Kansas City service. *KCS, Don Sarno Collection.*

Like nearly all other passenger-carrying railroads, KCS embarked on a postwar upgrading and expansion program for its passenger services. It bought more new lightweight cars, some secondhand cars, and refurbished and rebuilt several older cars. At mid-century, KCS made some big changes. Most notable was the addition of another K.C.-New Orleans streamliner, bringing the total to three daily K.C.-New Orleans trains each way (the *Flying Crow* was not considered a streamliner, however). Curiously, the new streamliner was nameless and known only by its numbers, 9 (southbound) and 10 (northbound). It was put into the *Belle*'s time slots while the *Belle* was shifted to an afternoon departure from both K.C. and New Orleans and its running times speeded up by more than four hours. At the same time, the *Belle* acquired a Shreveport-Port Arthur connection.

The investment in the new and upgraded services did not pay off as well as expected, and during the 1950s KCS trimmed some of its passenger services, including Nos. 9 and 10 as separate trains north of Shreveport. Nonetheless, the railroad kept some degree of faith in the passenger train, for during the second half of the 1950s it bought both new and secondhand passenger cars—a move which finally rendered the old *Flying Crow* streamliner status.

Interestingly, KCS passenger trains enjoyed a renaissance during the first half of the 1960s. The railroad still had a captive market—and a progressive passenger department that wasn't afraid to promote its remaining services. Special low coach fares and thrifty sleeping-car accommodation charges, low-cost meals, and friendly, reliable service produced increased ridership. For example, 1966 passenger revenues were a remarkable 15 percent higher than six years earlier. Underscoring its faith in its flyers, KCS ordered ten brand-new coaches from P-S in 1965, the last new streamlined, lightweight, intercity passenger cars built before Amtrak.

Unfortunately, Miss *Belle* and the *Crow* didn't last the decade. The U.S. Post Office carried out a nationwide mass execution of RPO and rail-hauled mail services, shifting a large volume of mail movement to planes and trucks. Furthermore, the discontinuance of a number of connecting trains that fed traffic to KCS passenger runs at Kansas City and New Orleans resulted in a rather sudden downturn in loadings. This one-two punch sent KCS reeling; in May 1968 the *Crow* vanished, and on November 2, 1969, the *Southern Belle* departed K.C. and the Crescent City for the final time.

A bit of the *Belle* survives in the form of KCS's business train, newly assembled during the mid-1990s. The roving mini-streamliner, which is used for on-site inspection of rail properties and to provide charter services, is pulled by classic Electro-Motive diesels of yore and wears black with yellow and red trim, mimicking the attractive garb worn by the *Southern Belle* and her kin of thirty years prior.

THE *REBEL*S OF GULF, MOBILE & OHIO

In 1935, little Gulf, Mobile & Northern introduced the South's first streamliner, the *Rebel* (Chapter 1) between Jackson, Tennessee, and New Orleans and Mobile. Five years later, GM&N merged with the Mobile & Ohio, thus forming the Gulf, Mobile & Ohio Railroad. Concurrent with this merger was the

KCS's nameless streamliner
Kansas City-bound train 10-16 is at Texarkana, Texas, in the mid-1960s. The double number reflects the train's operation as No. 10 out of Port Arthur and No. 16 (the old *Flying Crow*) out of New Orleans, the two having been combined at Shreveport. The *Crow* name had been officially dropped by this time, but the train still sported a classy ex-New York Central cafe-lounge observation car. The *Belle* by this time no longer boasted an observation. *Thomas Hoffmann.*

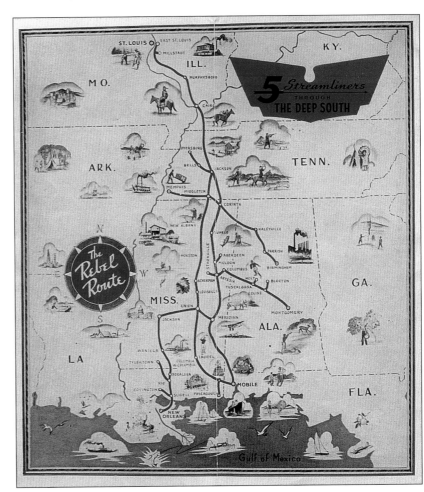

introduction of a big brother train for the little *Rebel*—the *Gulf Coast Rebel* (which quickly became known as the "Big *Rebel*")—which operated between St. Louis and Mobile. Although advertised as a streamliner, it was comprised of heavyweight coaches and lounge-coaches that had been modernized by the old M&O Iselin Shops at Jackson, and Pullmans modernized by the Pullman Company in Chicago.

The train operated daily on an overnight schedule between St. Louis and Mobile along the former-M&O route via Cairo, Illinois, Jackson, and Corinth and Meridian, Mississippi. Moving the *Gulf Coast Rebel* over the 648-mile run were new Alco-GE DL-series diesels. The chisel-nosed locomotives and their train wore the flashy silver-and-red scheme introduced by the original little *Rebel* trains of 1935 and 1937. In keeping with the *Rebel* tradition, the new big *Rebel*s featured hostesses.

In 1942, the early *Rebel* streamliners were removed from regional service, modified, and reconstituted as East St. Louis-New Orleans trains known simply as the *Rebel*. In this service, the trains operated overnight between New Orleans and Jackson and during the day between Jackson and St. Louis in both directions.

The new GM&O, a maverick in the solitude of Deep South railroading, merged with the Alton Railroad in 1947 thus doubling its (GM&O's) size and extending its reach to Chicago and Kansas City from St. Louis. Shortly after the merger, the railroad ordered new lightweight, streamline cars from American Car & Foundry, which permitted it to upgrade not only the *Gulf Coast Rebel* but the Chicago-St. Louis trains inherited from the Alton. These improvements included a through, lightweight sleeping car between Chicago and Mobile, southbound via the *Alton Limited* and *Gulf Coast Rebel* and northbound via the *Gulf Coast Rebel* and the streamliner *Abraham Lincoln*. By now, GM&O had adopted Alton's handsome maroon-and-red livery.

Despite the good intentions of GM&O, the *Rebel*s were early casualties, in no small part due to the fast, high-quality service afforded by competitor Illinois Central and its *City of New Orleans* and *Panama Limited* as well as by Louisville & Nashville's *Humming Bird*, all of which also linked St. Louis with the Gulf. The Little *Rebel*s were discontinued in 1954, and in 1958 the *Gulf Coast Rebel* also lost the battle, ending all passenger service on the GM&O south of St. Louis.

Gulf Coast Rebel

In a wonderful piece of 1940s-era advertising art (above left) provided by the American Locomotive Company for Gulf, Mobile & Ohio, the new *Gulf Coast Rebel* cruises through plantation country amid Spanish moss and swamps. Leading the modernized train is an Alco DL-series locomotive, Alco's 2000-hp answer to Electro-Motive's early E-series passenger diesels. GM&O predecessor Gulf, Mobile & Northern had already been an Alco customer when it purchased its *Rebel*s, whose power plants were supplied by Alco. Above, a GM&O timetable from 1941 included a map of the new (1940) railroad, noting it had "5 streamliners through the Deep South." *Both, Mike Schafer Collection*

Lone Star Streamliners

ROCKETS AND ZEPHYRS TO TEXAS

Almost a country unto itself, Texas has for decades been a favored destination for millions of travelers and tourists, making it a natural magnet for new streamliners. Intrastate streamliners (covered in the following chapter because of their regional nature) came first to Texas when, in 1936, Burlington reassigned *Zephyr* 9901 from Chicago-Twin Cities service to Fort Worth-Houston service as the *Sam Houston Zephyr*. The first long-distance streamliner to serve the Lone Star State, however, was Chicago, Rock Island & Pacific's *Texas Rocket*.

Using two streamliner trainsets powered by Electro-Motive and built by Budd in 1937 originally for Kansas City-Denver service (the *Denver Rocket*) and Fort Worth-Houston service (the original *Texas Rocket*), Rock Island established a 627-mile daylight run between Kansas City and Dallas, via Topeka, Oklahoma City and Fort Worth

in 1938. For the new daily speedsters, Rock reapplied the *Texas Rocket* name.

In 1940, Burlington subsidiaries Colorado & Southern and Fort Worth & Denver replaced their heavyweight Denver-Dallas *Colorado Special* with "The fastest, finest train service ever enjoyed between Texas and Colorado," the *Texas Zephyr*. At Dallas, the train connected with Rock Island's *Texas Rocket* to and from Houston.

In 1945, *Rocket* service to Texas doubled when the Rock Island introduced the *Twin Star Rocket* on its "Mid-Continent Route" between Minneapolis and Houston. At 1,370 miles, this would be the longest route for any of the railroad's growing fleet of *Rocket* streamliners. The train required a little over 24 hours to make the run via Des Moines, Iowa, Kansas City, Topeka, Fort Worth, and Dallas, and carried coaches, sleepers, diner, and a sleeper-lounge observation.

The euphoric post-World War II years brought a glut of new streamliners nation-

(Facing page) The northbound Twin Star Rocket *encounters a Fort Dodge, Des Moines & Southern interurban freight at Des Moines, Iowa, in April 1955. William D. Middleton.*

(Right) At Wichita Falls, Texas, E5s lead the northbound TZ *on July 30, 1967, only a few weeks before its demise. Tom Hoffmann.*

(Below) Morning sun baths one of the Texas Eagles *arriving St. Louis Union Station. Leading today's train is a set of Texas & Pacific E-units wearing the handsome* Eagle *streamliner scheme developed by Electro-Motive and Raymond Loewy in 1940. Al Schultz.*

wide, and in 1948 Texas got a bonanza of new trains. Three are of particular note here: the *Texas Chief*, *Texas Eagle*, and *Texas Special*.

THE *TEXAS EAGLE*

The *Texas Eagle* operated between St. Louis and Memphis and various Texas points over the Missouri Pacific and its Texas & Pacific and International Great Northern subsidiaries. The train entered service on August 15, 1948. Originally it was intended to operate through to Mexico City as the *Sunshine Eagle*, but the National Railways of Mexico was unable to purchase lightweight sleepers, dooming—temporarily—the international concept.

The *Texas Eagle* was a complex bird because of its multiple end points. For much of its life, the streamliner actually operated as two separate trains, departing St. Louis

simultaneously and running only minutes apart as far as Longview, Texas, where they split off in different directions. Trains 1 (southbound) and 2 (northbound), dubbed the "west *Texas Eagle*," ran between St. Louis and El Paso via Dallas and Fort Worth. Trains 21 and 22, the "south *Texas Eagle*," ran between St. Louis and Palestine, Texas, where it split into Houston and San Antonio sections—and vice versa northbound. Both *Eagles* initially had Memphis-Little Rock connections.

Beginning in September 1961, both trains would be combined between St. Louis and Texarkana, Texas, where a massive car-sorting took place in the small hours of the morning while passengers slumbered away in their coach seats and private rooms. Although the *Texas Eagles* were multi-car streamliners with all of the trimmings for most of their run, once in Texas the trains would fragment into individual consists as short as two cars heading for a number of different destinations. Through sleeping-car service from a variety of Texas points all the way to the East Coast was offered for a number of years via the Pennsy and the Baltimore & Ohio at St. Louis.

Coordinated connecting service was offered between San Antonio and Mexico City. Passengers could transfer between the *Texas Eagle* and the heavyweight *Sunshine Special* at San Antonio. St. Louis-Mexico City sleeping cars were added to the *Texas Eagle* beginning in December 1952 but ceased in April 1954. They were re-established in April 1962 and maintained until the end of 1968.

"Planetarium" domes came to the trains in the summer of 1952 with dome cars operating between St. Louis and Fort Worth and St. Louis and San Antonio. New sleeping cars were added in 1956, and in 1959, innovative Slumbercoaches offering low-cost sleeping accommodations began operating between Baltimore and San Antonio via B&O's *National Limited* east of St. Louis. They would be withdrawn in May 1964 and returned to builder Budd Company.

Drastic cutbacks occurred in the 1960s, first with the loss of through service to El Paso in 1964 and then with the axing of the Memphis connections the following year. The domes came off in 1967 as Mopac sold them to Illinois Central. But, all told, even in 1967 the train still served a remarkable diversity of destinations. It was possible to board *Texas Eagle* sleeping cars in St. Louis bound for Forth Worth, Houston, San Antonio, Alexandria (Louisiana) and even Mexico City. That would change. On December 31, 1968, MP terminated its remaining sleeping-car services due to the demise of the Pullman Company. In 1969, the Houston leg of the *Texas Eagle* was dropped as well as all service west of Longview, ending rail passenger service en total to Dallas and Fort Worth. In 1970, service was retrenched from San Antonio to Texarkana, rendering the remaining St. Louis-Texarkana coach-only run as more of a "sparrow" than an *Eagle*. That, like a lot of streamliners fallen from grace, finally ended when Amtrak began service, although that carrier would revive the *Texas Eagle* in the late 1980s as a Chicago-Texas train.

FRISCO AND KATY'S *TEXAS SPECIAL*

Two well-remembered regional railroads of south-central U.S., the St. Louis-San Francisco Railway ("Frisco") and the Missouri-Kansas-Texas (the "Katy"), teamed up in to introduce a dazzling new streamlined version of the 33-year-old legendary *Texas Special* on May 16, 1948.

Like its rival *Texas Eagle*, the *Special*'s north-end anchor city was St. Louis, the gateway between East and West. The main stem of the train operated via Frisco rails from St. Louis to Vinita, Oklahoma, where it entered Katy's Kansas City-Texas main line for the remainder of the trip to San Antonio via Muskogee, Oklahoma, and Denison, Dallas,

Waco, and Austin, Texas. Connecting service was provided between Denison and Fort Worth and Wichita Falls, Texas.

For the service, Frisco and Katy spared no expense, each ordering enough rolling stock from Pullman-Standard to equip two 14-car trains comprised of an RPO-baggage car, three coaches, coach-buffet-lounge, diner, seven sleepers, and a sleeper-lounge-observation car; E-series diesels from Electro-Motive provided power. All cars were sheathed in stainless steel accented with red roofs, window stripe, and underskirting making for an eye-catching streamliner. Even the locomotives sported stainless-steel fluted side panels, and the train name was emblazoned on the noses and sides of the diesels.

General Motors' Electro-Motive Corporation (Electro-Motive Division as of 1941) originally designed most streamliner paint schemes if Electro-Motive diesels were going to be used to power a railroad's first streamliner. In doing so, Electro-Motive provided the railroad with an art rendering that showed what the finished new locomotives would look like upon delivery. The above rendering by EMD's Ben Dedek showed how Katy's and Frisco's Texas Special E-units (and a bit of the train itself) were going to look upon their delivery for the new 1947 streamliner. These would be one of the few E-units to wear stainless-steel fluting.

The daily trains operated overnight in each direction, southbound departing St. Louis in the afternoon and arriving San Antonio early the next afternoon. And herein was a scheduling flaw that would soon haunt the operating department. A southbound *Texas Special* arriving San Antonio was scheduled out as the northbound *Texas Special* the same afternoon! Servicing crews had only two hours to turn, clean, restock, and reposition the train for loading before it left back for St. Louis.

The arrangement simply did not work; Katy and Frisco had to create a third trainset practically out of thin air. They did so by refurbishing several heavyweight cars, going so far as to paint their sides with "shadowlining" so that they appeared to be fluted stainless steel. These additional cars were pooled in with existing equipment, all of which was redivided into three sets. In September 1948, more-realistic schedules improved the *Texas Special* operation overall, including connections at St. Louis.

Business soon boomed, with 20-car *Specials* not uncommon in peak travel periods. As of 1950—the year *Railway Age* magazine claimed that the *Special* was one of the most profitable streamliners in the U.S—the train boasted through sleepers to and from the East Coast on Pennsylvania's *Penn Texas* and B&O's *National Limited*.

In the mid-1950s, Katy and Frisco ordered additional rolling stock. Also about this time the maverick little Katy was itself purchased by a conglomerate which had no interest in making certain passengers were having a comfortable ride to Texas—not that Katy freight trains were rolling smoothly along. By the end of the 1950s, deteriorating track conditions and air-conditioning malfunctions were resulting in *Texas Specials* that were running up to 14 hours late. In January 1959, a frustrated Frisco pulled out of the alliance, and the *Texas Special*'s northern terminus was shifted to Kansas City, with the train following an all-Katy routing south to San Antonio. St. Louis was left high and dry. In July 1964, the *Special* was discontinued south of Dallas, and nearly a year later the rest of the train vanished into history.

Bound for the Lone Star State, the Texas Chief *makes a grand entrance into Joliet Union Station behind new General Electric diesels in 1967. Mike Schafer.*

SANTA FE'S *TEXAS CHIEF, KANSAS CITYAN* AND *CHICAGOAN*

The most successful of Texas streamliners over the long run was, not surprisingly, a Santa Fe operation. The *Texas Chief* rolled into the hearts of travelers during the spring of 1948, carrying on popular traditions established by its *Chief* forebears on other routes—Fred Harvey dining-car service, courier nurses, recorded music, and wonderfully comfortable coaches with Ride Master seating.

When introduced, the *Texas Chief* was a Chicago-Galveston train operating entirely on the Santa Fe and the only direct Chicago-Texas streamliner. It ran via Kansas City, Topeka, Oklahoma City, Fort Worth, and Houston—a somewhat circuitous route of 1,410 miles. Running time in both directions was a respectable 26 hours and 15 minutes.

Rolling stock was a mixture of Pullman-Standard, American Car & Foundry, and Budd Company cars built new for the service as well as some cars that had been bumped from service on other, earlier *Chief*s. Aside from a full complement of dining and lounge cars, the train fielded a raft of Pullman sleeping cars, including a Chicago-Oklahoma City car, a Chicago-Wichita (Kansas) car, a Chicago-Tulsa (Oklahoma) car forwarded to that city on Santa Fe's Kansas City-Tulsa *Oil Flyer*, and of course Chicago-Galveston cars. In 1955, a connecting train out of Gainesville, Texas, was established to bring *Texas Chief* service to Dallas in the form of through Chicago-Dallas coaches and sleepers.

Throughout the life of the *Texas Chief*, it offered an evening departure westbound from Chicago, operating overnight to Oklahoma City thence on an all-day schedule through southern Oklahoma and Texas for a mid-evening arrival at Galveston. Similarly, the northbound train ran in daylight from Galveston and Houston to Oklahoma City, arriving Chicago the next morning.

The *Texas Chief* remained a healthy operation by 1960s standards, but it was cut back 53 miles from Galveston to Houston in 1967 when Santa Fe reluctantly embarked on a systemwide rationalization of train operations. Then in 1968 it lost its Dallas section; the good news that same year, however, was the addition of Big Dome lounges inherited from the *Chief*, which had been discontinued in May of that year.

The *Texas Chief* was not the only Chicago-Texas streamliner on the Santa Fe. In 1938 Santa Fe introduced the streamliner *Kansas Cityan/Chicagoan* between Chicago, Kansas City, and Wichita, Kansas. The *Kansas Cityan* name was applied to the westbound run and *Chicagoan* to the eastbound. Eventually these trains were extended to Oklahoma City and finally to Dallas. By day the two trains traveled between Chicago and Wichita, with the overnight portion of their trips between Wichita and Fort Worth/Dallas.

These were among the first of Santa Fe's trains to receive the new Big Dome lounge cars delivered by Budd Company in 1954. In 1968, the *Kansas Cityan* and the *Chicagoan* made their final runs, leaving the *Texas Chief* as the only surviving Chicago-Texas streamliner. The *Texas Chief* was one of the few trains selected by the new but meagerly capitalized National Railroad Passenger Corporation (Amtrak) for inclusion into the new national rail passenger system that emerged on May 1, 1971.

CHAPTER 6

REGIONAL FAVORITES

Regional Streamliners of the Northeast
A Southeast Streamliner Sampler
Mid-States Regional Streamliners
Postwar Experimental Streamliners
Second City Streamliners
Some Regional Streamliners of the American West

C&NW *Twin Cities 400*, 1939
A flash of yellow known as *"The 400"* captured the fancy of Upper Midwesterners when Chicago & North Western launched its new Chicago-Twin Cities streamliner—its first—in 1941. Here it poses for its portrait outside North Western Terminal in Chicago. *C&NW*

Not all streamliners were created equal. And certainly not all streamliners were long-distance runners on one- or two-night-out schedules with a long trail of sleeping cars. Indeed, for every transcon streamliner that departed Union Stations across the land, there were a bevy of short-hauls which never strayed more than a few hundred miles from their home port. These were the regional streamliners, the trains that brought people from small towns into the big city for a day of shopping; or the trains that linked major city pairs that were separated by a few hours, not days.

These were the streamliners that "belonged" to your home town. Rather than being impatient visitors from a distant part of America that streaked nonstop through your hometown (or stopped barely long enough to let off a passenger or two who had come a great distance), the regional streamliner was for the local folks. So with this closing chapter, we give a tribute to the regional streamliners of yore. No, they may not have been 20 cars long, and rarely did they boast of Pullmans with luxury private rooms. But they had their own interesting lounge cars, diners, domes, and observation cars— and they had a flavor all their own, one that prompted passengers to say, "Yup, that's *our* train!"

Regional Streamliners of the Northeast

With nearly 30 million people living along the Eastern seaboard in the 1930s between Washington and Boston—a 460-mile string of urban areas now collectively known as the Northeast Corridor— it's no surprise that this was one of the first regions in the country to receive streamlined passenger train service. The B&O, Reading, Jersey Central, New Haven, and the mighty Pennsylvania all had lines linking the great cities of this region which formed the cradle of democracy—Boston, New York, Philadelphia, Baltimore, and Washington.

The first streamliner to arrive on the Corridor came in 1935 from an unlikely source—the Baltimore & Ohio, traditionally an underdog in the market it shared with giant PRR. Since it was one of the first streamliners to roll on American rails, the *Royal Blue* is spotlighted in Chapter 1. The aluminum-alloy streamliner replaced the heavyweight *Royal Blue*, jointly operated with longtime B&O affiliates Reading and Jersey Central between Washington and Jersey City, New Jersey, 224 miles.

Apparently unsatisfied with the *Royal Blue* streamliner set, B&O sent it off to join its twin sister, the *Abraham Lincoln*, on B&O subsidiary Alton Railroad. B&O retained *Royal Blue* service with

Afternoon Congressional
The short-lived, ill-fated Penn Central Railroad (1968-76) was rarely associated with streamliners, but on this June evening in 1968, the Afternoon Congressional still appears to be very much a classy operation as it accelerates westbound from its Newark (N.J.) station stop. *Mike Schafer.*

Diesel-Era *Crusader*
Shiny clean two-tone green Reading FP7 locomotives hustle the *Crusader* along the Jersey Central main line at Bayonne, N.J., on a July evening in 1952. The train had an observation car at both ends, thereby obviating the need for turning at its terminals. The locomotives simply ran around the consist. *David Salter.*

The PRR-NYNH&H *Senator*
Running mate to the *Congressional*, the Boston-Washington *Senator* glides high above the Susquehanna River at Perryville, Maryland, early in its career. *Lawrence S. Williams, Joe Welsh Collection.*

modernized heavyweight rolling stock until its discontinuance in 1958.

The next carrier to introduce a lightweight train in the corridor was the Philadelphia-based Reading Railroad, of Monopoly® game fame. Reading ordered a new five-car conventional streamliner from hometown car-builder E. G. Budd Manufacturing featuring a tavern-diner, reclining-seat coaches, and not one, but two round-end coach observation lounge cars, one at either end of the train. In December 1937, the stainless-steel *Crusader* entered double-daily service on the 90-mile Philadelphia-Jersey City route in conjunction with CNJ.

"Clad in Shining Armor," as early advertising put it, the new train was powered by a Reading Pacific-type steam engine shrouded in fluted stainless steel. Later, Electro-Motive FP7 diesels would replace steam.

Wall Street brokers and others eager for a change from the Pennsylvania's stodgy heavyweight Philadelphia-New York "Clocker" trains could enjoy a full breakfast on their way from Philadelphia to New York in the *Crusader*'s cheery tavern-diner, whose menu featured such well-known Philadelphia staples as scrapple with eggs. After a strenuous day at the office or on the stock exchange, home-bound travelers could unwind with a drink in the train's tavern.

In 1964, the little streamliner was sold to the Canadian National Railroad which was experiencing record traffic demand. Reading continued to offer *Crusader* service, but with rebuilt heavyweight cars and later self-propelled Budd-built Rail Diesel Cars.

If the diminutive Reading was willing early on to experiment with short-haul corridor streamliners, giant Pennsylvania Railroad was reluctant. Rather, the sprawling carrier opted to focus on the long-distance market, ushering in its east-west "Fleet of Modernism" (Chapter 2) in 1939. Aside from the new prewar Seaboard and Atlantic Coast Line Florida streamliners which PRR handled north of Washington, conservative PRR offered no local New York-Washington streamliners as such.

However, in 1951 the railroad abruptly changed course, ordering brand-new trains from Budd exclusively for the Corridor. In many respects, they would turn out to be the finest trains ever run in the Corridor. On March 17, 1952, the PRR introduced the new equipment on its esteemed *Congressional* runs between

New York and Washington and, in conjunction with the New Haven Railroad, the *Senator* between Washington and Boston. Attired in gleaming stainless steel with Tuscan red letterboards and gold lettering, the streamliners were a radical departure from previous Pennsy corridor services. Their modern interiors reflected decorative motifs that were unabashedly patriotic. Shades of red, white and blue were the colors of choice throughout the train, and murals and etched glass reflected 18th Century colonial themes such as Betsy Ross and Old North Church. The curved bar fronts in the *Congressional*'s lounge cars were even decorated to resemble a colonial military drum. The theme was extended to include car names which honored Colonial heroes such as Molly Pitcher, Ben Franklin, and George Washington. Specially painted Tuscan Red GG1 electric locomotives pulled the *Congressional*s and, south of New York, the *Senator* as well.

Comprised largely of reclining-seat coaches (a rarity on PRR corridor trains), the new speedsters also offered parlor-car seating, maintaining a tradition that had dated to the beginning of *Congressional* service in the 1880s. There was even a seven-room "conference" car for enroute business meetings.

The formality of the train's diner was matched by the highly professional staff whom routinely greeted the first passengers by standing at attention. The crew was on good terms with the great of Washington and New York society who frequented the trains. Patrons could enjoy Pennsy specialties such as charcoal-broiled steak accompanied by fresh baked items like PRR's famous raisin

Congressional parlor car
Individual swivel seats were still the rule on railroad parlor cars when Budd built the *Congressional* and *Senator* in 1952. Some railroads digressed to stationary lounge-type chairs or 2-1 seating for their "parlor" offerings. *Lawrence S. Williams, Joe Welsh Collection.*

pie. For those seeking a less formal setting, the coffee shop car provided just the right atmosphere, duplicating the medium-priced urban lunch room of its day. Parlor-observation cars completed the train's offering.

Four complete trainsets, two for *Congressional* service and two for the *Senator*, were delivered. The *Morning Congressional*s departed New York and Washington in the early morning with a mid morning arrival at their respective destinations where they were turned to become the *Afternoon Congressional*s, leaving New York

and Washington in the late afternoon to arrive at their destinations in early evening. The *Senator*s left Boston and Washington around the lunch hour arriving at their termini in mid evening, making a single trip in one day.

In June 1956, the original 18-car *Congressional* sets were broken up and their cars were redistributed to other corridor trains, including a new *Midday Congressional*. After nearly two decades of service, the *Congressional* and *Senator* names and many of their cars passed into Amtrak service in 1971.

The legendary New York, New Haven & Hartford—the north-end anchor of the Northeast Corridor—was also one of the pioneers of streamlining, and its little *Comet* streamliner is covered in this book's first chapter. The double-ended, dolphin-nosed train entered Providence-Boston service in 1935 and remained in that assignment until the travel demands of World War II outstripped its capacity; in 1943 the *Comet* was bumped to local service. In 1949 it briefly returned to the Boston-Providence run, finally retiring in September 1951.

New Haven, working with Pullman-Standard and designer Walter Teague, also helped pioneer the design of non-articulated lightweight passenger equipment. Their collective efforts resulted in the "American Flyer" car (later so nicknamed after toy manufacturer A. C. Gilbert began offering models of the cars in its line of American Flyer electric trains). Built with lightweight metal alloys, the smooth-lined cars reduced the weight of a typical railway coach by $18^1/2$ tons. In 1934 the road began taking delivery of 205 American Flyer coaches and grill cars which would form the backbone of New Haven's passenger fleet through the war years.

Pleased with the equipment, New Haven returned to P-S in December 1945 with an order for 180 similar cars—but clad in stainless steel—in nine configurations including baggage-lounge cars, coaches, parlors, diners, grill cars, and observation cars. A follow-up order for 27 sleepers was placed in October 1946. Costing $20 million, the new cars were delivered between late 1947 and early 1950; still more cars were delivered in 1954. The stainless-steel cars carried the road's distinctive script herald and featured clean, modern interiors, plenty of leg room, and big picture windows to view the sights along the railroad's shore-hugging right-of-way.

New Haven's sizable order was not intended to re-equip just a couple of name trains but to democratically update much of its passenger fleet. No road had better reason to do so. In contrast to most American railroads which concentrated on freight, New Haven, as a result of serving some of the most populous areas in the country, was heavily oriented to passenger service. In 1946, for example, the railroad operated an amazing 545 pas-

senger trains daily. In 1947 the Yankee carrier derived nearly half of its gross revenues from its passenger trains.

Among the trains receiving priority in the postwar upgrade was New Haven's star train, the *Merchants Limited,* and its newer running mate the *Yankee Clipper,* both of which operated between Boston and New York's Grand Central Terminal. Between Boston and Washington via New York's Pennsylvania Station and the PRR between New York and Washington, both the *Patriot* and the *Senator* were upgraded as well. When in 1952 the *Senator* received new PRR equipment, the New Haven equipment was redeployed to other trains, among them the *Puritan,* the *Gilt Edge,* the *Colonial* and the *Connecticut Yankee.*

In addition to the regional flavor which railroads everywhere imparted to their trains through the design process, meals, too, offered a chance to sample the

diversity of America's regional culture. Dinner on board the New Haven was very much a New England event with featured menu items like Boston scrod and baked beans (in little brown bean pots emblazoned with the railroad's name) with brown bread.

The completion of the Connecticut Turnpike in 1958 and the appearance of a New York-Boston airline shuttle severely impacted New Haven passenger service. New Haven's trains struggled on through mismanagement, bankruptcy, and eventual inclusion into the ill-fated Penn Central Railroad in 1968, then Amtrak in 1971. Today, while the former New Haven route still hosts fast passenger trains and is undergoing complete electrification all the way to Boston in anticipation of true high-speed train service, in quality, diversity and frequency, today's service is a ghost of the New Haven's outstanding fleet of postwar streamliners.

New Haven streamliner
Laden with Pullman-Standard "American Flyer" cars from NH's postwar car order, the *Colonial* rips through Mamaroneck, New York, on a June morning in 1968 en route from Washington to Boston. The New Haven EP5 electric locomotive replaced the train's Pennsylvania GG1 electric at Pennsylvania Station in Manhattan. *Mike Schafer.*

A TRAIN CALLED *PHOEBE SNOW*

The *Phoebe Snow*

Few streamliners exuded human qualities
as much as Lackawanna's *Phoebe Snow.*
Here she is, a streak of gray and maroon at
Dover, New Jersey, a short distance into
her all-day sojourn through New York
State's Southern Tier. For many years
Delaware, Lackawanna & Western had
capitalized on the fictional maiden, so
Phoebe Snow became the obvious
choice for personification in streamliner
form. For equipment, Lackawanna chose
not one but three builders to supply
Phoebe's rolling stock: American Car &
Foundry, Budd, and Pullman-Standard. The
Budd-built tavern observation car—stainless steel but painted—was a fixture on
the streamliner and featured not one but
two drumheads heralding Phoebe's name.
John Dziobko.

At the turn of the century, a striking auburn-haired maiden appeared on the American advertising scene: Phoebe Snow. Attired in alabaster white, she personified the clean, fast service provided by Delaware, Lackawanna & Western's soot-free, anthracite-coal-burning locomotives. Sketched by numerous artists and heralded in a seemingly endless series of jingles alluding to her first-person experiences riding the Lackawanna, Phoebe Snow quickly became a part of local folklore. When the Lackawanna decided to introduce a modern streamliner on the daytime run between Hoboken, New Jersey (across the Hudson River from New York), and Buffalo after World War II, the name Phoebe Snow was a natural.

Lackawanna's principal competitor between New York and Buffalo was New York Central's *Empire State Express.* Overshadowed but by no means outclassed, DL&W offered competent, homespun service to the cities and towns of New York's Southern Tier and Pennsylvania's Pocono region with a catty-corner routing out of New Jersey to Buffalo. Although DL&W's route was geographically the shortest between New York and Buffalo—395 miles via Scranton, Pennsylvania, versus NYC's 435 via Albany—the Lackawanna route required a ferry or subway trip between Manhattan and Hoboken; thus handicapped, DL&W had long ago ceded the New York–Buffalo market per se to the Central.

Instead, the Lackawanna found a comfortable niche catering to those seeking passage to the many interme-diate points on its own route. Lackawanna's trains were populated with businessmen going to and from IBM at Endicott, New York, or Corning Glass in Corning, New York, with families visiting relatives in Upstate hometowns like Dansville and Mount Morris, and vacationers seeking the splendor of the Pocono Mountains.

On November 15, 1949, *Phoebe Snow* became a rolling advertisement, entering service with two light-weight consists on the morning-to-evening run daily each way between Hoboken and Buffalo. The new train replaced the time-honored *Lackawanna Limited.* The true dimensions of what made the Lackawanna special became apparent as one rode the line in daylight. Ambling through the Delaware Water Gap and the rural charm of the Pocono region, riding the Lackawanna was a lot like driving the country back road instead of the freeway. Nonetheless, the original running time for the *Phoebe* between Hoboken and Buffalo was just 8 hours and 15 minutes, only a few minutes longer than NYC's *Empire State Express.*

Behind maroon-and-gray Electro-Motive diesels, streamlined coaches provided service not only to Buffalo but through seating to Chicago via Nickel Plate's *Nickel Plate Limited* (see Chapter 2). These cars were drawn from two groups of 62-seat chair cars delivered in 1949 by ACF and Pullman-Standard. The DL&W had enough streamlined coaches to equip not only the *Phoebe* but the overnight Buffalo-Hoboken *New Yorker* and its westbound counterpart, the *Westerner.*

Behind the coaches was a Budd-built smooth-side stainless-steel diner seating 36 guests amidst indirect lighting, floral drapery, and snowy white table linen. Lackawanna cuisine was distinctly American. For dinner one might choose the Individual Chicken Pie, Yankee Pot Roast, or Baked Virginia Ham. The initiated would be certain to order a side dish known as "Krusty Korn Kobs," a delectable corn muffin baked in molds to resemble a small ear of corn.

Behind the diner, on the westbound run only, was a 10-6 sleeper of ACF manufacture operating through to Chicago via the Nickel Plate west of Buffalo. These sleepers carried names which reflected the Indian influence in Lackawanna territory, bearing the names of geographic points of interest along the line such as *Tunkhannock* ("small stream") or *Kittatinny* ("endless mountain").

At the end of the train was the train's signature car, the tavern-lounge observation. Forward in the car was the tavern section whose tables were presided over by an oval portrait of Miss Phoebe. Here, folks could sample from a list which ran the gamut from Genesee beer to New York State wines. For the cigar fancier "Lackawanna Specials" were available from the attendant. If tastes ran toward scenery, a selection of plump lounge chairs offered the traveler a fine vantage point from which to view Nicholson Viaduct, and other marvels of the Lackawanna route. The Budd-built beauties featured not one but two recessed maroon drumheads on which "*The Phoebe Snow*" was emblazoned in white script.

The early 1950's were good times for the railroad passenger business. Lackawanna promoted its trains assiduously, assuring summertime travelers that their vacation really started when they "stepped aboard the *Phoebe Snow*." To this day, some locals still remember Lackawanna's musical radio advertisements inviting them to "Ride the Route of *Phoebe Snow*."

As the decade wore on, however, Lackawanna discovered it was not immune to the ailments which were overcoming most of the railroad passenger industry. Business travelers and vacationers alike were abandoning the rails in favor of the convenience of the auto or the speed of the plane. The construction of government-subsidized Quickway 17 across the Southern Tier and other highways linking New York and Buffalo accelerated the disturbing trend.

On October 17, 1960, former rivals Lackawanna and the Erie Railroad merged to form the Erie Lackawanna Railroad. One of the direct results of the merger was the reduction of duplicative passenger services. As of April 30, 1961, the *Phoebe Snow* was consolidated with the *Erie Lackawanna Limited*—formerly the famous *Erie Limited*—between Hoboken and Elmira. Beyond Elmira, the *Limited* and *Phoebe* went their separate ways, the former to Chicago and the latter to Buffalo. On October 28 of the same year, the *Phoebe*'s equipment began operating to Buffalo on the old Erie route beyond Hornell, New York. Gone now were the *Phoebe* name and the distinctive tavern-observation cars. Things looked very bleak, indeed.

Enter William White who in 1963 became EL's new president. The new headman—who had been president of the DL&W from 1941 to 1952—hadn't been in office long before he had the ex-*Phoebe* tavern-observations reinstated on the *Erie Lackawanna Limited*. The response was gratifying. Aficionados of the old DL&W welcomed the resurrected cars—which still bore their *Phoebe Snow* drumheads—with placards, smiles, and even a bouquet of flowers for the surprised conductor of the *Erie Lackawanna Limited*. This caught the attention of the New York press, which incorrectly but happily reported that *Phoebe* had returned.

With the October 27, 1963, timetable change, however, *Phoebe* was indeed officially back as a train, her name replacing that of the *Erie Lackawanna Limited*. One of the most famous names in the business had returned, though on a largely different routing: Hoboken-Chicago by way of Youngstown, Ohio.

But a shadow still hung over the train. Despite gallant efforts to attract passengers for the 1964 New York World's Fair, deficits became the rule rather than the exception. During this time, the *Phoebe*, like many other trains, found itself depending more on mail and express revenue than passenger fares. Then, in early 1966, the U.S. Post Office notified EL of its intent to terminate the train's RPOs, which meant an additional significant loss of revenues. That was the final straw, and on June 15, 1966, EL filed notice with the Interstate Commerce Commission to discontinue the *Phoebe Snow*. On November 28, 1966, a beloved train which had symbolized the optimism of the railroad passenger business in the 1940's and the sad realities of it in the 1960's, died, leaving only sweet memories of an unforgettable streamliner dressed in maroon and gray.

Phoebe Snow tavern observation
Phoebe's Budd-built tavern-lounge observation had a smart, modern feel to it. The tavern section, toward the rear, was partitioned from the rest of the car with glass walls. A "real life" portrait of Phoebe in an oval frame adorned the wall at the forward end of the tavern section. *Bombardier Corporations, Joe Welsh Collection.*

Central of Georgia *Nancy Hanks II*

The original *Nancy Hanks II* streamliner was a gray-and-blue beauty built by American Car & Foundry in 1947 and powered by Electro-Motive E-units. In late summer 1958, the train gallops through Barnesville, Georgia, with a respectable-size consist. After CofG became a subsidiary of the Southern Railway, the *Nancy* received a former Wabash *Blue Bird* dome parlor-lounge car. *David W. Salter.*

Nancy Hanks II coach

The ACF coaches built for CofG were quite unusual in that they featured curtains instead of window shades covering only the lower half of the windows. *ACF Collection, St. Louis Mercantile Library.*

A Southeast Streamliner Sampler

CENTRAL OF GEORGIA'S KISSIN' COUSIN STREAMLINERS

The Southeast was hardly a bastion for streamliners. Most of the lightweights which plied their way across the likes of Georgia, the Carolinas, and Alabama were long-distance trains en route between the North and Florida—and often they passed through during nighttime hours. Aside from Florida East Coast's short-lived *Henry M. Flagler* streamliner between Jacksonville and Miami, the Southeast's principal regional streamliners of note belonged to the Central of Georgia Railway.

Central of Georgia (CofG), with a route-mileage of some 1,800 miles, was itself very much a regional railroad, webbing its namesake state with lines linking nearly every one of its major cities: Atlanta, Macon, Augusta, Savannah, Albany (All-BANE-ee), Athens, and Columbus. CofG also had lines reaching west into Alabama, principally to Montgomery and Birmingham. The railroad relied heavily on "overhead" or "bridge" traffic; that is, relaying traffic—both freight and passenger—that originated and terminated on other lines. CofG's involvement in the *City of Miami* streamliner operation aptly illustrated this: Cof G relayed the train between Birmingham and Albany, 251 miles.

The little carrier did not ignore its local constituents,

however. In 1947, it introduced not one but two of its own new streamliners, the *Nancy Hanks II* and the *Man O' War*. Named for famous race horses, the two trains were, interestingly, built by two different companies, although both trains were powered by Electro-Motive diesels. American Car & Foundry constructed ten cars—one baggage coach (combine), four regular coaches, four "divided" (segregated) coaches, and one grill lounge car for *Nancy Hanks II* service while the Budd Company delivered combine *Fort Mitchell*, coaches *Fort McPherson* and *Fort Oglethorpe*, and club-observation car *Fort Benning* for the *Man O' War*. All *Man O' War* cars were named for on-line locations.

The "*Nancy*" went to work on the 293-mile Atlanta-Macon-Savannah route, operating westbound out of Savanna in the morning for an early afternoon arrival in Atlanta; returning, the train left Atlanta in the evening for a just-before-midnight arrival back in Savannah. A connecting train known as the "Little Nancy" ran between Millen, on the big *Nancy's* route, and Augusta allowing for Augusta-Atlanta travel.

The *Man O' War* worked a shorter route, Atlanta-Columbus, 117 miles, and because of the brevity of the run it initially made two round trips per day. The train was based at Columbus, first making a morning/midday round trip to Atlanta and then a late-afternoon/evening round trip to Georgia's largest city. At Columbus, the train made connections the Chicago-Jacksonville *Seminole* and, to a lesser degree, with the *City of Miami*. In 1954, one of the round trips was dropped and the train was operated as a mid-day round trip out of Atlanta.

Both trains were well-received by the riding public, and the *Nancy* was especially well patronized although the "Little Nancy" was discontinued during the 1950s. By the end of the 1960s, the *Man O' War* had been rescheduled to provide travelers with a full day of shopping in Atlanta, but the train had shrunk to a two-car streamliner, sans observation car. The *Nancy*, on the other hand, enjoyed somewhat of a renaissance late in the decade when it was upgraded by CofG's then-parent railroad, the Southern, with a dome parlor-lounge car. In keeping with the racehorse theming, the lounge beneath the dome became the "Saddle & Stirrup" room when the car became a regular on the *Nancy*.

The *Man O' War* survived to 1970 before being discontinued; *Nancy* fared a little better, operating right up to the start up of Amtrak. *Nancy Hanks II* made her last race across Georgia on the evening of April 30, 1971, arriving Savannah amid newspaper reporters and well-wishers who had grown up with the train.

Central of Georgia *Man O' War*
Although the *Man O' War* was built the same year as the *Nancy Hanks II*, in 1947, the Budd Company was the contracted builder, not ACF. Though a smaller streamliner than the *Nancy*, the *Man O' War* featured a classy tavern observation car named *Fort Benning*, the well-known U.S. Army installation located on the CofG. The modern, all-stainless-steel *Man O' War* contrasted with the sleepy surroundings of Chipley, Georgia, as it paused during one of its double-daily Atlanta-Columbus trips in the late 1950s. *David W. Salter*

Mid-States Regional Streamliners

Missouri River Eagle, 1971
Just over 30 years old, MP's *Missouri River Eagle* had seen better days when it called at Sedalia, Missouri, for a scant few passengers on April 14, 1971. Two coaches were more than ample to handle passenger loads. In a little over two weeks, the new Amtrak will have replaced the train with a New York/ Washington-Kansas City long-distance run. *Jim Heuer.*

MISSOURI PACIFIC'S *EAGLES*

Some railroads had such success with streamliners that they developed whole themed fleets of them. There were Santa Fe's *Chiefs*, the *Zephyrs* of Burlington, and, of course, the *City* trains of Union Pacific among others. Missouri Pacific was one mid-states carrier that ushered in a single new streamliner, the *Eagle*, and wound up with a whole "sky" full of 'em. The original *Eagle* was styled by celebrated designer Raymond Loewy whose list of accomplishments included the Pennsylvania Railroad GG1 electric, the Coldspot refrigerator, Studebaker's Avanti, and even Skylab.

Mopac's blue-and-light gray beauties would eventually cover the road's network of steel stretching from St. Louis to the Gulf of Mexico and the Colorado Rockies, but most *Eagles* would be regional in nature.

The *Eagle* first flew on March 10, 1940, following the Missouri River for 478 miles between St. Louis, Kansas City, and Omaha on a daytime schedule. For the service, American Car & Foundry built two six-car *Eagle* consists, each featuring coaches with reclining seats, an attractive diner-bar-lounge, and a 26-seat parlor observation car. A mail-storage car and a mail-baggage car rounded out the consist, pulled by a reliable Electro-Motive E3 locomotive.

The new *Eagle* was an instant success. Ridership on the train increased an average of 150 percent in its first six months of operation. Indeed, passenger revenues for all trains on the Mopac's Eastern Division where the *Eagle* ran were up 225 percent compared to the same period in 1939.

The early success of the *Eagle* spawned an *Eagle* fleet serving a number of destinations. First to follow was the two-car *Delta Eagle*, built by St. Louis Car Company and introduced on May 11, 1941. Another river-hugger, this *Eagle* ran the 259 miles from Memphis, Tennessee, south along the Mississippi River to the unlikely outpost of Tallulah, Louisiana. Despite the odd routing, the train repaid MP's investment, although in the long run it did not prosper and in 1954 was discontinued. At the time of the *Delta Eagle's* introduction, the original *Eagle* was renamed *Missouri River Eagle* to distinguish it from future new *Eagle* streamliners.

Next in line was the *Colorado Eagle*, entering service in 1942 between St. Louis and Denver. World War II delayed further *Eagle* introductions until 1948 when three new *Eagle* services were instituted, notably the *Texas Eagles*, twin trains linking St. Louis with several Texas cities. As long-distance trains, the *Colorado* and *Texas Eagles* are covered in chapters 3 and 5, respectively.

The year 1948 also saw the inauguration of the *Louisiana Eagle* and the *Valley Eagle*. Operating overnight between New Orleans, Louisiana, and Fort Worth, Texas, 551 miles via MP subsidiary Texas & Pacific, the *Louisiana Eagle* in later years became a part of the *Texas Eagle* operation west of Marshall, Texas. In fact, the *Louisiana Eagle* drew from a pool of equipment purchased new from ACF and Budd by MP, T&P, and International-Great Northern (another MP subsidiary) for both *Texas* and *Valley Eagle* service.

The *Valley Eagle* made its first run on October 31, 1948, and, like the *Delta Eagle*, was another short-haul regional train. Unlike its brethren, though, the *Valley Eagle* had the distinction of being the only *Eagle* to operate entirely intrastate, in Texas, between Houston and Brownsville. Ten cars were built for the service by ACF for the St. Louis, Brownsville & Mexico Railway (yet another Mopac subsidiary), enough to provide two trainsets for daytime service in each direction between Houston and Brownsville, 372 miles.

From its inception in 1940 until 1952, the *Missouri River Eagle* offered largely the same accommodations as when it debuted. In 1952 the train achieved "domeliner" status when MP, T&P, and I-GN together purchased five Pullman-Standard dome coaches—known as "Planetarium domes" on Mopac lines—assigning two to the *Missouri River Eagle* (one for each train set) and the rest to the *Texas Eagle*. In later years the train would often carry the Budd dome coaches that once served the *Colorado Eagle*.

Impacted by declining revenues and rising costs, the *Missouri River Eagle* found itself fighting for its life in the 1960s. In 1962, the *Valley Eagle* had already been terminated, and in 1963 the MP unsuccessfully petitioned the State of Missouri for permission to discontinue the *Missouri River Eagle* between St. Louis and Kansas City; instead, the Kansas City-Omaha segment was dropped in 1965, and the remaining service somehow survived until Amtrak's arrival in 1971 when Amtrak replaced it with an extended *National Limited* operating through from Washington and New York to Kansas City. In the 1990s, Amtrak's westbound *Kansas City Mule* and eastbound *Ann Rutledge* perform nearly the same duties and operate on approximately the same schedules as the original *Missouri River Eagle* east of K.C.

Those who rode the Mopac in its glory years in the passenger business remember a friendly railroad which seemed to be able get you just about anywhere you wanted to go. But the *Eagle* fleet which had become a welcome part of everyday life in the American Midwest and South Central states vanished as that way of life changed. Today, memories of *Eagle* trains with lots of personality and a pretty-as-you-please paint scheme have left a host of devoted followers who keep the *Eagle* legend alive.

Diner-lounge, Missouri Pacific *Eagle* of 1940
With its portholed windows, wood-paneled walls, and trim in deep blue and stainless steel, the lounge section of the *Eagle*'s diner-lounge was an exceptional design execution. A local artist provided the eagle mural behind the bar, the original artwork of which resides at the St. Louis Museum of Transportation. *ACF*

Eagle parlor-observation car
A view from the observation lounge end of the *Eagle*'s parlor-observation car reveals two inviting rows of overstuffed, swivel parlor chairs, including two set up for card gaming. *ACF*

THE LEGENDARY *ROCKET*S OF THE ROCK ISLAND LINES

When the Chicago, Rock Island & Pacific introduced its first streamliners in 1937, it was only natural that they be christened as *Rocket*s. After all, the railroad's first train, which ran with much fanfare between Chicago and Joliet, Illinois, in 1852, was pulled by a little steam locomotive dubbed *The Rocket*.

Rock Island jumped onto the streamliner bandwagon in a big way, ordering not one but six *Rocket* trains for various routes. E. G. Budd Manufacturing built the cars while Electro-Motive built six 1200-hp TA-model passenger diesels—precursor to the phenomenally popular E-series locomotives—to pull the trains. Each train was semi-articulated; four sets had three cars (baggage-dinette-coach, straight coach, coach-parlor observation) and two had four cars (baggage-dinette, two coaches, parlor-lounge observation). Initial assignments were:

1. The *Peoria Rocket*, Chicago-Peoria, Illinois, 161 miles, a single set making two round trips per day.

2. The *Des Moines Rocket*, Chicago-Rock Island (Illinois)-Des Moines, Iowa, 358 miles, a single set making one round trip per day out of the Iowa state capital.

3. The *Texas Rocket*, Fort Worth-Houston, 283 miles, the set making one daily round trip.

4. The *Denver Rocket*, Kansas City-Denver, 637 miles on an all-day schedule, three round trips per week.

5. The *Kansas City Rocket*, Minneapolis/St. Paul-Kansas City, 493 miles; two sets providing daily service in each direction.

Not surprising, since nearly all other new streamliners throughout the U.S. were being universally embraced by the traveling public, the new *Rocket*s were a sensation, and the *Rocket* name soon became closely associated with the Rock Island. Assignments for some of the new little trains changed even-

Original *Rocket* streamliner
One of the original six *Rocket* streamliners of 1937 slips through the countryside in June 1941 behind one of the TA-type EMC locomotives. Although the exact location of the photo is unknown, the train appears to be on the Peoria branch. One of the original sets was assigned to Chicago-Peoria service making two round trips a day between Illinois largest and then-second-largest cities. The *Peoria Rocket*s were very popular and the longest lived of any of the *Rocket* streamliners, lasting from 1937 to 1979. *Dave Oroszi Collection.*

ROCK ISLAND LINES

tually. For example, in 1938 the *Denver Rocket* was reassigned to Kansas City-Dallas service and at the same time the *Texas Rocket* set was likewise put on the K.C.-Dallas so that daily *Rocket* service could be provided between the two cities.

The *Rocket* fleet soon grew. The *Rocky Mountain Rocket* was born in 1939 (as a true long-distance train, this *Rocket* is covered in Chapter 3), and in 1940 the *Choctaw Rocket* began overnight service on an unlikely route: Memphis, Tennessee, to Amarillo, Texas, 761 miles via Little Rock, Arkansas, and Oklahoma City, Oklahoma. The following year the joint CB&Q-Rock Island Minneapolis-St. Louis *Zephyr Rocket* joined the fleet. Nearly all these new *Rocket*s utilized Electro-Motive E-units pulling conventional streamlined equipment delivered by Budd and Pullman-Standard in 1939-40.

After World War II, more *Rocket*s began flying with the 1945 introduction of the most far-flung *Rocket* to date, the *Twin Star Rocket* between Minneapolis and Houston (Chapter 5). That was followed in 1947 by the *Corn Belt Rocket* on the 503-mile Chicago-Omaha route. After the war, the original six *Rocket* sets began to be broken up and their cars redistributed among the newer conventional streamlined cars being delivered, thus providing the railroad with greater flexibility in accommodating passengers.

The only other all-new *Rocket* to appear after the *Corn Belt Rocket* was the *Jet Rocket*, an experimental lightweight train built by American Car & Foundry for Chicago-Peoria service. Pulled by a futuristic Electro-Motive diesel known as an LWT-12 (for "Lightweight, 1200 hp; see sidebar), this low-slung train brought fixed

consists and all their associated problems back to the rails in 1955 for an unsuccessful two-year stint.

As was the case for most U.S. railroads, rising costs and dwindling revenues in the late 1950s and throughout the 1960s sent much of the *Rocket* fleet into low orbit, the most successful survivors being the *Peoria Rocket*s and those running on Rock's main line between Chicago, the Quad Cities (Davenport/Bettendorf, Iowa, and Rock Island/Moline, Illinois), and Omaha. Seemingly always beset by financial problems, Rock Island's slip into red ink in 1965 did not help matters, and much of what remained of the *Rocket* fleet unraveled in the late 1960s. Amtrak came along in 1971, but Rock Island by then was too impoverished to muster the necessary payment to join the new carrier and was thus obligated by federal law to continue operation of its remaining two trains on its own, the Chicago-Rock Island *Quad City Rocket* (a remnant of the erstwhile *Des Moines Rocket*) and one *Peoria Rocket*.

Those two remaining *Rocket*s limped along until December 31, 1978, when they made their final trips—an abandonment that was but a portent of things to come. Two years later, the 7800-mile CRI&P itself went out of business, the largest U.S. railroad ever to abandon service in total.

Des Moines Rocket

Looking quite unlike its original incarnation as a Budd streamliner, the *Des Moines Rocket* of 1965, leaving Chicago for its namesake, shows how railroads of that era had to rely heavily on mail and express traffic to offset dwindling passenger revenues. The Alco DL-series locomotive leading was originally built for *Arizona Limited* streamliner service in 1941 (Chapter 3). *Mike Schafer.*

Jet Rocket

Rock Island's experimental *Jet Rocket* arriving Chicago in the 1950s. *John Szwajkart, Robert P. Schmidt Collection.*

General Motors *Aerotrain*
Bound for Chicago, New York Central's *Great Lakes Aerotrain* slips out of Cleveland Union Terminal on August 15, 1956. The sleek train proved that looks weren't everything. After less than a year on the NYC, it was withdrawn from service. Though reasonably reliable (the space-age LWT12-type locomotive being little more than a high-speed version of a tried-and-proven standard Electro-Motive switch engine in prom clothes) the cars rode rough account of their single-axle arrangement versus conventional two-axle rotating truck assemblies of conventional cars. One of the three LWT12 locomotives built was also used to power Rock Island's *Jet Rocket* Talgo train. *John Dziobko.*

Postwar Experimental Streamliners

Streamlining represented a major revolution in the American passenger train during the 1930s, and during the 1950s several U.S. railroads attempted to, in a sense, re-invent streamlining itself. If nothing else, the noble experiments that followed proved that history does indeed repeat itself.

Despite a burst of postwar optimism that prompted railroads across the land to launch new streamliners, realities began to set in as the 1950s unfolded—the main fact being that Americans loved the freedom and convenience of the automobile more than almost anything regardless of the long-term costs and negative environmental implications. For railroads this meant an alarming slide in passenger revenues despite escalating costs. Major postwar developments like the Vista-Dome car only helped slow the decline. Railroads had to come up with yet a newer idea: trains that would attract people back to the rails and at the same time drastically reduce operating costs—in truth, the emphasis was on latter.

Enter the "super lightweights"—experimental trains of racy, low-slung design (in which low centers of gravity allowed for high-speed operation on existing track) and very lightweight construction pulled by matching locomotives of compact, efficient design. Such new trains theoretically would require less capital investment and could be operated at substantially less cost.

The first of this new breed was the "Talgo" train, three of which were built by American Car & Foundry in 1949. The moniker was an acronym: T = Train, A = Articulated, L = Lightweight, G = Goicoechea (the train's inventor), O = Oriol (the train's financier). In essence, the Talgo concept was a variation on articulation, a feature incorporated in early U.S. streamliners. In the Talgo train, each car had but one axle at

only one end of the car; the non-axled end was supported by the axled end of the adjoining car. Although cars could be added or subtracted, it was a laborious process.

Pullman-Standard built two Talgo trains in 1956-57, one for New York Central (*The Xplorer*) and one for the New Haven (the *Dan'l Webster*). The trains were powered by 1000-hp diesel hydraulic locomotives (facing page) built by Baldwin-Lima-Hamilton Corporation; New Haven's had one locomotive at each end to eliminate the need for turning the train at terminals. ACF also built a Talgo train for the New Haven in 1956, serving as the Boston-New York *John Quincy Adams*. At about the same time, ACF also built a five-car Talgo train, powered by a Fairbanks-Morse locomotive, for the Boston & Maine as well as one to serve as Rock Island's *Jet Rocket*.

The most-well-known of the postwar experimental breed was General Motors' *Aerotrain*. Its futuristic locomotive, whose design bore the unmistakable stamp of Detroit automobile stylists, was designated as a model LWT12 (for "lightweight, 1200 hp"). The cars were also of GM parentage and were in reality modified intercity bus carbodies—from GM's bus-body division—riding on two axles, one at each end of the car; the *Aerotrains* were non-articulated and their consists could be relatively easily adjusted to meet travel demands. Two *Aerotrains* were built in 1956 and tested on New York Central, Union Pacific, Santa Fe, and Pennsylvania before being sold to Rock Island circa 1958. A third LWT12 locomotive was built, also in 1956, to power Rock Island's Talgo-style *Jet Rocket* ACF Talgo trainset.

The Talgo concept caught on in Spain where it was greatly improved and still enjoys popularity. Americans preferred the comfort and spaciousness of conventional streamlined equipment and wound up shunning the little trains. Fraught with technical problems and poor ride quality, all U.S. experimental trains became, if you will, "doomliners," soon being pulled from service. Despite their more conventional nature, the *Aerotrain*s did not fare much better and wound up in Rock Island's Chicago-based suburban services until 1965 while the *Jet Rocket* and its locomotive were scrapped. Today, the two *Aerotrain*s can be seen at the St. Louis Museum of Transport and the National Railroad Museum at Green Bay, Wisconsin.

Interestingly, Amtrak began experimenting with vastly improved Talgo trains in the 1990s. They have been well-received by today's riding public, and more Talgo trains are under construction as this book goes to press.

New York Central, *The Xplorer*

The Xplorer and its twin, New Haven's *Dan'l Webster*, were both powered by hydraulic-transmission German diesels which were subject to frequent breakdowns. Below, the NYC train is shown westbound at Dayton (Ohio) Union Station while in Cleveland-Columbus-Cincinnati service circa 1957. Its Pullman-Standard cars bore a striking resemblance to Talgo trains being tested in the U.S. during the 1990s. *R. D. Acton Sr.*

American Car & Foundry Talgo train

In 1949, American Car & Foundry unveiled its Talgo streamliner, jettisoning rail passenger technology into realm of Buck Rogers (right). The difference between the Talgo train and its conventional kin is graphically illustrated in this scene, probably staged at builder ACF. Hip passengers enjoy conversation in the observation car as a conductor gives a "highball" signal to an adjacent regular streamlined coach under construction. *ACF Collection, St. Louis Mercantile Library.*

Second City Streamliners

C&O Pere Marquette, 1962
Chicago's backside forms an urban back-drop for Chesapeake & Ohio's *Pere Marquette* streamliner easing out of Grand Central Station on the south perimeter of the Loop in August 1962. The success of the original *Pere Marquettes*, launched in 1946 between Grand Rapids and Detroit, Michigan, by the Pere Marquette Railroad (absorbed by C&O in 1947) prompted C&O to establish another set of *Pere Marquettes* to operate west of Grand Rapids in 1948. *Bob Johnston.*

Chicago—traditionally the second-largest city in the U.S.—was the undisputed hub of the American streamliner. In terms of volume and variety, more streamliners strode in and out of Chicago's six major downtown terminals (counter-clockwise from the north, North Western Terminal, Union Station, Grand Central, La Salle Street, Dearborn, and Central Station) on a daily basis than in any other city.

Within the confines of about one square mile, one could sample the streamliners of Chicago & North Western, Pennsylvania Railroad, Milwaukee Road, Burlington, Gulf, Mobile & Ohio, Baltimore & Ohio, Chesapeake & Ohio, Rock Island, New York Central, Nickel Plate, Santa Fe, Wabash, Chicago & Eastern Illinois, Monon, Erie Lackawanna, Grand Trunk Western, North Shore Line, and Illinois Central.

Many of the trains of these carriers were, of course, famous-name transcons that carried passenger to all corners and coasts of America. However, most streamliners serving the "Second City" functioned as regional trains—usually running on day schedules—linking Chicago with major (and sometimes not-so-major) metropolitan areas that were but a few hours distant, places like St. Louis, Detroit, Cincinnati, Minneapolis/St. Paul, Omaha, Kansas City, and Milwaukee. Some of the city pairs, notably Chicago-St. Louis and Chicago-Twin Cities, were busy, well-populated, hotly contested corridors where more than one carrier vied for passengers.

Other city pairs, such as Chicago-Grand Rapids, Michigan, were captive to one carrier, in this case Chesapeake & Ohio (facing page). Regardless, the variety of Chicago's regional streamliners was fascinating and colorful. Herewith are some samples.

CHICAGO-TWIN CITIES

Some 400 miles of lovely rolling farmland and river valleys separate Chicago from Minneapolis and St. Paul. Burlington was the first of the three principal railroads linking Chicago with the Twin Cities to inaugurate streamliner service on that corridor, with the *Twin Zephyr*s in April 1935. Milwaukee Road followed suit in May 1935 with its *Hiawatha* trains. Covered in more detail in Chapter 1, both road's trains were enormously successful. In 1939 they were joined by North Western's *Twin Cities "400"*, a brand-new Pullman-Standard streamliner which replaced The *"400"*, an upgraded, high-speed, premium-service heavyweight train launched in 1935 in answer to the *Hiawatha*s and *Zephyr*s. North Western's train made the 400-or-so-mile trip in about as many minutes, hence the name.

Both Milwaukee Road and Burlington continued to upgrade their Twin Cities streamliner services, introducing new equipment and additional trains. Some consider the 1939 editions of the *Twin Cities Hiawatha*s to be the pinnacle of Milwaukee Road's service, with their stellar streamlined Hudson-type (4-6-4) locomotives, smooth-riding rib-sided passenger cars, Tip Top Tap lounge cars, and very Art Deco Beaver Tail observation cars. For Burlington, it was the 1947 *Twin Zephyr*s, whose regularly assigned consists included five Vista-Dome cars.

Eventually, Chicagoans could choose from the *Morning Zephyr*, *Afternoon Zephyr*, *Morning Hiawatha*, *Afternoon Hiawatha*, the *Pioneer Limited*, or the *Twin Cities "400"* if they were headed for Minneapolis/St. Paul—and vice versa, of course—with running times as fast as 6 hours, 15 minutes between Chicago and St. Paul.

Burlington's route struck west-northwest from Chicago across northern Illinois, then from Savanna, Illinois, north hugged the Mississippi River all the way to St. Paul. Burlington thus described the *Twin Zephyr*s' river-hugging portion as one "Where Nature Smiles for 300 miles." The route was fast, too. For several years, the *Morning Zephyr*'s westbound carding between Chicago and Rochelle, Illinois—83 miles in 68 minutes (including a scheduled stop at Aurora)—categorized it as one of the fastest streamliners in the country.

Milwaukee's line headed due north from Chicago,

Burlington *Morning Zephyr*, 1958
Nature was smiling over the passengers aboard northbound train No. 21, the *Morning Zephyr*, along the east bank of the "Mighty Mississip" near Maiden Rock, Wisconsin, on June 29, 1958, as the train breezed toward the Twin Cities. This day's train must be brimming with summer travelers, as there is an extra coach in the consist, behind the first dome car. A pair of Electro-Motive E5 locomotives, clad in stainless-steel fluting, are in charge of keeping the train on its tight schedule. *William D. Middleton.*

Milwaukee Road F7 Hudson

The 1939 edition of the *Twin Cities Hiawatha* is often considered the epitome of the whole *Hiawatha* fleet, before and since. Motive power for the '39 "Hi's" were streamlined Class F7 Hudson steam locomotives built by American Locomotive Company (Alco). Hudson No. 100 is just moments out of Chicago Union Station in September 1938. *Milwaukee Road.*

Twin Cities Hiawatha, final version

The view below of the Twin Cities-bound *Morning Hiawatha* rustling the calm of suburban Milwaukee early in the 1960s represents the 1948 edition of the *Twin Cities Hiawatha*s, including its most famous car, the Skytop parlor-observation. (A close examination reveals the conductor enjoying the very last seat on the train in the car's glass-ceilinged lounge area.) The Super Dome lounge, two cars ahead, had been added in 1952. *Jim Boyd.*

tapping Wisconsin's largest city, Milwaukee, before striking west to La Crosse, Wisconsin, from where it, too, followed the Father of Waters to St. Paul and Minneapolis. North Western's *Twin Cities "400"* also served Milwaukee, but its route northwest from there to the Twin Cities passed through pleasant farming country and little else. For this reason, and because the *Twin Cities "400"* never offered dome service as would its competitors, that train succumbed early on, in 1963.

Milwaukee Road also introduced overnight streamliner service on the route when it partially upgraded its *Pioneer Limited* in 1949 with new lightweight cars built by the railroad's skilled shop forces in Milwaukee. New lightweight, streamlined sleeping cars built by Pullman-Standard were added in 1953.

As was the case all over America in the late 1960s, the Chicago-Twin Cities trains became victims of rising

costs and dwindling revenues. The *Afternoon Hiawatha* and *Pioneer Limited* were discontinued in 1970; beginning several years earlier, one set of *Twin Zephyr*s was often consolidated with the *Empire Builder* and *Western Star* between Chicago and St. Paul. Both *Twin Zephyr*s and the *Morning Hiawatha* lasted until Amtrak.

NORTH WESTERN'S OTHER "400"S

The streamliner *Twin Cities "400"* spawned a whole fleet of *"400s,"* several of which fared better overall than the parent train. Most of the other "400s"—trains like the *Green Bay "400," Shoreland "400,"* and *City of Milwaukee "400"*—thrived within the densely populated, industrialized 200-plus-mile corridor between Chicago and Green Bay, Wisconsin, via Milwaukee, north of which the trains followed two different routes.

Two streamliners of note that plied this corridor

Twin Cities "400"

Strung out across Great Northern's James J. Hill Bridge across the Mississippi River in Minneapolis, the new *Twin Cities "400"* is a breathtaking sight. Elsewhere in America, Judy Garland was singing "Over the Rainbow" in MGM's new color spectacular, "Wizard of Oz," major exhibitions were dazzling people in New York and San Francisco, and Americans everywhere were emerging from a dusty decade that had gone from rags to riches. The Streamliner Era was in full swing. *C&NW.*

FAST *Daily* SCHEDULE

Northbound Read Down	CENTRAL STANDARD TIME	Southbound Read Up
11:30 am	Lv.......CHICAGO......Ar.	9:10 pm
11:44 am	Lv......Evanston.......Ar.	8:50 pm
12:06 pm	Lv......Waukegan......Ar.	8:25 pm
12:20 pm	Lv......Kenosha.......Ar.	8:10 pm
12:32 pm	Lv......Racine........Ar.	7:58 pm
1:05 pm	Lv......Milwaukee......Ar.	7:30 pm
1:35 pm	Lv....Port Washington....	Via Fond
2:05 pm	Lv.......Sheboygan......	du Lac
2:36 pm	Lv.......Manitowoc......	
3:35 pm	Lv......Green Bay......Ar.	4:25 pm
4:32 pm	Ar.......Shawano......Lv.	3:33 pm
5:09 pm	Ar........Eland......Lv.	2:49 pm
5:34 pm	Ar.......Antigo......Lv.	2:20 pm
6:22 pm	Ar........Elcho......Lv.	1:29 pm
6:32 pm	Ar....Pelican Lake.....Lv.	1:19 pm
6:50 pm	Ar........MONICO......Lv.	1:10 pm
Service	Ar......Three Lakes......Lv.	Service
during	Ar.....Eagle River......Lv.	during
Summer	Ar........Conover......Lv.	Summer
Season	Ar......Land O'Lakes.....Lv.	Season
only	Ar......WATERSMEET.....Lv.	only
6:50 pm	Lv.......MONICO......Ar.	1:10 pm
7:10 pm	Ar.....Rhinelander......Lv.	12:35 pm
7:35 pm	Ar....Lake Tomahawk.....Lv.	12:07 pm
7:50 pm	Ar......Woodruff......Lv.	11:55 am
8:11 pm	Ar....Lac du Flambeau....Lv.	11:40 am
8:28 pm	Ar......Manitowish......Lv.	11:23 am
8:34 pm	Ar........Mercer......Lv.	11:18 am
9:10 pm	Ar........Hurley......Lv.	10:33 am
9:20 pm	Ar......Ironwood......Lv.	10:42 am
9:49 pm	Ar........Saxon......Lv.	10:10 am
10:30 pm	Ar.......ASHLAND......Lv.	9:30 am

Also makes Flag Stops at Summit Lake, Lake George and Marlands.

Chicago and North Western System
PIONEER RAILROAD OF CHICAGO AND THE WEST—SINCE 1848

Flambeau "400"
"Flambeau" is French for a torch, which is a featured icon of this brochure for the *Flambeau "400"* issued early in the 1950s. Early French explorers in what is now northern Wisconsin discovered Indians fishing at night by torchlight. *Don Sarno Collection.*

"Take the Twins" to St. Louis
(Right) Once it had re-streamlined the *Green Diamond* and added lightweight, streamlined equipment to the *Diamond's* companion day train, the *Daylight*, IC referred to them as twin streamliners. *Joe Welsh Collection.*

were the *Peninsula "400"* and the *Flambeau "400,"* both of which operated beyond Green Bay to Michigan's Upper Peninsula and the Wisconsin North Woods. The *Peninsula "400,"* inaugurated in 1942, ran to Ishpeming, Michigan, in the heart of iron country nearly 400 miles due north of Chicago. Inaugurated in 1950, the *Flambeau "400"* served the popular tourist region of Wisconsin's North Woods, terminating at Ashland on Lake Superior 450 miles north-northwest of Chicago.

In 1958, Pullman-Standard delivered 13 new intercity bilevel cars including coaches, coach-bar-lounge, and parlor cars. Together with World War II-era single-level streamlined C&NW baggage-mail-tavern and dining cars that were rebuilt with false roofs to match the height of the new bilevel equipment, the *Peninsula* and *Flambeau "400s"* were re-equipped that year, making them the last streamliners to be upgraded with brand-new equipment prior to Amtrak.

North Western's most far-flung *"400"* was the *Dakota "400,"* which debuted in 1950 between Chicago and Huron, South Dakota, 653 miles via Madison and La

Crosse, Wisconsin, and Rochester, Minnesota—certainly a lengthy run that made it almost more of a long-distance train than a regional streamliner. The *Dakota "400"* was briefly extended to Rapid City, South Dakota, in 1957 and then went through a series of cutbacks that eventually truncated it at Rochester where, as the *Rochester "400,"* it catered largely to patients traveling to and from the famed Mayo Clinic.

Union Pacific's shifting of its *City* streamliner transcons from the North Western to the Milwaukee Road east of Omaha in 1955 prompted C&NW to fill the void on its east-west main line by introducing the *Kate Shelley "400"* between Chicago and Boone, Iowa, 340 miles via Cedar Rapids, Iowa. Initially the train used cars that had been a part of the *City* Streamliner/Domeliner pool. In 1957, the "Katy," as it was known to some local residents, was cut back to Clinton, Iowa, on the Mississippi River, 138 miles out of Chicago. The little streamliner lasted until May 1, 1971.

CHICAGO-ST. LOUIS

Like Chicago-Twin Cities, Chicago-St. Louis was another competitive corridor. Within, three railroads offered double-daily direct streamliner service (in addition to heavyweight trains) between the two cities: Gulf, Mobile & Ohio, Wabash, and Illinois Central. (One could also utilize a combination of lines; for example, in 1950 one could ride Illinois Terminal's electric streamliner *Mound City* from St. Louis to Peoria and connect at the latter with the Chicago-bound *Peoria Rocket*.)

First with a streamliner on the corridor was the Alton Railroad (merged into GM&O in 1947) with its *Abraham Lincoln* of 1935, covered in Chapter 1. In 1937 it was joined by its twin sister, which had been serving as the *Royal Blue* on the B&O; in Chicago-St. Louis service it became the *Ann Rutledge*. By this time, IC had, in 1936, introduced its "tomato worm" streamliner *Green Diamond* (also covered in more detail in Chapter 1) on its Chicago-Springfield-St. Louis route. In 1947, the *Green Diamond* and its heavyweight companion train, the *Daylight*, were upgraded with a combination of new Pullman-Standard streamlined cars and rebuilt-from-heavyweight streamlined cars, and the following year GM&O took delivery of

new streamlined coaches and parlor cars for Chicago-St. Louis service.

Wabash was last in the race to streamline the Chicago-St. Louis corridor, but ended up with what was arguably one of the finest regional streamliners in the Midwest: the *Blue Bird* of 1950. This handsome Budd-built train featured not one, but four Vista-Dome cars. (Never mind that Wabash's route between Chicago and St. Louis traversed some of the flattest countryside in all of Mid-America.) The six-car streamliner had a baggage-lunch counter-lounge, three Vista-Dome coaches, diner-lounge, and a beautiful Vista-Dome parlor-lounge observation car featuring a Pullman-operated drawing room.

The *Blue Bird* made one round trip daily, heading north from St. Louis in the morning and arriving Chicago's Dearborn Station in mid-afternoon where it was turned for a late afternoon southbound departure. The train was so popular that Wabash had to order an additional dome parlor car to meet the demand for first-class service; the Pullman-Standard-built car included a cocktail lounge beneath the dome section known as the "Blue Bird Room." The railroad even produced a campy promotional movie in which the *Blue Bird* played a central role; it was the type of movie that no doubt made all the rounds at central Illinois grade schools.

Since the days when both trains were heavyweight, the *Blue Bird*'s daytime counterpart was the *Banner Blue*. The *Banner* remained heavyweight until 1960 when it achieved streamliner status, albeit somewhat at the expense of the *Blue Bird* and Wabash's St. Louis-

GM&O *Abraham Lincoln*, 1966

Old and newer cars mingle on GM&O's northbound *Abraham Lincoln,* above, on the final approach to Chicago Union Station during the summer of '66. The last three cars on the train—a coach, diner, and the parlor-observation—were part of the original *Abe Lincoln* streamliner of 1935. Nearly every car ahead of those three elderly rollers were from the GM&O's postwar car order from American Car & Foundry. Note the difference in car height, too, between the old and the new. Below, a handsome fold-out brochure espoused the virtues of traveling on the "Gee-Mo"—the Alton Route. *Photo, George Speir; brochure, Mike Schafer Collection.*

Wabash _Blue Bird_

Hustling along out of Decatur, Illinois, on its flight to Chicago on March 22, 1953, the _Blue Bird_ shows in part its as-delivered 1950 appearance. The demand was so high for first-class parlor service on the Blue Bird that Wabash had to order a second parlor car. Because Budd was backed up with other car orders, the additional dome parlor came from Pullman-Standard in 1952, and it can be seen here as the next-to-last car. It didn't match Budd's fluting, but it did its intended job of accommodating demand. Also, one of the dome coaches is missing from this day's train and has substituted with a straight coach (third car) from the _Blue Bird_'s sister train, the _City of Kansas City. Sandy Goodrick. Ad, Mike Schafer Collection._

Kansas City streamliner _City of Kansas City_, from which cars were pulled for upgraded _Banner_ service.

IC's Chicago-St. Louis service unraveled early on with the discontinuance of the _Daylight_ in 1958, leaving the _Green Diamond_ as its only Chicago-St. Louis streamliner. In 1968, the _Green Diamond_ was truncated to a Chicago-Springfield train, the _Governor's Special,_ which lasted until Amtrak.

Wabash was leased by Norfolk & Western in 1964 after which the former Wabash cars were redistributed throughout the newly expanded N&W system. The _Banner Blue_ was dropped in 1968, and not long after that the _Blue Bird_ was cut back to a Chicago-Decatur train and renamed _City of Decatur._

GM&O's 284-mile Chicago-St. Louis route paralleling famous U.S. Route 66 was the most successful in the long run, no doubt due to the fact it served the greatest population base, including the state capital of Springfield and a number of on-line colleges, including three at Bloomington/Normal. Although the "Annie" was dropped in 1958, the _Abraham Lincoln_ and the partially heavyweight _Limited_ marched on providing double-daily daytime service, along with the overnight _Midnight Special_ (the _Limited_ and the _Special_ never officially achieved streamliner status) right up to Amtrak, which eventually revived the _Ann Rutledge_ name.

CHICAGO-DETROIT

Even today, Amtrak's Chicago-Michigan corridor enjoys relatively frequent service. During the classic streamliner era, New York Central almost exclusively held title to the 284-mile Chicago-Detroit route which served several key Michigan cities: Kalamazoo, Battle Creek, Jackson, and Ann Arbor. Pennsylvania and Wabash's joint Chicago-Detroit service via Fort Wayne, Indiana, ended shortly after World War II, and Grand Trunk Western's Chicago-Detroit services for the most part required a change of trains at Durand, Michigan. NYC had by far the fastest, with cardings of about five and a half hours.

The corridor's first streamliner was NYC's *Chicago Mercury* of 1939, a train built from surplus commuter coaches much like NYC's Cleveland-Detroit *Mercury* of 1936; a decade later both the *Chicago Mercury* and the heavyweight *Twilight Limited* received new lightweight streamlined cars then being delivered by the hundreds to Central. With reclining-seat coaches, a tavern-lounge coach, full diner, and a parlor-observation, the *Chicago Mercury* was a classy operation, and the new *Twilight Limited* had nothing to apologize for either, since it had nearly an identical offering of cars. Both it and the *Mercury* provided daytime streamliner service twice daily in both

directions, supplementing the *Wolverine,* a Chicago-New York train operating via Detroit and southern Ontario which also eventually received streamlined equipment. In 1958, the *Chicago Mercury* was given a rather austere new name, being rechristened as the *Michigan.*

GTW was a latecomer to the Chicago-Detroit streamliner market, introducing its high-speed *Mohawk* in the late 1960s and almost matching Central's timings despite a route that was nearly 40 miles longer. The train lasted until Amtrak's startup.

As the 1990s drew to a close, one could still ride a lightweight, streamlined *Twilight Limited* and *Wolverine* between Chicago and "Mo-Town," a legacy to NYC's streamlining efforts dating back almost 60 years.

CHICAGO-HOOSIERLAND

Though largely a rural state, Indiana could boast its own little fleet of streamliners. Although such famous names in the business as the *20th Century Limited, Capitol Limited,* and *Broadway Limited* sped across Hoosier soil on a daily basis, they nary paid attention to anything more humble than New York, Pittsburgh, or Chicago. Two regional railroads of note, Chicago & Eastern Illinois and Chicago, Indianapolis & Louisville—the Monon Route, offered streamliners to

NYC's *Chicago Mercury,* 1948
Train No. 75, the westbound *Chicago Mercury,* is on the last lap of its trip between the Motor City and Chicago as it cruises up the Illinois Central main line near Hyde Park on Chicago's south side. (Some NYC Chicago-Detroit runs utilized the old Michigan Central entrance to Chicago, which was by way of suburban Kensington, Illinois, thence to Central Station on IC trackage rights.) The date is September 1948, and the train carries newer streamlined equipment—the first five cars on the train—as a result of NYC's huge postwar car order. With the exception of the last car on the train, which appears to be a heavyweight office car for railroad officials, the remaining cars are the original Chicago Mercury equipment rebuilt from suburban coaches. *William D. Middleton.*

The *Whippoorwill*

Chicago & Eastern Illinois' had two of its own streamliners, the *Whippoorwill* between Chicago and Evansville, Indiana, and the *Meadowlark* between Chicago and Cypress, far downstate in Illinois. The *Whip* only lasted a couple of years, making color photos of that train extremely rare. This publicity photo of the train, colorized by the railroad to show off the train's eye-catching colors, shows its as-delivered look, complete with an Electro-Motive E7. *Mike Schafer Collection.*

Indiana locales. As the name implies, C&EI was more aligned to serving Illinois, but its main line between the Windy City and the Ohio River at Indiana's southernmost tip tapped three important western Indiana cities: Terre Haute, Vincennes, and Evansville. This was a line heavy with Dixie-bound limiteds, including the streamliner *Dixie Flagler*, but C&EI saw need for a "Chicagoliner" that catered to cities and local towns north of and including Evansville. It did so with a new streamliner called the *Whippoorwill*.

Delivered by Pullman-Standard in 1946 (making it one of the first new postwar streamliners), the *Whippoorwill* featured a baggage-mail-coach named *Turkey Run*,

four coaches (*Vigo Trail, Vincennes Trail, Vanderburg Trail,* and *Vermilion Trail*), diner *Shakamak Inn*, and parlor observation car *Chicagoland.* An early morning northbound departure from Evansville and a late afternoon carding out of Chicago's Dearborn Station gave travelers the better part of a shopping day in Chicago.

The *Whippoorwill* was short-lived, however. When the Louisville & Nashville added a Chicago leg to its Atlanta-St. Louis *Georgian* via the C&EI in 1948, the latter's schedule was similar to that of the *Whippoorwill.* As a result, C&EI dropped the *Whip* and assigned its rolling stock to the *Georgian* (and later the *Humming Bird*) pool. The eye-catching *Whippoorwill* was forever rendered into obscurity, save for the publicity scene at left, which was used on C&EI timetables well after the train had vanished. The train was reincarnated, in a very broad sense, when in about 1960 many of its cars were sold to Illinois Central, which used them mainly on its Chicago-Waterloo (Iowa) streamliner *Land O' Corn*.

A railroad more closely associated with the Hoosier State was the Monon, which in 1947 entered streamlining with a bang, introducing not one but three streamliners. What made these trains stand apart from others of the period were that they were created in Monon's own shop complex at Lafayette, Indiana. At the time, the Chicago, Indianapolis & Louisville was emerging from financial woes, so it could not afford brand-new trains. Instead, the spunky carrier, under the direction of its new leader, John W. Barriger III (a visionary mid-century railroader), purchased an armada of surplus streamlined cars from the U.S. Army. Lafayette Shops gutted the new ACF-built cars and turned them into streamlined express-mail cars, coaches, grill-parlor cars, diner-bar-lounges, grill-coaches, diner-parlor observation, and parlor observation cars.

In 1947, amid much celebration in Indiana because it was Monon's centennial, the railroad introduced the *Hoosier*, the *Tippecanoe*, and the *Thoroughbred*. The first two trains provided fast double-daily service between Chicago and Indianapolis via Monon, Indiana, 184 miles, while the *Thoroughbred* ran between Chicago and Louisville, Kentucky, via Lafayette, 324 miles. For a

time, the railroad even ran a fourth streamliner, the *Varsity*, between Chicago and Bloomington, Indiana, to serve numerous on-line colleges.

The trains were cherished by Hoosiers, but like streamliners everywhere, all fell victim to the times. The *Hoosier* and *Tippecanoe* were dropped in 1959, but the *Thoroughbred* lasted until 1967. Interestingly, Amtrak Chicago-Florida service for a time utilized the former Monon main to Louisville, and until the mid-1990s Amtrak operated a Chicago-Indianapolis train called the *Hoosier State*, which in part ran on ex-Monon rails.

Monon's *Thoroughbred*
Louisville-bound, the *Thoroughbred* has just crossed into the State of Indiana at Hammond on an afternoon in April 1958. The snappy crimson, gray, and white color scheme honored the school colors of Indiana University at Bloomington. In later years, Monon repainted its passenger locomotives and rolling stock black and gold, honoring the colors of Purdue University at Lafayette. *George Speir.*

Interurban streamliners

Even electric interurban lines got into the streamliner act. In 1941, the Chicago North Shore & Milwaukee introduced two articulated streamliners known as the *Electroliners*. The four-car, double-ended trains were built by St. Louis Car and featured coach seating and a tavern-lounge. They spent the next 22 years zipping back and forth between Chicago and Milwaukee, each train making at least two round trips daily and being integrated into North Shore's hourly departure pattern from each city. The trains were sprite, making the 85-mile run in less than two hours—remarkable considering they made about ten intermediate station stops and, at Milwaukee, negotiated several miles of street running as illustrated in this 1962 view by George Speir of a southbound "*Liner*." The trains entered Chicago's Loop via the rapid-transit "L." The *Liner*s were popular and reliable, but their reign ended when the whole North Shore Line was abandoned in January 1963. The *Liner*s migrated to Philadelphia where they served in suburban service as *Liberty Liners* well into the 1970s.

RIO GRANDE'S *PROSPECTOR*

The *Prospector*
Rio Grande's westbound *Prospector* is some 22 miles out of Denver, but the Mile High City is still clearly visible below on the plains as the train winds its way up the Front Range of the Colorado Rockies on May 15, 1967. Tonight's consist includes a dome coach observation car which more often worked the *Royal Gorge* between Denver and Salida, Colorado, and occasionally filled in on the *California Zephyr*. The low-profile dome was built for Chesapeake & Ohio's never-run *Chessie* streamliner in 1948. In less than two weeks, the *Prospector* will be history. *K. C. Crist*

"Through the Rockies, Not Around Them" was the motto of the Denver & Rio Grande Western Railroad. While the slogan was intended to demonstrate the railroad's can-do attitude, it also hinted at its geographic shortcomings. At 570 miles, the railroad's Denver-Salt Lake City line was substantially shorter than the Union Pacific's 628-mile alignment, but much of it involved stiff grades, twisting track, numerous tunnels, and trips through precipitous gorges.

Determined to improve its position in this market which contained its two largest on-line cities, but with severely limited funds, Rio Grande went to the Budd Company in 1940 to see what it could afford. Budd's answer was a lightweight, self-propelled "vest-pocket" streamliner only two cars long. Rio Grande said yes, and took delivery of two trainsets. Each was a fluted

stainless-steel streamliner in microcosm. The first car had an operator's cab, a luggage compartment, and a main seating area offering 44 modern, reclining coach seats and spacious washrooms. The second car contained sleeping accommodations including eight upper and lower berths and two "chamberettes." Squeezed into the rear of the car was a tiny buffet and a two-table dinette area where the Pullman-operated dining service dispensed delicious entrees. Rounding out the train was a small observation lounge. Power for the little streamliner was provided by two 192-hp Hercules diesels mounted horizontally under the floors of the cars.

The new train was named the *Prospector*. The road wasted no time prospecting for business with the new streamliner, and the train was dedicated on November 17, 1941. The *Prospector*'s schedule was faster than anything Rio Grande had ever offered on the Denver-Salt

Lake City route, and it was also faster than UP's rival *Pony Express* by about an hour.

Business was strong from the beginning, but the little trains became victims of their own technology. As fixed consists, they could not be expanded to meet demand. Underpowered, they experienced frequent engine overheating and breakdowns with the ignominious result being a late arrival—behind the steam locomotives they were built to replace. On July 5, 1942, after less than nine months of service, the *Prospector*s were withdrawn and returned to Budd which scrapped them.

Emerging from receivership in 1947, Rio Grande reentered the streamliner stage by participating with Western Pacific and Burlington in the 1949 debut of the *California Zephyr* (Chapter 3). D&RGW also needed to replace cars on its other trains and managed to garner a good price when it relieved the Chesapeake & Ohio of its responsibility to pay for streamlined cars it had overordered from Pullman Standard.

Rio Grande purchased eight coaches, four sleepers, three baggage-mail cars, three baggage cars, two baggage-coaches, three buffet-lounges, and two dining cars and also picked up three low-profile Budd dome coaches directly from the C&O. The bulk order allowed the road to completely reequip the heavyweight *Prospector* that had replaced the ill-fated Budd train of 1940 and to virtually re-equip, except for Pullmans, the Denver-Colorado Springs-Salt Lake City-Ogden *Royal Gorge*.

The first of the new cars entered service in March 1950 and soon the entire order had arrived. Attired in one of the most striking streamliner paint schemes of the era, the new trains and their Alco or EMD diesel power featured stainless steel and Aspen Gold sides set off with black stripes.

A ride on the postwar *Prospector* was memorable. Traveling west into the setting sun, the train climbed the Front Range of the Rockies offering spectacular views back at the endless Plains stretching eastward. In winter, the lights of Denver below would glow below like a luminescent carpet. In the diner, passengers were greeted at their table by a smiling crew and fresh Colorado carnations. Rocky Mountain trout, long a Rio Grande specialty, might be punctuated with a cup of coffee and chocolate covered orange sticks (a local favorite of Salt Lake City residents).

Tucked into a cozy Pullman berth or stretched out in a reclining coach seat, passengers slept as their train visited Rocky Mountain towns such as Glenwood Springs and Grand Junction (which the *California Zephyr* served in daylight). Dawn found the streamliner descending Soldier Summit with a breakfasttime arrival in Salt Lake City. While the *Prospector* and company enjoyed good patronage at first, increasing auto, bus and air competition spelled hard times for rail passengers. In 1954, UP's *Pony Express* was discontinued, killed off in part by the success of the upgraded *Prospector*. But soon the *Prospector* felt the pinch of declining passenger revenues and the withdrawal of mail contracts. On May 28, 1967, the train made its final run.

The *Prospector* served its passengers faithfully, symbolizing what was best about America's regional streamliners with its distinctive local cuisine and friendly western personality. Today, it remains a pleasant memory of a simpler time when Americans rode the train.

Prospector ad from 1950
The *Prospector* was one of the few trains that began as a streamliner, then was converted to a heavyweight train, and then reintroduced as a streamliner. This ad accompanied the *Prospector*'s second incarnation as a streamliner in 1950. *Joe Welsh Collection.*

Good *Service*

Good *Eating*

Good *Sleeping*

You'll enjoy service from America's friendliest railroad crew on your Prospector journey ...in the Pullman, coach, or diner-lounge your every travel need receives courteous, smiling attention...you're pampered to perfection!

Food prepared to your epicurean taste—including mouth-watering charcoal broiled steaks, and Rocky Mountain Rainbow Trout —is featured daily on the Prospector. Whatever your taste, there's a treat in store for you in this streamliner's cuisine.

You'll slumber like a child in the accommodation of your choice on the Prospector. *All-new* sleeping cars, featuring upper and lower berths, roomettes, bedrooms, and bedroom suites guarantee soothing somnolence on your starlight journey. You arrive at destination rested and refreshed, ready for a full day of work or fun!

Prospector....
....*Overnight Every Night*.... DENVER—SALT LAKE CITY

Daylight art, 1937 train
There weren't enough superlatives to describe Southern Pacific's first offering in world of streamlining—the *Daylight*. From the nose of its GS-class 4-8-4 Northern-type steam locomotive to the tip of its teardropped-shaped observation end, the *Daylight* was the best things to happen in the realm of stylish California transport. In letting the world know about its bold new train, SP issued a wonderful foldout that opened to reveal a rendering of the train in full glory (above), complete with the obligatory California mission. *Don Sarno Collection.*

THE *DAYLIGHT*S AND THE *LARK*

It has been said that the best way to judge the character of an organization is by how it responds to a crisis. Faced with declining passenger traffic as a result of the Depression, the Southern Pacific Railroad in 1933 launched an all-out effort to revitalize its passenger service. Working with car builder Pullman-Standard and locomotive manufacturer Lima (Ohio) Locomotive Works, the SP set incredibly high standards for design—and then refused to compromise them. The result was often called "The Most Beautiful Train in the World."

Inaugurated on March 21, 1937, SP's streamlined *Daylight* replaced a heavyweight train of the same name operating on the 470-mile Coast Line between Los Angeles and San Francisco. Aside from the name and train numbers (Nos. 98 and 99), the new streamliner borrowed little from its heavyweight predecessor. Wearing SP designer Charles Eggleston's unforgettable red, orange, and black color scheme, the lustrous new 12-car train featured state-of-the art design and interior accommodations. Passenger accommodations were the best money could buy. A combined coffee shop-tavern car offered low-cost meals for the budget-minded traveler, and a deluxe dining car and parlor car seating catered to the luxury-minded. Up front was a new streamlined GS-2-class 4-8-4 steam locomotive—a design so good it would spawn an entire family of dependable motive power to haul other crack SP trains.

If the equipment was beautiful, so was the scenery. SP's Coast Line followed "El Camino Real"—"The

King's Highway"—which linked a chain of California missions. And while that made for an interesting historical footnote, nature's handiwork stole the show. This was a California as yet unspoiled by development. Leaving San Francisco southbound in early morning, passengers had a panoramic view of the rich Santa Clara Valley, a major fruit-growing region. In spring, when miles of blossoms snowed the orchards, the sight was breathtaking. Up through the rugged Santa Lucia Mountains the *Daylight* climbed and twisted, the GS-2 on the head end barely breaking a sweat.

Shortly after descending the Santa Margarita Range via a series of loops into San Luis Obispo, the blue Pacific Ocean was suddenly alongside—and its white-sand beaches and lazy surf would be a constant companion for the next 113 miles. All too soon, beautiful Santa Barbara, with its magnificent white stucco and red-tile-roofed buildings, was in sight. At Ventura, the seaside adventure ended as the train headed inland, reaching Los Angeles at the dinner hour. After it was opened in 1939, the new Los Angeles Union Passenger Terminal provided a fitting terminal to a memorable ride.

Within days of the *Daylight*'s inauguration, SP knew it had a winner. Demand for a seat on the new train was so high that the railroad routinely operated a second section (using older non-streamlined equipment) to handle as many as 400 overflow passengers per day. To nearly everybody's amazement, traffic studies showed that, rather than being the result of a fickle public's temporary fascination with something new, the demand was likely to continue. By 1939, the *Daylight* was offi-

cially the most heavily traveled single-section intercity train in the country, averaging 370 passengers per trip. Seeing the handwriting on the wall, as far back as early 1938 SP had begun planning to add a second stream-liner to handle the record-setting demand.

Also constructed by P-S, this second *Daylight* was introduced on the same route in early January 1940. The two new 14-car trains replaced the first two *Day-light* equipment sets as the *Morning Daylight*. Newly

refurbished, the original 1937 streamliners became the *Noon Daylight*.

May 1940 found SP ordering yet more equipment for the *Daylight*s and to create a "*Night Daylight*," as it were. That equipment ended up entering overnight San Francisco-L.A. service on the existing heavyweight train, the *Lark*, which officially became a streamliner on July 10, 1941. The new all-Pullman train offered the most modern overnight sleeping accommodations to SP's

Coast Daylight

Cruisin' the Coast Line, the southbound *Coast Daylight*—20 cars strong in this 1950s scene—makes a strong case for SP's claim that the *Daylight*s were "The Most Beautiful Train(s) in the World." *Southern Pacific Lines.*

well-heeled business and celebrity patrons using the Coast Line. The swank new triple-unit Lark Club diner-tavern-lounge was a festive gathering place and it wasn't uncommon to find a celebrity like Bob Hope here enjoying the ride.

The popular *Daylight*s spawned other whole new day trains. Operating on the inland route via Stockton, the SP *San Joaquin* between Oakland and Los Angeles received some streamlined equipment from the *Daylight* pool and the name *San Joaquin Daylight* in July 1941. The train became a virtual streamliner on January 5, 1942, when it inherited cars of the *Noon Daylight* which had been terminated for the duration of the war because it provided a near-duplicate service to the *Morning Daylight*. The *San Joaquin Daylight* gained a Sacramento section in 1946 (operating between Sacramento and Lathrop as the *Sacramento Daylight*). SP's distinctive homebuilt "three-quarter" dome lounge cars were added to the train in 1955.

Despite the investment in new trains, the late 1950s and '60s were unkind to SP's passenger department. The railroad's former customers transferred their allegiance to the automobile as the interstate highway system restructured the American way of life and the jet airliner rose to prominence. The SP, which had invested millions of dollars introducing a fleet of the handsomest trains in the country, lost money as spectacularly as it had spent it. Disillusioned, it dropped the nickname the "Friendly SP" and set a course to get out from under the burden of money-losing passenger operations.

An early casualty was the *Lark*. Partially re-equipped in 1949, the conservative two-tone gray train operated as an all-Pullman run until 1957 when it was combined with SP's *Starlight*, a streamlined overnight coach train which linked the same endpoints as the *Lark*. With the consolidation, the *Starlight* lost its identity and the *Lark* lost some of its status. A victim of the jet airliner and the superhighway, which inexorably stole its predominantly expense-account clientele away, the *Lark*'s last run came in April 1968.

The original *Daylight* was a little luckier. Although the *Noon Daylight* had been discontinued back in 1949, the former *Morning Daylight* was renamed the *Coast Daylight* in 1952 and upgraded with new coaches in 1954. When Amtrak started in May 1971, it selected SP's *Coast Daylight* and *Cascade* (Oakland-Portland) for inclusion into its new, though skeletal, system. Under Amtrak, the *Cascade* briefly became a nameless triweekly Portland-Los Angeles train combined with the now-nameless daily *Coast Daylight* south of Oakland. Late in 1971, the *Coast Daylight* name reappeared while the L.A.-Portland train became the *Coast Starlight*—which ultimately became the surviving name.

Today, Amtrak's *Coast Starlight*, considered by many as the best long-distance train in the U.S., still shows passengers the wonders of the Shasta Route (see the *Shasta Daylight* story in Chapter 4) and the Coast Line, keeping alive a tradition of unbeatable service and scenery established when the Friendly SP ran the "Most Beautiful Trains in the World."

The *Lark*
The overnight Oakland/San Francisco-Los Angeles *Lark* was a businessperson's train as well as a popular run for Hollywood celebrities. When this scene was recorded of the Lark's arrival at Los Angeles Union Passenger Terminal on September 10, 1957, it had become a coach-and-Pullman train, but it still featured its Lark Club lounge and full dining car, both exclusively for Pullman passengers. Coach passengers could avail themselves of the train's snack-lounge car. The Oakland section of the train, sometimes known as the *Oakland Lark*, featured coaches, sleepers, and a buffet-lounge sleeper. The two sections were split/combined at San Jose. *John Dziobko.*

Where'd they go, the streamliners? If you've read most or all of the capsule passenger-train histories featured in this book, you'll know that an alarming number of streamliners never made through the 1960s, and that many of those that did were discontinued when Amtrak began operations on May 1, 1971. (Underfunded, Amtrak could only continue operating about half of the 300 or so intercity passenger trains that had survived to 1971.) A few streamliners belonging to carriers that at first opted not to join Amtrak marched on, but within a dozen years or so, they were gone too or had finally been turned over to Amtrak.

During its early years, Amtrak inherited a huge assortment of cars from the railroads; many of them are featured in this book when they were newly delivered from Pullman-Standard and Budd. During Amtrak's infancy, one could still ride a former New York Central tavern observation car, an *Empire Builder* Ranch Car, a Union Pacific 11-double-bedroom car, a Southern Pacific Audubon diner, a Santa Fe "Top of the Cap" Hi-Level lounge, and zillions of CB&Q Vista-Domes. (Did any railroad have as many domes as Burlington?) Eventually, though, most of these cars were supplanted by new equipment, much in the manner that these first-generation streamlined cars replaced heavyweight rolling stock.

Union Pacific special at Sherer's Falls, Oregon, 1996. Jim Thomas

So, do streamliners still link America's great cities? If your definition of "streamliner" means a matching train of lightweight rolling stock, wearing a distinct paint scheme—Red and orange, perhaps? Or maybe Royal blue and gray?—with a variety of equipment like Vista-Dome coaches, Sun Lounge sleeping cars, Pleasure Dome lounges, and Skytop parlor observation cars . . . well, we're sorry to say, no. On the other hand, if you loosen the definition a mite to include any train comprised of lightweight equipment aerodynamically designed to minimize wind resistance, well then, there is some good news. Nearly all of Amtrak's new passenger cars are of lightweight, stainless-steel construction. And Amtrak's new locomotives? *Very* streamlined. So, by those counts, yes, streamliners still roll the steel boulevards of America. They've just gone through another stage of evolution beyond the "classic" period featured herein.

In fact, there *are* survivors from the "classic" period, in terms of names and routes if not appearances. You can still board the *Capitol Limited* at Washington, D.C., and step off a *Chief* at Los Angeles Union Passenger Terminal. Never mind that the two trains look exactly alike (in fact, as of 1997, Amtrak's *Capitol Limited* equipment set actually continued to California as the *Chief* after a short layover in Chicago.) Like much of the rest of America, the trains have become homogenized. Fortunately, the inherent ambiance, comfort, and excitement of streamliner travel is still there. And that's what really counts.

But if you're wondering just what did happen to some of the trains and

rolling stock of the classic streamliner period, there are some surprises there, too. The photo featured on this page underscores this. At a glance, it appears to be the new, domed version of Union Pacific's *City of Portland*, probably photographed circa 1955. In reality, it's UP's roving goodwill Domeliner on a public excursion run in 1996. Although a number of UP Streamliner and Domeliner passenger cars scattered to the four corners of the country after 1971, the railroad fortunately kept a modest roster of its 1950s-era streamlined for charter service and employee outings.

Here are some other entries in the "Where Are They Now?" series:

● As of the late 1990s, Burlington Northern & Santa Fe maintained a modest fleet of ex-Santa Fe cars, including a Big Dome, for business-train operations. Warbonnet-painted locomotives often pull the train, and if you squint your eyes a bit, it looks an awful lot like the *Chief*.

● The two GM *Aerotrains* survive, one at the National Transportation Museum in Green Bay, Wisconsin, and one at the National Transportation Museum near St. Louis.

● Also at the St. Lous National Transportation Museum, one can see Burlington shovelnose 9908-*Silver Charger* and one of the parlor observation cars built in 1935 for *Royal Blue/Abraham Lincoln* service.

● A streamlined GS-4 *Daylight* steam locomotive, SP 4449 owned by the City of Portland, Oregon, has on occasion operated with a *"Daylight"* set of equipment, some of which actually were cars built for *Daylight* service.

● The first dome car built in the U.S., Burlington's homebuilt *Silver Dome*, reposes at the Mad River & Nickel Plate Railroad Museum in Bellevue, Ohio.

● You can ride a North Shore *Electroliner* at the Illinois Railway Museum at Union, northwest of Chicago, and also view Burlington's *Nebraska Zephyr*, which was built in 1936 as one of the second *Twin Zephyr* sets.

● As of 1997, the State of North Carolina owns and operates, in public service, several KCS *Southern Belle* cars and a former *Hiawatha* Super Dome.

● Dozens of various individual lightweight, streamlined (and a few modernized heavyweight) passenger cars built in the 1940, 1950s, and 1960s have been saved by numerous private parties, companies (including some railroads), and museums. Some are stored; some are in static use or on display, and a few still enjoy operation in private excursion service.

● And finally, you can still see one of the two trains that started it all—Burlington's *Pioneer Zephyr*—a.k.a. *Zephyr* 9900—whose home since 1960 has been Chicago's famous Museum of Science & Industry. Coincidentally, as this book was being written in 1996-97, the *Pioneer Zephyr* was receiving a complete makeover at a shop near Milwaukee as part of the Chicago museum's plans to enhance its *Zephyr* exhibition.

INDEX